Southern Living®

2004
Garden
ANNUAL

Dutch Iris, tulips, poppies, and pansies thrive in an Atlanta garden. (See page 220.)

Southern Living®

2004
Garden
ANNUAL

Oxmoor
House®

Southern Living®
2004
Garden ANNUAL

©2004 by Oxmoor House, Inc.
Book Division of Southern Progress Corporation
P.O. Box 2463, Birmingham, Alabama 35201

ISSN: 1048-2318
Hardcover ISBN: 0-8487-2810-6
Softcover ISBN: 0-8487-2811-4
Printed in the United States of America
First Printing 2004

Southern Living®
Executive Editor, Homes and Gardens: Derick Belden
Garden Editor: Gene B. Bussell
Senior Writer: Stephen P. Bender
Associate Garden Editors: Ellen Ruoff Riley, Charles Thigpen
Assistant Garden Editor: Edwin Marty
Assistant Garden Design Editor: Troy H. Black
Senior Photographers: Jean M. Allsopp, Ralph Anderson,
Van Chaplin, Joseph De Sciose, Allen Rokach
Photographers: Tina Cornett, William Dickey, Laurey W. Glenn,
Meg McKinney
Production and Color Quality Coordinator: Katie Terrell
Editorial Assistant: Lynne Long
Production Coordinator: Jamie Barnhart
Contributing Editors: David W. Marshall, William C. Welch

Oxmoor House, Inc.
Editor-in-Chief: Nancy Fitzpatrick Wyatt
Executive Editor: Susan Carlisle Payne
Art Director: Cynthia R. Cooper
Copy Chief: Allison Long Lowery

Southern Living® ***2004 Garden Annual***
Editor: Susan Hernandez Ray
Contributing Copy Editor: Adrienne S. Davis
Contributing Designer: Rita Yerby
Editorial Assistant: Terri Laschober
Proofreader: Jacqueline B. Giovanelli
Contributing Indexer: Lauren Brooks
Director of Production: Phillip Lee
Books Production Manager: Larry Hunter
Production Assistant: Faye Porter Bonner

To order additional publications, call 1-800-765-6400.

Oxmoor House®

For more books to enrich your life, visit
oxmoorhouse.com

Contents

*Angel trumpets
(page 148)*

*Piedmont azalea
(page 81)*

*Japanese maple
(page 170)*

Crowned tickseed (page 141)

*I*f you do one thing this year, share your passion for gardening with your friends and family. Teach the kids in your neighborhood about plants. Show them how you grow your tomatoes. Sow a flower garden of zinnias. Go pick a bucket of blackberries. Let them know there is more to life than television and video games. As they all travel down the garden path, they will learn that the journey is more important than the destination.

Consider the *Southern Living® 2004 Garden Annual* a celebration of our year. Here are all the wonderful people, places, and plants we came to know in 2003. While thumbing through these pages, we hope you will find ideas and inspiration for creating your own garden. The monthly checklists and letters to the editor will provide timely guidance and answers to your gardening questions. Also included is a plant hardiness zone map, page 240.

As always, we are grateful to the many folks who have welcomed us into their gardens over the past year and have allowed us to share them with the South. Thanks to all.

Garden Editor

*Tiny tomatoes are easy to grow
(See pages 82–84.)*

*Primroses brighten
dreary
winter days (See
pages 18–19.)*

January

garden checklist
JANUARY

Editor's Notebook

PHOTOGRAPH: VAN CHAPLIN

Hey, everyone, I have a favor to ask. Could each of you visit my garden this week and cover my flowerbeds with dollar bills? What do you mean, that's a waste of money? You weren't worried about money when you raked all your leaves into the gutter last fall. Those leaves are USDA Prime organic matter, the kind of stuff you'll pay big bucks for at the garden center this spring. Cheapo that I am, I never waste fallen leaves. Instead, I rake them into huge piles, gleefully run over them twice with my mulching mower, and then place them between perennials and shrubs in my planting beds. The chopped leaves make an attractive mulch that doesn't blow or wash away. As they break down, they turn into nutritious soil that keeps my plants fat and happy. Best of all, I feel at peace with my conscience knowing I'm saving precious landfill space for more deserving garbage. So if you'd like to feel better about yourself, chop up your leaves—or send me some dollar bills. —STEVE BENDER

■ **Garden notebook**—A new year is beginning, and there is absolutely no better time to start a garden journal. Note the weather, plants in bloom, chores completed, and plants added. Over time these monthly observations will sharpen your gardening skills.

■ **Greens**—Continue to harvest collards and kale; cooler weather sweetens the leaves. Harvest regularly from the bottom of the plants so they will continue to grow.

■ **Houseplants**—Foliage plants thrive in bright light near windows. Turn your houseplants every few weeks to keep growth straight and even. Chinese evergreens *(Aglaonema modestum)* and peace lilies (or spathiphyllum) do well in locations that receive less light. In bright areas, large weeping fig *(Ficus benjamina),* mother-in-law's tongue *(Sansevieria trifasciata),* and corn plant *(Dracaena fragrans)* are easily grown. Apply a water-soluble fertilizer every four to six weeks.

■ **Seeds**—It's a great time to think about seeds for spring sowing. Order now for the best selection, and you'll be prepared to plant your garden when the weather warms.

■ **Shade trees**—Increase real estate values and reduce energy use year-round with trees. Shade cast on the south and west sides of a home reduces air-conditioning costs in summer. Deciduous trees lose their leaves in winter and allow the sun to warm homes. Place large trees, such as pecan, bur oak, lacebark elm, and Chinese pistache, 15 to 20 feet from the house; set small ones, such as crabapple and redbud, as close as 4 to 6 feet.

■ **Citrus**—In Florida, this is the height of the ripening season. Don't fertilize plants now. If temperatures are expected to drop to 30 degrees, protect your lemon and lime trees.

Plant Supports

Hold up forced hyacinths, daffodils, and crocus as they begin to bloom. Pepperwood (used here with these white hyacinths) or curly willow can be purchased from your local garden center. However, your own backyard may provide the greatest inspiration. Branches of winged elm, sweet gum, dogwood, and oakleaf hydrangea offer interesting bark with distinctive texture and form.

■ **Camellias**—In the Middle, Lower, and Coastal South, purchase camellias *(Camellia japonica)*, and add them to your garden while they are blooming. Beautiful early-flowering selections include 'Debutante,' 'Lady Clare,' and 'Professor Charles S. Sargent.' Midseason selections include 'Kramer's Supreme,' 'Nuccio's Pearl,' 'Pink Perfection,' and 'Swan Lake.' Late-blooming selections, which will extend your flowers, include 'Purity' and 'Governor Mouton.' Add them to your garden when the ground is no longer

camellia

frozen. Container-grown plants have an easier transition into the garden. Camellias prefer well-drained soil that is rich in organic matter. When you're choosing a planting location, be sure to find an area that is sheltered from sun and drying winds.

■ **Vines**—Add vines to your garden for vertical color. Good choices include Carolina jessamine *(Gelsemium sempervirens)*, 'Tangerine Beauty' crossvine *(Bignonia capreolata* 'Tangerine Beauty'), and 'Magnifica' trumpet honeysuckle *(Lonicera sempervirens* 'Magnifica'). These are excellent for climbing on arbors, fences, walls, or simple strands of wire.

■ **Winter lawns**—Sow ryegrass to fill in bare spots or to green a brown lawn. You can sow up to 10 pounds of seed per 1,000 square feet of lawn. After the

petunias

seeds sprout and the ryegrass is growing, keep it mowed at the same height you mowed your permanent grass. The ryegrass will die in the spring about the time your permanent grass starts growing strong again.

■ **Blueberries and figs**—In Florida, plant both in full sun. To ensure fruit set on blueberries, interplant two or more of the following plants : 'Tifblue,' 'Climax,' 'Powderblue,' 'Woodard,' or 'Brightwell.' Suitable fig selections include 'Brown Turkey,' 'Celeste,' 'Alma,' 'Magnolia,' 'San Piero,' and 'Green Ischia.'

■ **Flowers**—In Florida, set out petunias, geraniums, nasturtiums, pansies, dianthus, stock, sweet peas, lobelia, violas, and snapdragons.

■ **Flowering trees**—In Texas, small ones, such as crepe myrtle, vitex, Mexican plum, and redbud, can be planted as close as 4 to 6 feet away from the house. These grow 12 to 18 feet tall and can be placed 15 to 20 feet apart. Select container-grown trees for easy transplanting. Water well.

■ **Fruits and nuts**—In Texas, peaches, plums, pears, figs, and pomegranates begin producing in two to three years. Consult your local nursery to learn the best selections for your area. Set out pecans now while they're dormant. Place container-grown or bare-root trees where they will have at least 40 to 50 feet of open area to spread. Thornless blackberry selections include 'Apache' and 'Navaho.'

PRUNE

■ **Crepe myrtles**—Remove branches that are too close together or that cross or rub each other. It is important not to prune the tops of crepe myrtle trees to make them bloom. Topping may yield larger flowers but does not increase the overall volume of blooms. Extreme topping often results in weak growth that tends to bend or break in summer rains.

■ **Fruiting vines and shrubs**—Remove last year's growth on muscadine grape plants, leaving only a few short spurs coming from main vines. Cut spurs back to several inches, leaving three buds per spur. Remove or cut back old blueberry canes that have little strong growth.

pruning a crepe myrtle

Tip of the Month

I use a black felt-tip marker and a yardstick to mark the handles of my garden tools (trowels, weeders, hoes, shovels, etc.) in 6-inch increments. Now I can easily estimate depths and distances.

DORIS J. STARLING
ROCKVILLE, MARYLAND

Welcoming
the Birds

BY CHARLIE THIGPEN
PHOTOGRAPHY VAN CHAPLIN

Gardening and birding are the top two outdoor activities among Americans. Combine them to make your landscape more attractive and entertaining.

During winter, when the landscape is dormant, let our winged friends become your gardening focal points. They offer beauty and life to the yard, and the songs they sing can brighten even a gray, blustery day.

As temperatures dip, natural food supplies dwindle, and birds must scratch the leaf-littered ground in search of seeds and insects to sustain them. Now's the time to give them a little help. Try these tips on attracting and feeding birds.

Richard Melton of Tuscaloosa, Alabama, and his mother-in-law, Bev Vogt, know a lot about birds. Richard designs gardens to attract them, and Bev owns a Wild Birds Unlimited store in nearby Northport. In fact, Richard built a habitat garden behind Bev's store that attracts a great number of birds daily. The garden seems to be in perpetual motion as birds dart around the feeders and plants.

Bev says the most effective way to attract birds is to feed them. Richard stresses that to keep them in and around your yard, you must create a bird-friendly environment. They need four elements to stay healthy, happy, and wanting to hang around.

left: Richard Melton has a deck full of feeders and potted plants. He designed his backyard garden to attract birds.
above: Bev Vogt and Richard work together to bring in the birds.

Food for Birds
Just like everything else, birdseed has become specialized. Bev's shop carries 15 different types of feed. In addition to that, you can buy suet cakes, dried fruit, peanuts, and even mealy worms. Her premium-blend seed is very popular with customers, but if you're confused about what to buy, look for black oil sunflower seeds. These attract many different types of birds. Remember, buying the cheapest birdseed isn't always a bargain. Inexpensive seed can contain filler, which birds won't eat. So you end up with unused seed.

To prevent the little green weed patches that appear in your lawn, use a No-Mess blend, which has little or no waste and won't sprout in your yard. If you really want to spoil the birds, put out fruit or shelled peanuts.

Along with an assortment of foods, Bev also sells different types of bird feeders. She has squirrel-proof feeders and cone-shaped baffles to prevent raids by these pesky rodents. Hang feeders at least 5 feet off the ground and 10 feet away from trees, shrubs, fences, or houses to keep squirrels at bay and eliminate ambush areas for cats.

Water for Drinking and Bathing
"To attract birds, it's critical to have flowing water," Richard says. "Mosquitoes can't reproduce in moving water, and babbling or splashing water sounds like a natural running creek, so the birds are drawn to it."

Richard builds shallow wading areas only 1 or 2 inches deep. They give birds a perfect place for bathing, which helps them clean their feathers of dirt and mites. Once the birds visit Richard's backyard stream, they remember the water source and return.

Shelter and Nesting Sites
Birds need protection from the elements. Thick, bushy evergreen plants that block the wind and rain shield

HELP TRACK BIRDS
Each year the National Audubon Society and the Cornell Lab of Ornithology host the Great Backyard Bird Count. It helps determine populations and migrating habits of birds around the country. For more information visit the Great Backyard Bird Count Web site at www.birdsource.org/gbbc.

birds from cold or wet weather. Such cover also helps create escape routes to get away from predators. Shrubs with tight branching habits make good nesting sites. Birdhouses can also be placed around your home to provide secure spots for birds to raise their young. House wrens nest in hanging baskets filled with plants.

Plant Diversity
A large selection of plants will entice many different species. Brightly colored flowers attract hummingbirds, while fruiting plants, such as holly, mahonia, and pyracantha, lure migrating cedar waxwings.

As we build more subdivisions each year, we take away bird habitat, so we should incorporate more native plants into our landscapes. Many of these plants, such as coreopsis, ferns, hydrangeas, native azaleas, and upright yaupon hollies, arc easy to grow and can add great beauty to a garden.

Birds are truly our feathered friends; they pollinate flowers and reduce bug populations. So return the favor by making your yard a place where birds can feel at home. ◆

Raking leaves will keep your yard tidy and can help your upper body gain valuable strength.

Tool Time

For physically friendly tools, call the Life with Ease at 1-800-966-5119, or visit their Web site at www.lifewithease.com. Another good source is Lee Valley Tools. Call 1-800-267-8735, or visit www.leevalley.com.

Growing Goodness

This season offers plenty of opportunities to work outdoors—stimulating body, soul, and garden to grow healthy and strong.

Crisp days are upon us. Enjoy the exhilarating cool air and clear days by working outside. Gardening during the winter months prepares your yard for spring and can give your body a form of exercise that will help you stay fit for a lifetime.

The Goodness of Gardening

Many fitness enthusiasts consider gardening to be moderate exercise, and 30 minutes of moderate exercise per day can lower cholesterol; drop blood pressure levels; and help prevent type 2 diabetes, strokes, and heart disease. Gardening also contributes to muscle endurance, flexibility, and strength.

Equally rewarding, the gardening life often lowers stress, alleviates depression, and can improve your self-esteem. Gardeners of all ages enjoy the chance for self-expression and creativity, as well as accomplishing a task. The garden's sensory extravaganza also reduces tension: The colors, sounds, and fragrances can make you forget the cares of a dreary day.

■ **Prune.** Now is a good time to prune evergreens, summer-floweringshrubs, and trees. The bare branches of dormant deciduous trees make it easier to evaluate the situation.

■ **Prepare the soil.** This is a great time to turn your soil as harmful insects and their eggs will be exposed

to the cold and to hungry birds. Mix in compost, manure, or other organic materials for a lush planting bed in the spring.

■ **Plant.** Trees and shrubs set out in January have extra time to establish healthy root systems before spring.

■ **Mulch.** Add a thick layer of mulch to protect new growth. Pine straw, fallen leaves, and composted pine bark are good choices. Mulch provides protection for roots and helps conserve moisture.

■ **Clean containers.** Soak your collection of leftover clay pots overnight in a mixture of 1 cup white vinegar and 1 cup household bleach per gallon of warm water. If your pots are

Adding pine straw or mulch to a flowerbed helps protect tender plants, and it stretches your tense muscles.

upside down to prevent water collection. If the water freezes, the containers could break.

■ **Prevent disease.** Many fruit trees and roses will benefit from an application of dormant oil spray, which kills overwintering insects and diseases. It can also reduce the scorching effects of drying winter winds.

■ **Think ahead.** After working in the yard, take time to plan and dream. Draw a small map of your garden, and make a list of plants and seeds you'd like to order from your favorite garden catalogs. LYNNE LONG

still crusty, try scrubbing with a steel wool pad after they have soaked for 12 hours. Rinse with warm water, and allow the pots to air-dry.

■ **Ready tools.** Shovels, shears, and mowers should be sharpened and oiled. Paint tool handles bright colors, such as yellow or red. This will help preserve the wood and will make these items easier to spot when you set them down on the lawn.

■ **Relocate accessories.** Bring garden ornaments, such as jars or urns, into your basement to prevent damage from falling temperatures. If they cannot be moved, cover or turn them

Boost Your Benefits

■ **Stretch.** Begin your gardening tasks with a warm-up. Gently stretch the muscles you will be using most—arms, shoulders, and back. Add some trunk twists.

■ **Vary your activity.** If possible, divide 30-minute sessions into 8-minute intervals. Break up strenuous chores with lighter ones. For instance, swap between digging and easy watering.

■ **Alternate positions and limbs.** Using different muscle groups reduces soreness and helps achieve a more balanced workout.

■ **Lift safely.** Remember to bend your knees, and use your legs instead of your back when lifting heavy pots or sacks of potting soil.

■ **Take small trips.** You'll gain more from making several short trips to the compost pile than carrying one large load. The extra distance will burn more calories, and you'll be less likely to try to haul or lift too much.

Pot Toppings

Try using different materials as mulch to give your containers a finished look.

Potted plants are a great way to dress up your home both inside and out, but, let's face it, the containers they come in can look pretty boring. We found some creative ways to perk up those plain pots. The result? A variety of unusual mulches that look terrific and help keep your potted plants from drying out quickly. It's like the icing on the cake.

Most soil mixes are full of little white round balls called perlite, which are added to the soil for better drainage. When you water your plants, these white balls rise to the top. Cover them with ceramic tiles, seashells, or any other finds to add interest to your containers.

The Natural Touch

As an alternative to mulch, which washes away, or Spanish moss, which can be a problem when watering the

below: Sweet gum balls and pinecones cover the soil in this planting of variegated Japanese sedge.

plant, consider using sweet gum balls or pinecones collected from around your yard. They're free and add shape and form to your containers. Prickly sweet gum balls and pinecones can keep dogs, cats, or kids from digging around your potted plants.

Small stones such as pea gravel can also be used. Many florist shops and garden centers sell small bags of polished rocks or smooth, rounded pieces of colored glass. You can also collect rocks from around your garden or from a nearby streambed.

For an even more natural look, lay sheet moss over the soil. It's easy to work with and available at most garden centers. Often used to line hanging baskets, it's a nice topping for your pots. Bulbs look great sprouting through a carpet of moss.

Make Your Own

Brightly colored ceramic tiles are inexpensive and come in a wide range of shades to accent any pot. Broken into pieces, they work great and won't decompose or wash away. To break tiles, wrap them in a towel or rag, and tap them with a hammer. Wear gloves and safety glasses to protect yourself. Unwrap the cloth, and set the tiles around the base of a potted plant. Use one color, or mix them together so these bright tiles complement your plants.

Another idea is to save broken terra-cotta pots. When pots crack, break them into 2- to 3-inch pieces, and reuse them as mulch. With time, the orange-brown color will become stained with green moss, giving your containers an aged look.

Create a Theme

Take the idea one step further, and create many different effects. For instance, seashells scattered across the top of a pot of tropical plants add a

BY CHARLIE THIGPEN
PHOTOGRAPHY VAN CHAPLIN

left: Broken tiles scattered around these burgundy bromeliads add a decorative element. **inset:** Many soil mixes are full of little white balls called perlite, which can make plantings look unnatural. **top:** Tiles shine brightly in this small planter of variegated euonymus. **above:** Seashells look right at home around the base of a palm.

coastal look. If you use shells collected from the beach, be sure to wash them thoroughly. In fact, it might be a good idea to boil them in water to remove any salt, which could leach into the soil and harm plants. Other ideas include colorful marbles, glass beads, or buttons.

As these examples prove, mulch doesn't have to be boring. Use your imagination to cover your soil and perk up your potted plants. ◆

Promising PRIMROSES

Bring home these colorful flowers—they're springtime in a pot.
A little-known surprise: The yellow ones are fragrant.

The promise of this flower is simple—easy care, irresistible color, and the assurance of a smile. These cool-weather blooms, abundant now, bring a big splash of sunshine indoors. Which shade and selection should you choose? Good news—primroses are inexpensive, so you can indulge in an assortment.

Who's Who

The Pacific Giants Series (*Primula* x *polyantha*) has deep green leaves that hug the pot's rim in a thick rosette. Quarter-size flowers form a central cluster topping a short stem. A remarkable palette includes bold Mardi Gras gold, red, hot pink, and purple at one end of the color range. There are also soft sunset oranges, peaches, and creamy yellows. And if you're a true blue lover, this is the flower for you.

Prissier in appearance is fairy primrose *(P. malacoides)*. Loosely clustered flowers perch atop long, delicate 6- to 8-inch stems. Bluish-green, slightly ruffled leaves whorl at the base. Shades range from lavender to soft pink and pure white.

A third type resembles fairy primrose with larger blooms and hairy leaves. German primrose *(P. obconica)* has salmon, purple, or pink blossoms about an inch wide. Handling the textured leaves may cause skin irritation.

top: Pacific Giants Series primroses adorn this front door. Placed on a saucer, this wreath would also make a colorful centerpiece. **above:** Old Fiesta ware perfectly cups a single primrose. Water these drainless containers carefully to avoid soggy roots.

Bring Them Home

Turn your front door into a blooming party with a wreath of Pacific Giants. Purchase a plantable wire form, line it with moss and potting soil, and tuck primroses around the circle. If kept moist and cool, it will last for months.

If you have room for only a few, plant primroses in colorful coffee cups. Without drainage, water may collect in the container, causing the plant to die. Keep soil moist but not excessively wet.

Fairy and German primroses pair well, so fill a plant stand with them. Vessels such as an old breadbox can harbor many containers, and the fairy type displays beautifully en masse, giving their delicate flowers collective impact.

Tender Loving, Easy Care

Primroses dwell happily in a cozy winter home for several days but then require an equal dose of moist, chilly air. Place them outdoors in morning sun, protected from harsh winter winds. Keep soil watered—small pots dry quickly. If plants wilt, place them in the sink, mist foliage, and saturate the soil. Then put the containers in a cool, dark place overnight.

The truth about primroses is this—they're one of the easiest, most cheerful flowers you can have this time of year. They aren't a splurge; they're the path to the promise of spring.

BY ELLEN RUOFF RILEY / PHOTOGRAPHY RALPH ANDERSON

This plant stand holds a trio of German primroses on the top shelf, along with a breadbox full of fairy primroses below.

Blooming jonquils, azaleas, dogwoods, and viburnums in a South Carolina garden (See pages 30–33.)

February

garden checklist

Editor's Notebook

PHOTOGRAPH: VAN CHAPLIN

In my ever so humble opinion, no rational gardener should be without nun's orchid *(Phaius tankervilliae)*. Unlike cattleya and other fussy orchids, this terrestrial one (meaning that it grows in the ground and not in trees) is easy, easy, easy. You can grow it outdoors in Central and South Florida. Elsewhere, it makes a great houseplant, thriving in bright, indirect light. It combines very handsome, large, pleated leaves with tall spikes of showy blossoms in late winter and spring. The petals are creamy white outside and dusty rose inside, while the "lips" are striped with rose-purple. Nun's orchid is available from greenhouses, but mine started as a division I got from Senior Photographer Van Chaplin. It quickly grew into a beautiful plant I keep by my bedroom window. Last week, Van told me his nun's orchid had died, and he asked if I would give him a division of mine. Sorry, man, I'd like to help, but that's just not my habit. —STEVE BENDER

TIPS

■ **Forcing branches**—Forsythia, quince, spirea, and redbud will bloom indoors with a little help. Choose stems with flowerbuds that have begun to swell. Cut the stems at an angle, and place in a container of water. Once indoors, recut the stems, and place them in tepid water. Place the container in a cool spot with indirect light, and watch the blooms begin.

■ **Horticultural oil**—Apply a dormant oil, such as SunSpray, to fruit and nut trees to combat scale and other pests. Horticultural oils are also useful for controlling scale insects on camellias, hollies, citrus, and other ornamentals. Be sure to direct spray to the undersides of foliage on evergreen plants. For best results, complete coverage is recommended. Dormant oils should be applied before spring growth begins.

■ **Lawns**—A little work now can save you a lot of work later. Spot-control weeds in dormant warm-season lawns by hand pulling or applying a broadleaf weed control such as Weed-B-Gon or Weed-Stop. To prevent crabgrass seeds from finding a happy home in your lawn, apply a granular crabgrass preventer such as Scotts Halts or Sta-Green Crab-Ex.

■ **Testing soil**—Alkaline soils, which have a high pH, can cause problems in growing many types of plants. If you are having trouble, test your soil to determine the pH. You may need to use different plants.

■ **Watering**—During prolonged dry or windy conditions, monitor moisture of shrubs and trees, especially evergreens. Replenish mulches to reduce water loss. Wrap trunks of newly set out trees to protect them from rotating cycles of freezing and thawing.

■ **Citrus**—In Florida, remove or shorten limbs that pose problems for maintenance activities. Cut all shoots or suckers that arise from below the graft, as these will be nonproductive limbs.

PLANT

■ **Vegetables**—In the Lower South, start setting out transplants of cabbage, broccoli, cauliflower, and onion sets. You can continue sowing seeds of spinach and lettuce. In the Middle, Lower, and Coastal South, sow English peas or sugar snap peas in your garden. Plant seeds now while the weather is cool to give them time to grow, flower, and set seed before the weather turns too hot. (Try 'Maestro' English peas and 'Super Sugar Snap' peas.) In the Lower and Coastal South, plant cool-weather vegetables.

Camellias

Continue to choose common camellias *(Camellia japonica)* while they are in bloom. Many colors and flower shapes are available, from singles to peony forms with many slender petals and more formal types such as 'Kramer's Supreme,' 'Pink Perfection,' and 'Purple Dawn.' They do best in partially shaded areas with acid soil. If you don't

have those conditions, use camellias in containers on porches and other sheltered areas. Select pots that are 18 inches in diameter or larger, and fill with soil that is highly organic. Sphagnum peat moss combined with compost and a small amount of coarse sand makes a good mixture. Keep the soil evenly moist, and turn the container periodically so plants grow symmetrically.

Roses

Now is the ideal time to set out bare-root or container-grown roses. For landscape impact, choose a few climbing roses placed to accent fences, walls, arbors, or trellises. Outstanding choices include antiques such as 'Cl Souvenir de La Malmaison' (pink), 'Reve d'Or' (yellow), 'Cl Cramoisi Supérieur' (red), and 'Cl Old Blush' (pink). Select a sunny location with room for the canes to spread at least 10 to 12 feet. Prepare the soil by mixing organic material, such as compost, peat, or composted pine bark, in a hole 18 inches deep and across. Water well at planting, and mulch to protect against cold and drying winter winds.

■ **Annuals**—In Florida, set out snapdragons, petunias, dianthus, alyssum, or calendulas for early-spring color. Wait until late March to plant flowers that are sensitive to the cold, such as impatiens. The average last-frost date is around mid-March.

■ **Flowering trees**—In Florida, plant in sunny areas to brighten late-winter days. Taiwan flowering cherries, saucer magnolias, redbuds, and Japanese maples will bloom in February. Add Chickasaw and American plum, crabapple, dogwood, and fringe tree *(Chionanthus virginicus)* to extend the flowering period into late March. After planting, use an organic mulch, and water every other day for six to eight weeks. Then water only twice a week.

■ **Spring color**—In Texas, plant pansies, violas, petunias, snapdragons, stock, alyssum, and hollyhocks. Combine these with soon-to-bloom flowering bulbs to extend seasonal color. Arrange in elongated or teardrop masses of compatible colors. Keep in mind the potential size and spread of individual plants as they mature. Before planting, spade in 3 to 5 inches of compost or other organic material, and broadcast 3 to 5 pounds of balanced, slow-release fertilizer per 100 square feet of bed.

PRUNE

■ **Evergreen shrubs**—Evergreen shrubs, such as hollies or wax myrtles, should be pruned as needed. Wait until after bloom for spring-flowering shrubs such as azaleas.

■ **Liriope and mondo grass**—Now is a great time to trim foliage before new leaves emerge. Cut small plantings by hand; for larger ones, use your lawnmower with the blade set at $2^{1}/_{2}$ to 3 inches high. Be careful not to cut too short, as you may damage the new growth. You can check the height of the new growth by gently pulling apart existing leaves near the base of the plant.

liriope

■ **Roses**—In Texas, mid-month is the ideal time to prune everblooming shrub roses everywhere except the Panhandle, where this should be done in late March. Begin by removing dead or weak wood. Shorten healthy canes to 18 to 24 inches, and remove any crossing limbs. Make cuts at a 45-degree angle above outwardly facing leaf buds. Maintain a rounded or natural shape for an informal effect. Prune shrub roses and vigorous climbers such as 'New Dawn' and 'Lady Banks's' after their spring display.

Easy Angel-Wing *Begonias*

These colorful houseplants will lift your spirits during the cold months of winter.

When the chilling winds of the season are knocking on your door, invite the simple beauty of angel-wing begonias into your home. Handed down and cared for by many generations of gardeners, these true pass-alongs will charm you with their grace and cheer you with their radiant leaves and flowers.

Someone To Watch Over Me

JoAnn Breland, a horticulturist, treasures her collection of angel-wing begonias. When she was growing up in South Georgia, she helped her mother care for the ones that grew out on their porch. She says, "Now, when I take care of them, it's as if she is still around. Angel-wing begonias help me stay connected with my mama. I love the foliage, whether the plant is blooming or not."

So Many Begonias, So Little Time

There are numerous selections of angel-wings. They are also known as cane-type begonias, because their stems grow tall and have bamboo-like joints. They vary in size and have different combinations of foliage and flower colors. Leaves, shaped like angels' wings, appear in greens, maroons, and silvers. Richly veined or covered with spots, they can be striking—each a tiny tapestry of color. As varied as the leaves, flowers cascade in pinks, whites, reds, and oranges. Some are everblooming, while others flower from spring through autumn. "In winter, when there's not much in bloom, there are

left: 'My Special Angel' adds a splash of color to a living room.
right: 'Bubbles,' 'Corliss Engle,' and 'Tom Ment' are everblooming selections that offer flowers all year.

BY GENE B. BUSSELL / PHOTOGRAPHY VAN CHAPLIN / STYLING LISA POWELL

top, left: The silver spots in the leaves of 'Good 'n' Plenty' complement the pearls along the edge of the picture frame.
above, right: 'Kismet' is a miniature with silver foliage. The tin bucket on the left repeats the color in the leaves.
above, left: 'Polka Dot' (*Begonia maculata* 'Wightii') may seem like an angel, but it is actually classified as a fibrous begonia.

the angel-wings. When you're having a bad day, seeing the colorful foliage just makes you feel better," JoAnn says. These angels of winter will brighten icy months.

Feet of Clay

Steadfast plants, angel-wing begonias thrive in clay pots and bright, indirect light. They are especially easy to grow and prefer to be kept slightly dry. Use a soil mix that is rich in organic matter, contains some perlite, and is very well drained. Be sure not to overwater, as this can cause leaf drop. Water only when the soil is dry to the touch, and use a balanced liquid fertilizer. Inside, avoid placing plants near cold or warm drafts. In the early spring, prune back older canes to two leaf joints, and let them spend the season outside in light shade. The cuttings can then be rooted easily in water or potting soil. Bring them back inside in fall when the temperature drops into the 50s.

Keep them in their clay pots when you bring them indoors, and use decorative plates as saucers. Relate the colors of the saucers to the colors of the leaves to tie everything together. The clay pots serve a practical purpose as well; the weight of the terra-cotta helps keep larger growing selections such as 'Sophie Cecile' and 'Cracklin' Rosie' from toppling over.

Let your angels take flight by passing a few along to friends. With their polka dots, stripes, and spots, the begonias will become a joy for others to behold. Remember, everyone needs an angel-wing. ◆

ANGEL-WING BEGONIAS

NAME	FLOWERS	LEAVES
'Sophie Cecile'	rose-pink	green with silver spots, underside maroon
'Orange Rubra'	orange	light green with silver spots
'Cracklin' Rosie'	pink	dark green with pink spots, underside maroon
'Good 'n Plenty'	white-pink	dark green with silver spots, underside maroon
'My Special Angel'	pink	green with silver spots
'Tom Ment'	coral-pink	green with silver spots
'Mandarin Orange'	orange	dark green with white spots, underside maroon
'Corliss Engle'	salmon	dark green with silver spots
'Esther Albertine'	pale pink	apple green with white spots

Fragrance and Flowers

When winter daphne blooms, you know spring is in the air.

This shrub has a neat, rounded form and grows 3 to 4 feet high. White or pink waxy blossoms appear in showy clusters during late winter. The spicy-sweet fragrance of winter daphne is legendary. Plant it near sitting areas, paths, and entryways so you can enjoy the scent.

"If only they made an ice cream that tasted like those blooms smell." That's the best description I've ever heard of winter daphne's intoxicating fragrance. Sometimes the perfume seems honey-sweet, sometimes citrusy, and other times spicy like cloves. But whatever version shows up that day, your mouth waters just the same.

Native to China, winter daphne *(Daphne odora)* forms a dense, tidy mound 3 to 4 feet high and wide. Its handsome evergreen foliage consists of slender, glossy leaves about 3 inches long. While the straight species has solid green leaves, variegated selections sport leaves edged in creamy white or yellow. Boutonniere-size clusters of small, waxy flowers appear atop the foliage for several weeks in late winter, at about the same time that camellias bloom. The flowers are pink in bud, then open to either white or pale pink. So powerful is the scent that you'll often smell a daphne in bloom well before you see it.

If it drives you nuts to constantly battle rank and unruly shrubs, you'll love this one. Well-behaved, slow-growing, and refined, it seldom needs pruning. Take advantage of the fragrance by planting it near sitting areas, entryways, porches, and paths. Or use it in foundation plantings and rock gardens. Selections include 'Alba' (green foliage and white flowers), 'Aureo-Marginata' (yellow-edged leaves and blush white flowers), and 'Leucanthe' (green foliage and light pink flowers).

Great fragrance, good foliage, nice behavior—with all this going for it, you may wonder why more people don't plant winter daphne. The answer is that it is fickle, to say the least, and it has a nasty habit of dying on you just as you've decided you can't live without it (you can, but it's hard). What's the secret to its long-term survival? Louise Wrinkle of Birmingham, who owns the beautiful daphne you see above, says, "I think it needs absolutely the sharpest drainage you can give it." She grows hers on a raised garden terrace that contains mostly limestone gravel. She doesn't water or fertilize it. Although daphne will grow in acid soil, the use of limestone in this case indicates that neutral to slightly alkaline soil may be even better.

You don't have to plant it atop a terrace or raised bed. Instead, select a slightly sloping spot, where excess water quickly runs off. Dig a hole as deep as the root ball, but three times as wide. Discard any clay. Place the root ball in the hole so that the top inch sticks above the soil surface, and then fill in around it with a mixture of half topsoil and half pine bark or gravel. Water well, and cover the root ball with mulch. STEVE BENDER

WINTER DAPHNE
At a Glance

Size: 3 to 4 feet high and wide
Light: light shade, especially at midday
Soil: slightly acid to slightly alkaline; no clay; excellent drainage
Water: only during periods of extended drought
Fertilizer: seldom needed
Pruning: rarely needed
Range: Middle, Lower, and Coastal South (hardy to 5 degrees)

PHOTOGRAPHS: ALLEN ROKACH / STYLING: ROSE NGUYEN

Add water to these dehydrated pellets, and you'll have an easy way to plant seeds.

PHOTOGRAPHS: WILLIAM DICKEY

After planting, cover the damp pellets with plastic wrap to speed germination.

As seeds begin to grow, keep the pellets slightly moist and in bright light.

Transplant seedlings to larger pots when roots emerge from the Jiffy Pellets.

Start Seeds Now

The February gardener is a restless soul, with weather teasing the planter's spirit. One day it's chilly; the next it's solicitously springlike. Then, without a conscience, cool weather sneaks back. One way to soothe the psyche is the simple task of starting seeds.

If cold weather is still a possibility in your area, check the calendar and plan to plant about six weeks before your last frost date. Seedlings tend to grow rapidly within this time frame and soon reach the right stage for moving into the garden. Check out seed displays in stores, and peruse catalogs for the selections you want to try. The seasoned gardener might look for an exciting new introduction, while the novice can have grand success with something simple, such as morning glories or tomatoes. I always grow a moonflower crop for garden gifting—another reason to start your seeds indoors.

In a Jiffy

An easy, neat, and tidy way to start seeds is in Jiffy Pellets. These Oreo cookie-size, dehydrated brown wafers are a gardening marvel. Place them in a shallow dish, sides not touching, and moisten each one. Within 30 minutes they'll grow into soft, moist planting containers ready to harbor treasured seeds. If you require instant success, growing the Jiffy Pellets provides immediate confidence.

Gently push one or two seeds into each container, within the preformed planting hole. Nudge the seeds just below the soil's surface, using your fingertip or a dull pencil. Water them lightly, and cover the dish with plastic wrap to retain moisture.

Place the dish in bright light, out of direct sun. Germination time varies with each type of seed. Consult the package for information on when to expect signs of life. As the first nodding heads emerge, remove the plastic wrap to increase air circulation. If only a portion of the seedlings have sprouted, fold back the wrapper, continuing to cover the late arrivals.

Without the wrap, Jiffy Pellets dry out quickly. Check moisture daily, keeping the seedlings slightly damp. Put the dish in morning sun, turning it occasionally so stems grow straight.

Up and Out

As each plant matures, roots emerge from the pellet's bottom. Gather small clay or plastic pots, no larger than 4 inches across, and some moist potting mix. Fill each container half full with soil, place a seedling in each, and then surround the Jiffy Pellet with additional potting medium. If you've started a climber, such as a moonflower, push a small stake into the vessel for support. Place the pots in morning sun, and keep them damp. When frost danger has passed, transplant them into the garden.

ELLEN RUOFF RILEY

A Courtyard To Celebrate

This backyard is more than just eye candy. It's fun and functional year-round.

With many areas to explore, this courtyard's modest dimensions don't feel limiting.

Whenever friends gather at Van and Carolyn Rose Temple's home, the party always seems to drift out into the back garden. Although most guests probably don't give much thought to what draws them into the courtyard, the Temples know that it's no accident. The inviting space was actually the calculated plan of landscape architects Rick Griffin and Clifton Egger of Jackson, Mississippi.

Van and Carolyn Rose had purchased their home nearly 10 years earlier, but they hadn't gotten around to landscaping the backyard. When they finally decided to do something about the narrow 112- x 30-foot space, one of their first requirements was that the area lend itself to outdoor entertaining. They didn't envision theme park-size crowds. They simply desired cozy spaces to gather with their circle of friends. "They also wanted to make it inviting no matter what the season," Rick says.

Rooms To Roam

"Space constraints were a concern, but, working with Rick, we came to understand that a small space can be breathtaking with a little creativity," Van says. Although the original yard was basically flat, Rick created some ups and downs for more interest. "Different levels add to the room effect," Carolyn Rose says. "For about four months they pushed dirt this way, and then for the next four they pushed it the other way," she jokes. Then Rick designed several rooms that provide gathering spaces for friends or quiet niches for the couple.

Order in the Courtyard

With so much going on in the small space—paths, plants, a pergola, a fountain, a fire pit, and a summer house, Rick and Clifton wanted the design to have some element that established order. "We needed to tie it all together," Rick explains. "We used a strong axis down the center from the entrance of the summer house to the gate at the other end of the yard. Crossing in the other direction, there's another axis coming off the back porch and going through the pergola. I love to use sculptures as focal points, so we placed a big urn at the end of the pergola."

Material World

Another subtle element that makes the courtyard come together is the variety of materials Rick and Clifton selected. To liven up the plain stucco home, they used brick, concrete, stucco, wood, and iron in the courtyard, but they were careful not to overdo it. "Too much wood is not good, and too much iron is not good. The same goes for brick, concrete, and anything else," Rick cautions. "If someone has a brick home, they might first think they want a brick patio, until I explain you have to balance your materials."

For added interest, Rick and Clifton chose a varied palette of plants. Most of the trees, shrubs, and ground covers are evergreen, and those that aren't, such as oakleaf hydrangeas, have textured bark for interest in

Unique garden structures connected by spacious paths and an abundance of evergreens make this courtyard perfect for entertaining in any season.

winter. Tree-form evergreen shrubs such as yaupons, yews, privets, and Hollywood junipers help break up what would have been an 8-foot-high wall surrounding the backyard.

Because Jackson rests comfortably in the mild Lower South, even the Temples' winter parties are often held out in the garden. But Van and Carolyn Rose don't require a special occasion to host a get-together. Whenever good friends gather within the confines of their alluring new garden, there is cause for celebration any day of the year.　GLENN R. DINELLA

labor
of love

The flowers that fill this South Carolina garden reflect the enduring care of three generations of family and friends.

When Southerners set plants in the ground, they bury more than just roots. Memories, wisdom, laughter, love, gossip, and advice also go into the hole, to reappear another day and a galaxy of days thereafter.

So it is at a garden in Ridge Spring, South Carolina, dotingly cared for by Emily Lide Wheeler and her mother, Eulee. On this cool, clear February morning, they admire Lenten roses, a gift from their friend Peggy Garvin. As the season goes on, they'll witness the blossoming of Hattie Watson's magic lilies, Becky Beck's ginger lilies, Winkie Hartley's spider lilies, and Ron Porter's grandmother's purple phlox. "The garden is a collection of our friends," says Emily, "and I see each and every one of them in everything blooming out there."

Emily represents the third generation of Wheeler women to work

in this garden. The first, Emily Noterman Wheeler, arrived here with her family in 1930. The damming of the Saluda River to create Lake Murray, northwest of Columbia, had flooded their farm, forcing them to relocate. Fortunately, the waters spared the old house and its immediate surroundings, enabling "Mrs. Wheeler" (as the younger Emily called her) to move many of her treasured plants to the new house in Ridge Spring. "Now I can look out and see the very same crepe myrtles, magnolias, nandinas, and spireas she had at her place," says Emily. "It means a lot to know they were part of her original stock."

By the 1950s, Eulee Wheeler, the younger Emily's mother, had taken the reins of the garden. Eulee, now well into her eighties, truly has a way

left: Chinese snowball *(Viburnum macrocephalum)* is a favorite old shrub. Its white pom-poms cascade over azaleas in early spring. **top:** The Wheeler garden peaks with the blooming of jonquils, dogwoods, azaleas, and viburnums. **above:** Emily (left), Eulee (center), and Emily's niece Anne hold daffodils collected from the yard.

with plants, but a bigger garden didn't come easily. For one thing, money was tight. "I remember as a child going with Mother up to Miss Mitchell's in Johnston to buy an iris for 50 cents. That was big money," recalls Emily. For another, there weren't big nurseries and home centers selling plants like there are today. Eulee relied on

BY STEVE BENDER / PHOTOGRAPHY ALLEN ROKACH

above: Eulee considers Lenten roses *(Helleborus orientalis)*—seen here blooming at the foot of azaleas—the garden's most important plants.

mail-order catalogs, "wish books," and shared plants from neighbors to obtain the many camellias, althaeas, bearded iris, and daylilies that put on a glorious show even to this day. Each spring, Eulee dug clumps of jonquils growing wild along the roadside and brought them home to multiply.

A Winning Combination

The gardening bug bit the younger Emily during the mid-1980s, and she's been tending the garden ever since. She and Eulee won the very first daylily competition they ever entered and then proceeded to take blue ribbons for bearded iris all over the state. "It got so that the other contestants hated to see us walk through the doors," Emily states matter-of-factly. Now the bug has also bitten her niece Anne Wheeler Jordan.

Emily added azaleas, rhododendrons, viburnums, and other plants to the garden, all with the goal of having something pretty to look at in every month of the year. And she continued Eulee's tradition of transplanting homeless jonquils to a garden that

needed them. Lafonde Lindler's cow pasture, about 10 miles up the road, proved to be a gold mine. He had razed an old home site to create more pasture and, in doing so, scattered its Campernelle jonquils *(Narcissus odorus)* all over the field. The cows would not eat the bulbs, but they happily fertilized them, resulting in a sea of thriving jonquils Lafonde didn't want. "He said to me, 'Honey, you come and get every one of 'em,'" recalls Emily. "Well, I've been digging them for seven years, and I know I'll never get them all."

There's a trick to successfully moving jonquils in bloom, claims Emily. Use a long trenching shovel to trench around the clump. Then dig deep enough beneath the clump so that it all comes up in one piece without any damage to the bulbs and roots. "My brother and I once dug a clump so big we couldn't even lift it together," she says. "We had to *roll* it to the car."

As the Wheelers' garden acquires shared plants, it continues to dispense them. "Everybody who comes here usually walks out with a sackful of this or that," remarks Emily cheerfully. "Iris is a real favorite." Some folks even help themselves. Emily once discovered a note that read, "I came. I saw. I coveted. And I swiped one of your plants." Emily didn't miss it. To her, it was simply placed in the care of another.

The Garden's Lesson

This is what gardens like Emily's teach. More than just dressing up the countryside, they connect mother and daughter, friend and stranger, people we've forgotten and people we can't forget. These points hit home as I listened to Emily describe her friendship with Orene Stroud Horton. Shortly after Orene came to write for *Southern Living*, she was diagnosed with cancer. Throughout her long, trying battle, Orene remained purposeful, inquisitive, and upbeat, always looking for the next great garden. She recently passed away.

This story I'm writing was to have been her next great garden.

Emily told me that not long before Orene's death, the two of them had competed at a camellia show; Orene's stunning sasanqua had taken first prize. Afterward, Orene did something that was so characteristic of her—something any other gardener would have done. She pressed to the ground a lower branch of that sasanqua to root a piece of it for Emily's garden.

"I can't wait to get it," says Emily, "because if there's one plant that really says Orene, it's that sasanqua."

below: Over the years, Eulee and Emily dug hundreds of jonquils growing wild and planted them in islands and drifts.
below, left: The trick to moving jonquils in bloom is to dig the clump without damaging the bulbs or roots.
right: *Narcissus jonquilla*

*a container brimming of blue salvia
and purple aster (See page 45.)*

March

Editor's Notebook

Okay, here's a question that could quite possibly make the difference between enjoying the rest of your life or feeling like you've gone to heaven only to discover they let in lawyers. What do you do if your daffodils are in full bloom and a freeze is expected later that night? Well, if you have the IQ of a hamster, you quickly forget about it and go to bed. The next morning, you discover crumpled daffodils that will never stand tall again. What happened is that when the air temperature falls to about 28 degrees or lower, water inside the cells of the stems freezes, expands, and explodes them. Any daffodil in bloom or in bud is subject to such disaster. Suitably chastened, you must now resolve never to repeat this horrifying mistake. The next time a freeze threatens to cut your daffodils off at the legs, beat it to the punch. Cut blooming or budded daffodils that night, stick them in water, and bring them inside. You'll get to enjoy spring up close, and so will that hamster.

—STEVE BENDER

Azaleas

They're blooming now, making it a great time to select and add them to your garden. For the best results, plant in masses of one color. Azaleas like acid soil that is moist and well-drained. They also prefer high, filtered shade like that under pine trees. Mulch with pine needles, pine bark, or similar material to protect their fine, fibrous roots. Low-growing evergreen selections include 'Gumpo' (1 foot or less), medium-growing Kurume Hybrids (2 to 4 feet), or large-growing Indica Hybrids (4 to 8 feet). Add deciduous natives for fragrance and color.

TIPS

- **Clay soils**—Use gypsum to help break up compacted soils. It will make the particles of clay clump together, opening up spaces for water to penetrate and allowing easier growth for roots.
- **Lawns**—Plugs, sold in trays at nurseries, can be used to fill in damaged areas.
- **Perennials**—Divide and reset crowded bloomers, such as chrysanthemums, Shasta daisies, and black-eyed Susans. Replant in prepared beds that have rich, well-drained soil and receive at least six hours of sun daily.

PLANT

- **Figs**—Now is a good time to plant a fig *(Ficus carica)*. These fast-growing plants will mature into large shrubs. They can also be grown in containers or trained as espaliers. Though not particular about soil, they do prefer full sun. Great selections include 'Brown Turkey,' 'Alma,' and 'LSU Purple.'

mint

- **Herbs**—Plant thyme, mint, and oregano now so they can get a good start for the season. Wait till danger of frost has passed before planting dill, fennel, and basil.
- **Star magnolia**—Add flowers and fragrance to your garden with *Magnolia stellata*. This small deciduous tree provides dependable bloom and makes a great specimen. Place near pathways or entry points in your landscape so you can fully appreciate the fragrance. Reliable selections include 'Royal Star,' 'Pink Stardust,' and 'Waterlily.'

lantana

- **Trees and shrubs**—Large-growing trees should be planted no closer than 15 to 20 feet from a structure. Small-growing types, such as crepe myrtles and redbuds, can be set as close as 3 to 5 feet. Prepare planting holes about twice as wide as the root ball but no deeper than the level at which the tree grew in its container. Replace the fill area with original soil, and then mulch with several inches of bark, hay, pine needles, or similar material. Water well, and stake.

- **Ornamental grasses**—In Florida, use large ones, including maiden grass *(Miscanthus sinensis)*, as corner plantings in beds; plant singly or in clumps of three. Plant smaller ones, such as purple muhly grass, in masses of at least three. Place ornamental grasses in areas that receive sun for most of the day.

magnolia

- **Warm-weather flowers**—In Florida, by the 15th of the month, the probability of a freeze is low. Set out warm-weather flowers such as angelonia, gomphrena, ageratum, impatiens, melampodium, begonia, coleus, wishbone flower, marigold, salvia, lantana, cleome, and zinnia.

New Guinea Impatiens

- **Perennials**—Central, East, and South Texas gardeners can set out daylilies, purple coneflowers, autumn sage, 'Indigo Spires' salvia, coreopsis, garden mums, verbenas, lantana, ruellias, and gaura. Keep in mind the mature size of the plants as you set them out.

PRUNE

- **Everblooming roses**—Prune existing canes to between 18 and 24 inches, and remove any dead or weak wood, leaving three to five healthy canes. Climbers such as 'Don Juan,' 'Cl. Peace,' and 'New Dawn' should be secured horizontally to trellises or other supports when possible to encourage flowering. Wait until after they bloom in spring to prune climbing roses.

- **Shrubs**—Prune deciduous shrubs such as spirea, quince, and forsythia once they finish blooming.

FERTILIZE

- **Lawns**—Wait to fertilize warm-season lawns, such as Zoysia, Bermuda, and St. Augustine, until after they turn green. If you have centipede, use a product that contains iron and is specially formulated for that type of grass. Fertilize cool-season lawns, such as Kentucky bluegrass, tall fescue, and perennial ryegrass. Feed with a slow-release, high-nitrogen fertilizer, such as 29-3-4.

- **Roses**—Feed roses monthly with a light fertilizer such as Lesco 15-0-15 or Scotts 18-9-18 All-Purpose Plant Food. To control black spot, spray with Immunox fungicide. For thrips or aphids, use Immunox Plus Insect + Disease Control.

- **Shrubs and small trees**—In Florida, use a fertilizer such as Lesco 15-0-15 or Scotts 18-9-18 All-Purpose Plant Food at a rate of no more than 2 teaspoons per foot of plant height. Spread over a 3-x 3-foot area.

March notes:

Tip of the Month

I used a file to put a sharp edge on one side of my garden trowel. Now it does great double duty—either for digging or for chopping small roots and tough weeds.

VERN DAILEY
WILLS POINT, TEXAS

BY STEVE BENDER
PHOTOGRAPHY GARY CLARK
STYLING ROSE NGUYEN

March Madness

Feeling the urge to plant? Here's what to do now
to guarantee surefire spring success.

Meet my next-door neighbors, the Pokeweed family, who just moved down from their previous digs in Fish Emulsion, Tennessee. That's Ficus Pokeweed on the right; his radiant wife, Honeydew, in the center; and their two lovely children, Humus and Tansy. This delightful, if somewhat zany, group just can't wait for spring. At the first sight of all the flower and vegetable transplants overflowing greenhouse benches, they pursue the only logical course. They raid the kids' college fund to buy as many annuals, perennials, shrubs, and supplies as can be crammed into a rusted minivan without violating the laws of physics.

After zooming home at Mach 1.2, they set out transplants in neat little rows, heedless of an oncoming cold front. Upon waking the next morning to find that frost has turned their transplants into disgusting goop resembling strained peas, they vow never to be so foolish again and promptly invest in a pyramid scheme.

The Pokeweeds may be a bit fargone, but there's a little of them in most of us. We have a pretty good idea of when it's finally safe to set out tender plants, but we're also seduced by the combination of bright flowers begging to be bought and sunny, unseasonably mild weather. So we temporarily jettison our common sense and hope we don't pay for it later.

left: It's hard to know where to stop when spring fever strikes. Some folks are fit to be tied.

PLANT NOW

broccoli	petunia
cabbage	seed potatoes
English pea	snapdragon
kale	spinach
lettuce	sweet William
onion sets	viola
pansy	

PLANT LATER

ageratum	impatiens
begonia	marigold
caladium	pentas
celosia	pepper
coleus	tomato
eggplant	zinnia

If you're unsure which transplants can be planted now and take a light frost and which ones need to wait until the danger of frost has passed, refer to the lists above. But don't go nuts if you've already set out tender plants and hear that a frost is coming. There are easy ways to provide temporary protection. You can place an empty flowerpot over a plant for the night. (Make sure it's big enough to fit over the plant without squashing it.) A plastic milk jug with the bottom cut out will do the same job. Or drape plants with a floating row cover or lightweight shade cloth. Covering plants with pots or jugs will ward off a light frost, while the use of a row cover or shade cloth should protect plants subjected to temperatures as cold as 27 or 28 degrees.

Other Early-Spring Chores

Of course, for many folks in the Coastal and Tropical South, frost is no longer a concern. That leaves time for plenty of gardening activities that they and other Southerners should pursue this month.

■ **Planting trees and shrubs**—March is a great time. The weather is cool, and there's usually plenty of rain, so root systems can grow without being stressed.

■ **Pruning**—Now is the time to prune summer-flowering trees and shrubs, such as crepe myrtle, Rose-of-Sharon *(shrub althaea)*, chaste tree, butterfly bush, gardenia, cape plumbago, and hibiscus. Remove dead, diseased, or spindly growth. You can also prune most shade trees except for maple and birch. (You should wait until summer for them.)

■ **Fertilizing lawns and seeding or sodding**—Do this for cool-season lawns, such as Kentucky bluegrass, tall fescue, and perennial ryegrass. Get it done now before hot weather.

■ **Preparing soil**—As soon as it is dry enough to work without getting muddy, use a garden fork or tiller to loosen the soil of an empty bed to a depth of about a foot. Work in lots of organic matter, such as garden compost, chopped leaves, composted manure, ground bark, and sphagnum peat moss. Add any necessary lime, sulfur, or other nutrients as indicated by a soil test. If your bed is already planted with perennials, spread a thick layer of compost or chopped leaves around plants. ◆

Spring Lace

A profusion of blooms brings this shrub's branches to life.

Billowy, white clouds of bridal wreath spirea rise from the soil, creating fluffy mounds across the Southern landscape. This shrub's long, arching branches appear lifeless in the cooler months. By late winter or early spring, a few warm days force pearly white buds to swell on the woody stems. Then, like magic, the shrub is clothed in delicate lace, gracing the garden like a well-dressed bride. This old-fashioned shrub is dependable and dedicated, returning to the garden faithfully each year.

Bridal wreath (*Spiraea prunifolia* 'Plena') is one of the first shrubs to flower in the spring along with forsythia and quince. Its blooms are small yet numerous. Flowers appear by the thousands before foliage leafs out. The tiny clustered rosettes of pure white petals line the whiplike stems, making the branches great for cutting and using in arrangements.

This plant will look showy for several weeks until the tiny blooms shatter and dust the garden in white. As the flowers fade, new foliage begins to cover the naked stems. The small rounded green leaves give the shrub a fine-textured appearance from spring through summer. In fall, foliage often turns red before dropping off.

Although spirea looks delicate, it's extremely durable and long-lived. It performs best in rich, well-drained soil but will tolerate poor soils. Once a plant is established in the landscape, it requires little water. The more sun spirea receives, the more it blooms; this shrub will grow in shade, but blooms will be sparse.

Bridal wreath needs space to thrive. Old, established plants are rangy; growing 6 to 8 feet tall and wide. Its mounding form is great for creating a broad hedge. Although not an evergreen, its numerous branches create impenetrable thickets, so it can be used as a screen to hide undesirable views. Spirea can also be planted on slopes to sprawl across a difficult-to-landscape hillside. It is usually planted en masse, but a single shrub may be placed on the back side of a flower border for early-season blooms.

Spirea benefits from an evergreen backdrop. When planted in front of hemlocks, Leyland cypress, Southern magnolias, or broad-leaved hollies, they become more visible and showy. Their fine, wispy texture stands out against the dark green background.

Don't forget this old-fashioned shrub. It's extremely easy to grow and will fill the garden each year with its elegant, lacy white blooms.

CHARLIE THIGPEN

SPIREA

At a Glance

Size: 6 to 8 feet tall and wide
Range: Upper, Middle, and Lower South; performs best in Upper and Middle South
Light: better in a sunny to partially sunny location
Soil: grows best in fertile, well-drained soil, but will tolerate many poor soils
Flowers: Numerous small white blooms arrive in late winter or early spring on leafless stems.
Pruning: Cut one-third of the tallest woody canes to the ground in spring after bloom. This will keep shrubs full and bushy with new growth.

PHOTOGRAPHS: SYLVIA MARTIN

PHOTOGRAPH: JEAN ALLSOPP

left: Spirea blooms are small but plentiful. Each flower has swirled white petals that form tiny rosettes along cinnamon-colored stems.

A Fence With Rustic Charm

This handsome wooden fence wraps the backyard and keeps the dogs in.

PHOTOGRAPHS: VAN CHAPLIN

above: The new fence and gate look right at home in this wooded side yard.
above, right photos: A weight-and-pulley system automatically closes the gate. For the weight, we used a metal pot filled with concrete.

After 10 years of thinking my two dogs were full-blooded English setters, I found out they had a little bit of Houdini in them. My furry friends, Mac and Spud, turned into escape artists and began to disappear from the backyard. The old fence was only 4 feet tall and had developed a few low spots, making it easy for the dogs to jump over. The time had come to put up a new one.

I decided it had to be at least 6 feet tall to prevent the dogs from getting out. The taller fence would also create a little privacy. Plus, I wanted it to have a rustic look to match the tree-covered setting.

Many houses in our neighborhood have split-rail fences wrapping their lots. I thought it might be neat to buy cedar split rails and attach them vertically instead of horizontally. The rough-cut cedar rails have lots of knots, and their irregular look adds character to any yard. Here's how to install this simple fence.

Place pressure-treated 4 x 4s in concrete to make sturdy and long-lasting posts. Position two posts 3 feet apart for the gate. That opening is wide enough to allow a garden cart or wheelbarrow to maneuver through it, yet keeps the gate easy to operate. Then space the rest of the posts 7½ feet apart.

Once the concrete hardens and all the posts are secure, stretch 6-foot-tall wire fencing, and nail it to the posts. Attaching fencing to posts is a two-person job, unless you have a come-a-long (handheld winch puller) to help pull and hold the fence in place. Use U-shaped nails to tack the wire to the posts.

Attach 1 x 6 pressure-treated boards horizontally to the top and bottom of each post with wood screws to complete the framework.

Add the cedar split rails to the 1 x 6s with wood screws. Space the cedar strips 1 foot apart on center. Cedar rails are available at many hardware stores and home centers. They usually come in 10-foot lengths. Cut them into 6-foot pieces with a saw.

Don't waste any scrap cedar; use it to top the small arbor over the gate. Cut 2 x 4s at a 45-degree angle, and nail them to the top of the gateposts to frame the pitched arbor. Then nail the cedar sections to the 2 x 4s. To tie it all together, tack a salvaged piece of copper to the front of the arbor. An arched gate, built of 1 x 6s and Z-braced on the back side with 2 x 4s, makes a nice entry point. Hang the wooden gate with heavy-duty hinges.

Use a steel cable, a large eye-screw, an S-hook, and a pulley to make a homemade weight to close the gate automatically behind you. Our weight is an old tin pot filled with concrete.

After the construction is over, you can complete the project with whatever detailing you wish. Inexpensive terra-cotta pots would make great finials to top the 4 x 4 posts and give a finished look.

Note: When purchasing pressure-treated lumber, check the label on the wood to see if it was treated with arsenic, which can contaminate soil. If this concerns you, select another wood such as cedar or redwood that is not treated with arsenic. Look in the marketplace in the near future for lumber not treated with arsenic.

CHARLIE THIGPEN

Fun Veggies, Unique Look

They might seem a little different, but they have great flavor
and add a splash of color to the garden.

If you're getting tired of growing the same old produce year after year, it may be time for a change of pace. As an alternative, you can nurture vegetables that you don't see every day at the supermarket. Last summer, in a relatively small garden, we grew red okra, purple bell peppers, white eggplants, and 20-inch-long asparagus beans.

Most Southerners love to gobble up okra that's been dipped in batter and fried till golden brown and crunchy. And nothing in the world is better than fresh okra. The unusual colors of red or burgundy okra may surprise you, but the plants produce excellent yields of the delectable pods. They stay tender even when they reach 6 to 8 inches long. Most of the green pod selections must be harvested when they are 3 to 5 inches long. Once cooked, the red okra will turn green.

Besides the colorful pods that they produce, red okra also creates large green foliage with red veins. Even the stems of this distinctive plant are burgundy. Beautiful, soft yellow, hibiscus-like flowers make this okra more than worthy of any flower border.

A Rainbow of Options

Today's gardener can grow bell peppers in a wide assortment of colors. They come in yellow, green, orange, red, and purple. These purple bells, aptly named 'Purple Beauty,' are so dark, they almost appear to be black. Their flavor isn't as strong as that of the more familiar green bell peppers. Because of their mild, sweet taste and unusual look, these vegetables will make a colorful addition to any summer salad.

White eggplants hanging on 3-foot-tall plants are guaranteed to turn heads. 'Cloud Nine' is a selection that's never bitter, so you won't have to soak it in salt water before cooking. The plant's fruit is 6 to 7 inches long and about 3 inches wide. White eggplants are easy to grow and will produce large yields. Because the fruit is so heavy, you will need to support the plants with 3- or 4-foot-long wooden stakes or metal rebar. Put the stakes in at planting time, and then secure the stems as they mature.

Asparagus beans produce super-long, thin, tender green pods. They are sometimes called yard-long beans. These snap beans might grow up to 20 inches in length, but they are most tasty when harvested at 12 inches. Asparagus beans are great climbers, so they will need a trellis or some other type of structure on which to grow.

This spring, look for transplants of purple bell peppers and white eggplants. If you can't find them at your local nursery or garden center, you can start them from seed. Red okra and asparagus beans are simple to grow by directly seeding rows of them in the garden, but don't plant them too early in the spring. They require warm soil to germinate and grow.   CHARLIE THIGPEN

Thanks to plant breeders all over the world, we can now grow exotic-looking vegetables that come in all shapes, sizes, and colors, such as these white eggplants, purple bell peppers, asparagus beans, and red okra.

Blackish-red stems and pods as well as whorled, soft yellow blooms make red okra a showstopper.

the
southern
gardener

Container Gardening

everyone can have a garden, even if it's only one small pot on a tiny terrace. Planting in containers is enormously appealing and terribly contagious. Have success with one, and you'll find umpteen reasons for adding another, then a few more. Consider these benefits.

- quick and easy color right where you want it
- great-looking front door dress-ups
- instant success
- herbs at your fingertips

We've consulted experts throughout the South for advice. On the following pages, you'll read their tips, which will help you grow confidence as well as beautiful container gardens.

The Southern Gardener Special Section was coordinated and written by Ellen Ruoff Riley;
photographed by Ralph Anderson, Van Chaplin, William Dickey, and Karim Shamsi-Basha;
designed by Patricia Hooten; and edited by Libby Monteith.

Easy Colorful Containers

Choose your palette, and tackle it with confidence.

A spiky dracaena highlights this arrangement of chartreuse coleus, yellow lantana, Persian shield, angelonia, red pentas, and salvia.

The stems of Swiss chard mirror the red pansies; sweet flag also works well with the palette.

Perennials play beautifully in a galvanized tub. Their easygoing look fits the container's casual nature, with flowers in bloom throughout the summer.

Color—it can make us feel cool, hot, jazzy, or serene. And, more often than not, it's the first thing we think about when choosing plants for containers. Don't let color intimidate you—it's easy and fun to work with.

Cues and Clues

We face important choices with containers, especially those placed in prominent locations such as an entrance. Flower shades, foliage hues, and even a pot's glaze can be vital in determining a container's design success in the landscape.

Look to your surroundings for color clues. House and trim paint are important factors to take into account. Choose plants that complement the facade with similar shades for a quiet look, or take a contrary position with vibrant opposites. The first approach creates a dressy, disciplined assembly, while the second look is more casual and fun loving.

Architecture also factors into this equation. A bungalow is more attuned to riotous color, while a home with a classic facade benefits from the single-shade approach.

This planter, arranged by Austin, Texas, garden designer Sharon St. John, overflows with long-lasting color. Blue salvia establishes the focal point, with purple asters filling in the middle. Bright green 'Margarita' sweet potato tumbles easily over the side, softening the container's slender base.

This container, which illustrates the impact of colorful foliage and texture, was designed by B.B. Barns garden shop in Asheville, North Carolina. The dark color of elephant's ears is repeated in the middle of the pot by the coleus, with 'Blackie' sweet potato anchoring the base, balancing the texture.

Mix and Match

Color comes in numerous forms. Flowers are the instant inclination, but foliage also offers a broad palette of options. The beauty of coleus, Persian shield, caladiums, and other lively leaves is their constant, never-out-of-bloom growth pattern. Combine these plants with flowers for tremendous nonstop seasonal splash.

Vary the sizes and shapes of the foliage. Use light and dark leaves, as well as smooth and textured ones. "Great interest is created by choosing different textured leaves. For example, pair the fuzzy foliage of a begonia with a lacy fern for a fascinating effect," says Tracy Sumney at B.B. Barns in Asheville, North Carolina.

Color Care

It takes maintenance to keep color constant throughout the season. Feed your flowers with a liquid blossom-boosting fertilizer, such as 15-30-15, every other week. At the same time, remove all flowers past their peak to encourage new bud formation.

"Don't be shy about taking the clippers to some plants," Tracy recommends. "Things like coleus must be pruned back throughout the season so you don't lose the planting's original shape." ◆

Convenient Contained Herbs

Bring the garden to your back door, and keep your clippers handy.

everyone loves them; they offer an enormous array of aromatic foliage, flavorful culinary benefits, and an easy-growing attitude. Whether you're a first-time planter or a seasoned veteran, herbs offer grand opportunities for gardening success. Plus, they flourish in containers, adding to their versatility and value.

Container Logic

Truth is, there is an ongoing relationship between homeowners and their herbs. Basil may be a summertime food group in itself, and every stroll past the rosemary invites a gentle caress of its Mediterranean perfume. While herbs can flourish in a garden, chances are you won't use them very

Keeping flower buds clipped discourages seeding and prolongs your harvest.

often if they're halfway across the yard. Big containers right outside the back door are far more convenient, and their contents stand ready for harvest at a moment's notice.

Choose pots that are large enough to harbor plants from spring through fall. For instance, basil is vigorous and needs a deep container for root development. Thyme and oregano, with their short, spreading habit, prefer one with room to cascade over the edge. Small pots are labor-intensive, requiring frequent watering; a 12-inch-diameter container is better to carry your plants through summer.

Easy Rules, Instant Success

The basic container concepts apply to herbs, regardless of which ones you are growing. The pot must have a large drainage hole and be filled with lightweight, moist potting mix. Choose a growing medium with little or no sphagnum peat moss to aid air circulation throughout the pot—all-important for healthy roots and long-lasting plants. Or blend your own potting mix, adding bonemeal and a little sand to a purchased product. Include a granular timed-release fertilizer, choosing a balanced formula such as 14-14-14. A blend with a higher middle number has more phosphorus, which encourages herbs to flower, diminishing their flavor.

Plant pots with only one type of herb, or treat your containers as small mixed gardens. Combining them makes a pretty display if you choose compatible selections. Light and water requirements vary, so pair those with similar attributes for success. Here are a few good combinations we've found work well.

■ **Aromatic collection:** Plant oregano, sage, thyme, rosemary, and bay together to make a great-looking container. These Mediterranean herbs

require a lot of sunlight and fairly dry soil. Remember, though, pots dry out faster than the garden, so water is still a must.

■ **Basil:** Choose several different selections for an interesting arrangement. Mix the common sweet kind with 'Purple Ruffles,' 'Siam Queen,' and lemon basil. If you're short on space, the petite selections of 'Spicy Globe' and 'Piccolo' pair nicely.

■ **Lemon herb garden:** For wonderful citrusy fragrance, try lemongrass, lemon thyme, lemon geraniums, lemon basil, and lemon verbena. ◆

It's a toss-up which aspect of growing herbs in containers is the best: They're right outside the door, and they make a great-looking display.

A moss-lined wire produce basket becomes a window box filled with 'Spicy Globe' basil, parsley, and a few flowers. This container receives sufficient morning sun for healthy growth and requires water every day.

At the Pategas residence in Winter Park, Florida, sculptural agaves are the stars in simple terra-cotta pots. The container color complements the roof tiles and is a nice contrast to the cool green of the plants.

A Grand Entrance
Enhance your front door with fabulous pots and plants.

In an Asheville, North Carolina, home, a large container placed to one side of the door is planted in a colorful, casual manner.

Welcome. It's a sociable Southern attitude we all try to convey in our homes. Expressing this hospitable point of view begins at the front door, where function and style come together with containers.

Size and Style
Pots of plants can embellish the front door or define the path to it. Decide the purpose of your containers; then choose the best size and design. A common mistake is using ones that are too small. Kristin and Stephen Pategas, owners of Hortus Oasis in Winter Park, Florida, offer these tips.

■ Start with cardboard boxes. Get several sizes, and place them where your containers will be. This helps you determine the correct scale.

■ If you're placing multiple pots in the same vicinity, vary their heights and widths. Use cardboard boxes as stand-ins, or fill plastic trash bags with newspaper for the same effect.

Define the dominant materials, paint colors, and established plantings used in and around your home. "Complement your house and the materials used in the landscape, and repeat them when you can," Kristin says. "If you've got terra-cotta roof tiles, then terra-cotta pots are nice."

Choices
Look to your home's facade for planting cues. "If it's a cottage-style home, find a broad mix of plants and create a small garden in that container,"

Kristin says. A home with more contemporary lines lends itself to containers with only one or two plants that are architectural in character. "Choose something with strong texture, or use a standout specimen plant," Stephen says.

Three's Not a Crowd
The placement of pots, especially at an entrance, can be frustrating and tricky. A common approach is to just flank the front door with a pair of containers and be done with it. While this is okay, consider adding a third container. Kristin advises people to employ a classic design technique: "Always put things in triplets."

If pots are on each side of the front door, place the third on a step or the edge of a walkway to complete the shape. Or place two containers at the edge of a landing, adding the third element to one side of the door. ◆

EXPERT ADVICE
Containers lining a path can direct guests to the entrance. Philip Morris, a Birmingham, Alabama gardener, shares his wisdom and experience on making this treatment effective and easy.

■ Sink a container halfway into the ground. Practically speaking, this increases the pot's stability and protects the plant's roots from a hard winter freeze. Design-wise, the container appears to have been there for years.

■ Installed under established trees, containerized plants don't compete for moisture and nutrition with large roots. They appear to share the same soil while actually living separate lives.

the southern gardener

Hang Around With Color

For fabulous flowers anywhere, fill a basket. It's quick and easy.

a hanging basket is an instant garden, suspended where color would otherwise not exist. A small one occupies little space, while a large collection might become a virtual wall of flowers and texture. Scot Thompson, owner of Southern Gardens in Vestavia Hills, Alabama, has perfected this style of

This front porch becomes a private garden space with a screen of hanging baskets. Suspended at varying heights and planted in a flower-and-fern assortment, these arrangements are stylish and easy to care for.

container gardening. Here he shares his planting process.

"First, decide if your basket will be in full sun, partial sun, or shade," Scot says. Choose your flower-and-foliage assortment based on its light requirements. "Start with one upright plant, and then add some bushy and trailing ones and a green one, too," he suggests. A fern or an ivy serves as a color anchor, allowing brightly colored flowers to show off around it.

Step 1: Place a coco-fiber liner in the wire basket, molding it to fit snugly.

Step 2: Fill it halfway with moist potting soil, pressing down to remove air pockets. "If you're making a basket for full sun, add a water-retaining polymer at this point," Scot says. Follow the package directions for the correct amount—don't use too much. Add a healthy handful of timed-release granular fertilizer to the potting mix.

Step 3: Place your plants, centering the tallest one and surrounding it with the shorter and trailing selections. Add more moist soil around the roots, pressing it into place. Keep soil at least ½ inch below the liner edge to prevent washout when watering. Hang the basket, and water it thoroughly. "Even though you planted with a timed-release fertilizer, use a water-soluble blossom-booster once a month. Twice is even better," Scot suggests.

Voice of Experience

"Next to watering, pruning is the most important thing," Scot says. As the season progresses, many plants become overzealous. Without an occasional cutback, asparagus fern, verbena, coleus, and impatiens grow out of control. "If you prune your basket, it will be neat and compact, blooming much more than if you leave it alone," he advises. ◆

RECIPE FOR SUCCESS

A Shady Basket

1 (12-inch-wide) wire basket with coco-fiber liner
1 (6-inch) pot caladium
2 (4-inch) pots double impatiens
1 (4-inch) pot Boston or Dallas fern
1 (4-inch) pot rex begonia
1 (6-inch) pot ivy

How-to: Prepare basket according to Scot's instructions at right. Put the caladium in the middle, surrounding it with the impatiens and fern. Tuck the rex begonia along one edge; divide the ivy into two or three smaller plants, arranging them on the sides. Fill in with moist potting soil.
Care: Water plants as needed. Feed at least once a month with a blossom-boosting, liquid fertilizer. Trim impatiens and ivy occasionally to maintain shape.

Water Wisely

Take the worry out of this important garden task with these simple solutions.

This bubbler-style head distributes water into the pot without a lot of excess spray. The tiny tube comes over the back edge and remains hidden in foliage as the plants mature through the summer.

Successful container gardens depend on many factors: light, good potting mix, and proper plant choices. But, the essential ingredient is water. Too little is bad, too much is disastrous, and family vacations can be nightmares for pots—or so you might think. Here are a few tips to take the guesswork out of watering and maintenance.

Worry-Free Water

Irrigation systems aren't just for turf and flowerbeds. Do-it-yourself watering kits adapt to containers, turning this maintenance chore into a thing of the past. Look for a complete package that includes a pressure regulator among its parts. This small item screws onto your faucet and steps down water pressure so the tiny sprinkler heads won't pop off. If your kit does not come with this feature, you can find it separately in a garden center's irrigation department.

Follow the kit's instructions, running the tubing inconspicuously behind containers. Bring the hose over the back edge of the pot, and anchor the head centrally within the planting so water is distributed evenly. You can also run the tube up through the drainage hole so it is not visible around edges. Do this before the pot is planted. The drainage hole must be large enough to accommodate the tube and still allow water to escape

A plastic deck protector raises a pot off the surface. Cut the round disk into two separate supports, and place them under the containers.

EXPERT ADVICE

Here are some extra tips from landscape architect Stephen Pategas and landscape designer Kristin Pategas. Their thoughts are particularly valuable for those living in areas where rainfall is scarce during summer.

- If you place saucers under containers, turn them up during summer months to hold water, and upside down in winter so water drains.
- Containers installed in garden beds need a concrete stepping-stone underneath. In addition to preventing tipping, the stone helps the drainage hole stay open and functional.
- Using pot feet prevents deck stains and decay.

Battery-powered timers, available with many programming options, are the ticket to watering freedom. You'll pay $20 for a simple model and $50 for an elaborate one.

freely. Raise the pot to avoid crushing the pliable hose.

Consider leaving a 12-inch hose length extending from the pot's bottom, attaching it to the main water tube with a connector. If you choose to move the container, simply disconnect it from the system, and reattach it in its new location.

You can complete the system with a battery-powered timer. These devices connect to the faucet and offer many programming options. Available at garden centers, they provide freedom from everyday watering duty as well as vacation insurance for containers. Test it several days prior to your trip to ensure its accuracy.

Elevated Awareness

Pot feet are those paw-shaped chunks of clay or concrete protruding from a container's base. They raise the pot off a surface and assist in drainage. Elevating the vessel will give moisture a clear path as it travels through the hole. "Debris also can get under containers and clog drainage holes," says Stephen Pategas, landscape architect with Hortus Oasis in Winter Park, Florida. "When you use pot feet, it keeps the area underneath clean and keeps water draining freely." ◆

the southern gardener

Dress Up Your Windows and Walls

Let your personality blossom, and give your home a distinctive appearance.

A wall fountain becomes a decorative planting pocket on this covered porch. Garden designer Jan Feamster planned the unit as the focal point of an otherwise blank space.

Window boxes and containers that hug the house get color up close and personal. They put tiny gardens in unexpected places and are a fun expression of individual style. Follow our tips for great-looking combinations and placement ideas.

Window Dressings

Cottages, bungalows, and casual entrances lend themselves to window boxes. Their nature invites casual plantings overflowing with color and texture. Here are some things to remember when planning and planting.
- Drainage is a must. If your box is not predrilled, add holes, each at least a ½ inch in diameter. In a container more than a foot long, make multiple openings, spacing them a foot apart.
- A 1-inch layer of foam peanuts in the bottom prevents soil from escaping and adds insulation for roots.
- Add moisture-retaining polymer to the potting mix in hot, sunny boxes. This decreases daily water needs.
- Feed your box weekly with a liquid, flower-boosting fertilizer such as 15-30-15. Watering the container prior to feeding will prevent fertilizer burn.

Added Benefits

Place a window box container to give privacy to a room in public view. Plant the container lush and full for impact. In our example, a terra-cotta box fits nicely on a wide window ledge, creating a living screen for a bathroom window. Clay pot feet slide under the front edge to level this container, which is on a sloping surface.

Impatiens cover the front of the box in colorful profusion, and tall cast-iron plant *(Aspidistra elatior)* adds height and year-round foliage to fill out the back.

Recycle Containers

Jan Feamster, a garden designer in Mooresville, North Carolina, has found a new use for her old wall fountain. Tired of having pump and maintenance problems, she transformed the former water feature into a wonderful wall planter. She has planted the wide, shallow pocket with low-maintenance caladiums, impatiens, 'Gold 'n' Pearls' bacopa, and variegated sweet flag. Because this unconventional container does not have a drainage hole, Jan simply waters the plants sparingly whenever they require a drink. ◆

A terra-cotta box resting on the ledge gives this bathroom window a wonderful floral view and added privacy. The pot feet under the front edge level the container and improve drainage.

This cottage-style collection is filled with geraniums, petunias, and caladiums. A common mistake with window boxes is making the container too small for the site—notice how large these are (each is 38 inches) and how well they suit each window's proportions.

This trio of painted pots and shady plants turns the unplantable space beneath a tree into a garden. Elevating two different size containers on the bench establishes much-needed height. Plants include variegated white impatiens, caladium, and calathea (a houseplant).

Shady Characters

Add dynamic impact to dark places with bright, colorful containers of dependable plants.

Y ou really can use the words "colorful" and "shade" in the same sentence. Better yet, take these two ideas—a bright palette and low-light plants—and apply them to the same container. It's all a matter of knowing what to look for and how to put it together.

Glazed pots enhance readily available houseplants in an entryway. Corn plants, alocasias, horsetails, and philodendrons, used in an unexpected manner, celebrate every aspect of green.

Colorful Combinations

Consider this when choosing plants for shady containers: Light colors, such as white, pastel pink, salmon, and brilliant green, stand out as sunlight diminishes. A dark palette of red, purple, and blue recedes, fading into the background. Choose the lighter palette to shine and sparkle in your garden's darkest corners.

Impatiens are the hands-down favorite flower for shade. Easy to grow, they require little care once established. Seek out the newer double selections and others with variegated foliage for added pop. While it's easy to take this reliable plant for granted, using it in containers with interesting foliage produces a great, fresh look.

Look to houseplants for outstanding texture. These tropical troopers have brilliant foliage in myriad shades, along with bold leaves in fascinating shapes. Tuck them in 4- and 6-inch pots; then add impatiens for a vibrant combination. Most houseplants in these sizes are inexpensive and available at garden centers.

Pot Color

Another aspect is container color; light-hued pots add impact when complementing the plant palette. In our example (shown below, left), white-glazed containers mirror foliage hues and become an artistic focal point leading you into an otherwise dark entrance.

Paint Your Containers

While glazed enamel pots offer numerous options, you can easily customize them. Follow these simple instructions.

■ Start with clean, dry terra-cotta containers, and brush on an even coat of flat latex paint.

■ For subdued color, dilute paint by half with water, and apply it with a rag or sponge.

■ Don't wash off the nice mossy patina that terra-cotta gets as it begins to age. ◆

In the largest pot, New Guinea Hybrid impatiens flourish with variegated ivy trailing over the edge. In the container to its right, nandina's graceful foliage catches dappled light. Below is a collection of succulents.

Containers by Design

Use pots to punctuate your garden.

Planning a landscape is a lot like interior design—you are dividing up outdoor space into rooms, furnishing it with plants, and accessorizing it with containers. Pots and their plantings give a garden personality and turn ordinary space into an inviting outdoor retreat.

We talked to several experts who all have something to say about the significance of containers in garden design. Here are their experienced opinions.

Focal Points

Jan Feamster, a garden designer in Mooresville, North Carolina, artfully placed an old birdbath as an eye-catching feature in her garden. As you look through the arbor, this simple, shallow container draws your interest into another garden room and provides a visual stopping point.

Consider other ways to use containers as the focus of a garden.

- Place a pot at the end of a path to accentuate where the walkway stops.
- A large urn or substantial container centered in a round bed draws attention to that spot. Without it, the garden lacks a clear starting point.
- Use a container at the end of a low wall to give weight and architectural detail to the stopping point.

Define Spaces

Set boundaries in an undefined space with containers. Arranged in clusters of three or set as cornerstones, they function as portable walls in a garden room. "Pots are accents, but they also delineate space," says Barney Bryant, with B.B. Barns in Asheville, North Carolina. "Use containers to define a garden room's area. They are focal points and stop the eye," he says.

Large containers lining a walkway easily define the space as a promenade. An allée of crepe myrtles, berried hollies, or palms in large pots becomes an inviting

left: This birdbath beautifully illustrates the significance of a simple container as a focal point. Garden designer Jan Feamster of Mooresville, North Carolina, placed it to accent the view through the arbor and invite you into another garden room.
below: A blank wall becomes an artistic garden with this iron planter. The simple flower assortment allows the iron's architecture to star with the planting.

right: This tall urn filled with red fountain grass and petunias adds a striking vertical dimension to a bed of black-eyed Susans and cleomes.
below: A shallow flower-filled bowl at the end of this low wall acts as a finial.

passageway of live plants. Place them on opposite sides of the path in pairs or zigzagged down its length. Either way, an odd number of containers on each side is the most visually appealing arrangement.

Accessories

One of container gardening's most underutilized benefits is portability. Small pots can be moved easily, while a lightweight dolly is invaluable in relocating larger ones. Why move them around? "Containers are like accessories," says landscape designer Kristin Pategas, in Winter Park, Florida.

Think of your pots as you would furniture. Move them seasonally with changing light, or rearrange them for an event to direct foot traffic or hide a view. "Occasionally a plant will put on a spectacular show. Put it by the front door for a wonderful welcoming element through its bloom time," Kristin recommends. "A lot of people think that once they place a container, that's where it remains, but it doesn't have to stay put." ◆

EXPERT ADVICE

Here are some additional tips for container success.
■ "A windy location can be a challenge when your container is planted with something tall. Use a square-bottomed pot—it's less likely to tip over," says landscape architect Stephen Pategas.
■ "When you need height, place an obelisk or trellis in the container," Kristin Pategas says. "Plant a flowering vine on it for an easy focal point."
■ "Use a glazed pot as a distinctive addition to the garden. The container becomes as much a part of the design as the plants in it," says Kristin.

Simple sculptural plants have a big impact in a potentially overlooked area. Varying pot sizes and plant textures make for an interesting, heat-tolerant collection in designer Sharon St. John's Texas garden.

Plant It Right

Follow these easy steps for growing success.

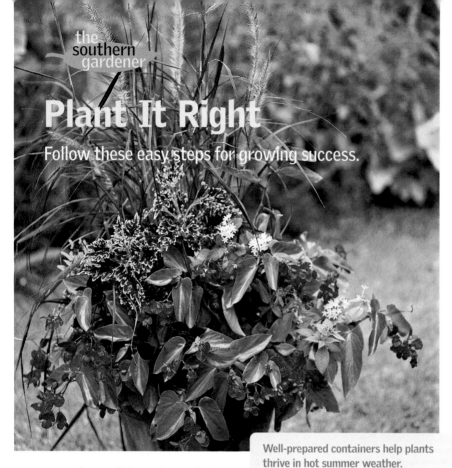

Well-prepared containers help plants thrive in hot summer weather.

When talking about design, you've heard it said that rules are meant to be broken. But planting is a different story. According to one expert, garden shop owner Barney Bryant with B.B. Barns in Asheville, North Carolina, successful container gardens are those put together by following a few simple rules.

The Pot

"I'm really picky about drainage," Barney says. "I insist each pot have a ¾-inch-diameter hole." To keep that drain free-flowing, add a shallow layer of foam peanuts.

When selecting pots, think big. "If I were to choose one size pot for successful container gardening, it would be 18 x 18 inches. From there, I would only go larger," Barney says. Small containers dry out quickly.

The Soil

"Potting soil is so important. If you don't use the proper mix, you're going to have problems," Barney warns. How do you know what good soil is? Try this B.B. Barns recommendation: Pick up a handful of soil, and hold it tight. When released, it should fall apart quickly. If not, there's too much sphagnum peat moss in the mix.

Moisten the mix prior to putting it in the container. Barney also suggests, "Hose down clay pots before planting. If you don't, the dry pot absorbs the moisture in the potting mix."

Placing Plants

Decide how the container is to be viewed—either against a wall, where it will have a flat side, or out in the open where it will be seen from all sides. Position the tallest plant as the focal point, to the pot's back if the arrangement is three-sided or in the middle if it is a circular situation.

Treat the rest of the arrangement like stairsteps. Place medium-size plants close to the tall focal point, and set trailing ones close to the container's edges. Once everything is in place, surround the roots with additional moist potting soil.

Water and Feed

As summer's heat increases, so must moisture. When plants mature and pots fill with roots, the daily water regimen must increase. "If your lifestyle makes frequent watering a problem, consider a drip irrigation system to maintain plants," he says. (See "Water Wisely" on page 49.)

Feeding your container garden is an essential part of its success. When planting, mix granular timed-release fertilizer with the soil. Choose a balanced mix such as 14-14-14, or increase your bloom power with an 11-40-6 blend. "We also tell our customers to water with a liquid blossom-boosting fertilizer, such as 15-30-15, every two weeks. You must do both to keep containers in top condition," Barney recommends. ◆

left: Place the tallest plant first, in the center if the container is to be viewed from all sides, and to the back if the pot will be up against a wall. We used red fountain grass.
middle: Add mid-size plants, such as red 'Dragon Wing' begonias, next to the tall focal point. Place trailing ones, such as yellow moss rose, around the edges.
right: Water every two weeks with a liquid blossom-boosting fertilizer.

ANNUAL FLOWERS

periwinkle
celosia
zinnia
purslane
portulaca
lantana
million bells
sweet potato vine
verbena
pentas

Color abounds in heat-loving succulents.
Black gravel covers the soil to help
contain moisture and keep pots neat.

Some Like It Hot

When summer heats up the South, consider
these plants for container success.

plants aren't terribly different from people—some of us are cool-natured, while others run on the warm side. It is a well-known fact that, come May or early June, most Southerners must give up cold-hardy pansies and snapdragons. The region's warm nights and toasty soil are more than they can bear.

Summer does take its toll on flowers—even more so when they are planted in containers. A pot sitting in full sun has no respite from intense temperatures, so the plants held within must be tough as nails. We went to Austin—a Texas hot spot—to ask Pat Swanson, owner of Pots & Plants Garden Center, for his best ideas on beating the summer heat.

Two Seasons

Container gardening requires flexibility. "You can't plant your container in March and expect it to last until September," Pat says. "In Texas, plant your pots in spring with selections that like cool evenings. When June comes, replant with the heat-lovers." Resist the temptation to purchase your summer plants early. Cool soil and sultry plants don't play well together; fungal problems, stunted growth, and bad results almost always ensue.

See our lists at right for seriously heat-tolerant plants—perfect for containers and tough enough to flourish through summer. ◆

Blanket flower carpets the
garden in steadfast color.

PERENNIAL FLOWERS

blackfoot daisy
(*Melampodium leucanthum*)
red bird of paradise
(*Caesalpinia pulcherrima*)
butterfly weed (*Asclepias tuberosa*)
Russian sage (*Perovskia atriplicifolia*)
Mexican flame vine (*Senecio confusus*)
blanket flower (*Gaillardia pulchella*)
coneflower (*Rudbeckia* sp.)
stonecrop (*Sedum* sp.)
salvia

TEXTURE
purple heart
red fountain grass
(*Pennisetum setaceum
'Rubrum'*)
coleus
caladium
ajuga

Coleus provides nonstop color
from planting day until frost.

A blank slate is the easiest way to begin; plan garden rooms for easy access from the home.

Before

At one end of this long, narrow deck, a chaise longue invites relaxation. Pots along the railing provide privacy, while the potted Japanese maple in the far corner brings the surrounding landscape closer to home.

Divvy Up the Deck

Put every inch of space to its absolute best use.

a deck plays an important landscape role. With smaller lots, it may be the yard, garden, and outdoor entertaining area rolled into one. So it's especially important to make effective use of this limited space and place containers for maximum impact.

Divide It Up

Often, a deck runs straight as an arrow down one side of the home. If that's the case, it's a good idea to partition it into several distinct sections.

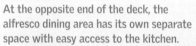

At the opposite end of the deck, the alfresco dining area has its own separate space with easy access to the kitchen.

Take into account how you want to use each one: a quiet reading nook, a dining spot, or a place for grilling. Decide which area to make a priority, and give it ample space. The largest, most used room should be the most accessible. For example, place the entertaining area near a doorway so guests can come and go with ease. But tuck a private reading niche in a low-traffic corner.

Portable Partitions

Planted containers provide an easy way to compartmentalize. Consider using some good-looking plastic pots that resemble terracotta and concrete; they don't weigh as much and are a lot easier to move. Unlike their counterparts, they can also withstand temperature extremes.

Use a couple of big ones clustered together to separate one area from the next. Group large containers near a wall. Movement around them is easy, but they still create a visual divider between areas.

Fill the pots with bold, tall plantings to add impact. For a long-term commitment, consider using small trees and shrubs, such as yaupon holly, Leyland cypress, and Japanese boxwoods. They will flourish for several years in containers and then can be moved to the yard. Repeating a plant that's already in your landscape adds continuity to the design. For an instant summer garden, large, inexpensive houseplants are great. Note which areas are sunny or shady, and choose plants accordingly.

Place a collection of smaller pots opposite the large ones to frame a passage. This is a great way to introduce seasonal plants, grouping numerous containers to maximize the effect. Raise the concentration of color above floor level by elevating a few of the planters.

You can also use containers to enhance privacy. Screen a view or cushion a cozy nook by placing pots along the deck's railing; fill them with dense foliage and flowers for an effective buffer. ◆

Choose the Right Mulch

Pine bark or hardwood?
Consider wisely, or you'll
be caught red-handed.

Clockwise from top, dyed mulch, pine bark mini-nuggets, and shredded hardwood. Which one is right for your garden?

Some things are just too shocking to be believed—such as hearing that Lassie was a KGB agent or that Katie Couric chews tobacco. So, at the risk of sending you into a coma, let me very gently reveal one of gardening's hidden truths—there is more than one kind of wood mulch.

Easy, easy! You're hyperventilating. Just breathe into this paper sack while I continue. Yes, it's true. Depending on where you live, you may encounter shredded hardwood, pine bark, cypress, and even that new dyed mulch you often see decorating finer service stations.

Now we all know the benefits of mulch—it beautifies, reduces erosion and compaction, discourages weeds, insulates roots, and conserves soil moisture. And we all know not to pile wood mulch up against tree trunks (this causes pest problems) or let it get more than 3 inches deep (this robs the soil of nitrogen and does bad things to plants). But what are the different pros and cons of these various mulches?

Kinds of Mulches

Shredded hardwood mulch is popular in the Upper South, where these trees dominate the forest. Good hardwood mulch consists mainly of shredded oak and maple bark. It is naturally dark brown and knits together well, so it usually stays in place during a hard rain. But it also packs down easily, which can rob nitrogen from the soil and cause other problems if mulch is deeper than a few inches.

Pine bark is probably the most popular wood mulch in the Middle and Lower South, where pines are ubiquitous. It's medium to dark brown. Although you can get it shredded, many people prefer it in chip form, sold as large nuggets and mini-nuggets. Large nuggets are several inches across. They won't pack down and smother things, and they decay slowly. But, they're big and coarse and tend to float during heavy rain like barges on the Mississippi. I prefer mini-nuggets. Their texture is nice, they stay in place better, and they're great for containers.

Shredded cypress is the wood mulch of choice for Florida and the Coastal South. Made from the bark of bald cypress, it's naturally decay resistant, so it lasts for a few years. Plus, it stays put. But not all cypress mulches are equal. The best kind is made from the bark of trees used for timber. It has a rich auburn-brown color. Cheaper cypress mulch just doesn't last as long.

Mulch To Dye For

What about the dyed-red mulches? Well, I don't want to offend anyone, but—oh, what the heck—I hate them. For one thing, why are they the color of Lucy Ricardo's hair? Secondly, you can't handle the stuff without getting red dye all over your hands, making you look suspiciously like an ax murderer. Finally, anytime the strongest color in your garden comes from mulch, you need to rethink your design.

STEVE BENDER

Inspired by memories, a Texas couple
created the garden of their dreams.

Reclaiming
a Family
Garden

above, left: Rain lily stars in this field of colorful wildflowers. **above, middle:** Mary Anne and Bob Pickens kneel on their lawn of coreopsis and Indian paintbrush in front of a pergola of 'Fortuniana' roses. **above, right:** This climbing Lady Banks's rose flourishes with little care on a weathered trellis.

For Mary Anne and Bob Pickens, the greatest joy of gardening is having their small troop of grandchildren look forward to spring, when they hunt Easter eggs in the coreopsis, chase lizards along the gravel paths, and watch wrens build nests around their home. Summer brings its own rewards, such as collecting caterpillars and playing with june bugs. The family's past lives on in their garden, and the future looks bright with this new crop of gardeners growing strong.

Mary Anne inherited this property north of Columbus, Texas, from her grandparents. The land was near the site of the old Pearfield Nursery, which was founded by her great-grandfather J.F. Leyendecker. The house had burned down in 1981, and the garden had long since grown over. Nevertheless, when the couple retired, they were committed to moving from Houston to the rolling hills of Colorado County. Mary Anne, a teacher, and Bob, a geologist, both had deep Texas roots, so they wanted to re-create a place that their family would cherish for generations to come. Today, they live in a farmhouse

left: A front lawn of coreopsis, bluebonnets, and Indian paintbrush provides a peaceful setting for the Pickenses' house.

built in the same *fachwerk* style as the original 1840s home and surrounded by a lovely country garden.

A Garden for Generations

Mary Anne remembers her grandmother's yard as a delightful place during her childhood. "The front was enclosed by a picket fence and had a center gate hung with a hand-wrought latch and hinges," she says. "The walk, lined on either side with English boxwoods, led straight to the front steps. On both sides, there were beds of assorted sizes and shapes, all lined with either sandstone or large, smooth river rocks. Paths throughout the garden were swept dirt, but in time, as things seeded, the paths became hard to find. A distinguishing feature of that garden was a large yucca on the side of the center walk.

Almost as striking as that was an enormous clump of pampas grass with plumes my grandmother cut to grace a 2-foot-tall carnival-glass vase.

"Less dramatic but even more wonderful," she continues, "were the numerous bulbs scattered around the garden and bordering the flowerbeds. There were summer snowflakes *(Leucojum aestivum)*, narcissus, Byzantine gladiolus, oxblood lilies, and my favorite little grape hyacinths that just seemed to pop up everywhere." Even after the old house burned, the bulbs kept coming back each spring, reminding her of her grandmother's garden. Mary Anne collected many of these and transferred them into the new design.

Because her grandmother also grew Barbados cherries, larkspurs, lantanas, crinums, Louisiana phlox,

BY WILLIAM C. WELCH / PHOTOGRAPHY ALLEN ROKACH

poppies, calendulas, and Johnny-jump-ups, Mary Anne wanted to incorporate them into her garden as well. "Grandmother enjoyed trying new things, but the old standbys were never discarded," Mary Anne remembers. "Pecans were the trees of choice to shade the corner swing and rocking chairs on the porch. Summer was a time for watching hummingbirds gather nectar from Turk's cap and red salvia, while I ate watermelon on the porch. Life had a slower pace then, and I look back on it with fondness."

Passed Down Memories

"I recalled all these things as I began planting, so I guess my garden does have a past," she says. "Bob and I designed a house that resembled my ancestral home, and I planned my garden hoping that someday our grandchildren would know and remember it as a special place."

Mary Anne is proud that she was able to establish cuttings of a Pearfield Nursery boxwood in the new garden. Other originals from her grandmother's yard include yucca, Turk's cap, four o' clocks, and bridal wreath.

Many relatives, too, have provided heirloom plants, which may have originally come from Pearfield Nursery. These include a beautiful flowering almond, a small white althaea, old double orange daylilies, and a sago palm of Pearfield Nursery origin.

Mary Anne also wanted to bring back some of the roses that her ancestors had sold. Because there were none left in the garden or in the old growing fields, she used nursery catalogs as guides and found a number of roses that were originally in the garden. "I am currently growing two roses that my great-grandfather J.F. Leyendecker advertised: 'Cécile Brunner' and 'Duchesse de Brabant.' My conditions are extremely harsh, but I've had the most success with a found rose known as 'Caldwell Pink.' China roses, such as 'Louis Philippe,' 'Cramoisi Supérieur,' and 'Ducher,' or tough old ones such as 'Fortuniana,' Lady Banks's, and Cherokee are also doing very well."

top: A gated arbor welcomes you into the vegetable and herb garden. **above:** Colorful wine bottles line a path accented by masses of white cilantro and Texas star *(Lindheimera texana)*. **right:** Wide porches provide inviting space to enjoy the yard.

left: The yucca blooming in the front garden was grown from a shoot of an original plant, which was prominent in an 1863 painting of the garden. **below, left:** The garden features heirloom plants, such as Johnson's amaryllis, prairie phlox, and 'Fortuniana' roses.

A small orchard behind the house holds pear trees and Japanese persimmons grown from cuttings of old trees left in the pastures at the original home site.

In Good Hands

"While we were planning the home," she says, "Bob and I also became interested in learning more about native plants. So, in addition to the heirloom plants from my grandmother's garden, we have included many that are native to our immediate area, as well as some drought-tolerant South Texas species such as Texas pistachio and Anacacho orchid tree."

While Mary Anne's domain is around the house, Bob gardens in the pasture. When cattle were taken off the land, he was thrilled to have so many types of wildflowers and grasses appear. After much trial and error using native grasses in the garden, Bob and Mary Anne decided to make a simple border or mini-prairie of grasses and wildflowers along one side of the fenced enclosure. Most of these plants were moved in from the pasture. Bob has identified grasses in the mini-prairie as little and big bluestem, Indian grass, gulf muhly, silver bluestem, brownseed paspalum, and broom sedge.

The Pickenses are both dedicated to conserving water in the landscape. Turf is not included, so they don't have to water a lawn. The front garden flows into an open meadow that is mowed as needed. They use drip irrigation on the fruit trees when getting them established and then only during extreme drought. Buried tubes with upright emitters water the beds.

Mary Anne and Bob have truly created the garden of her memories. Along the way, they have added their personal touches, a gift for the generations to come.

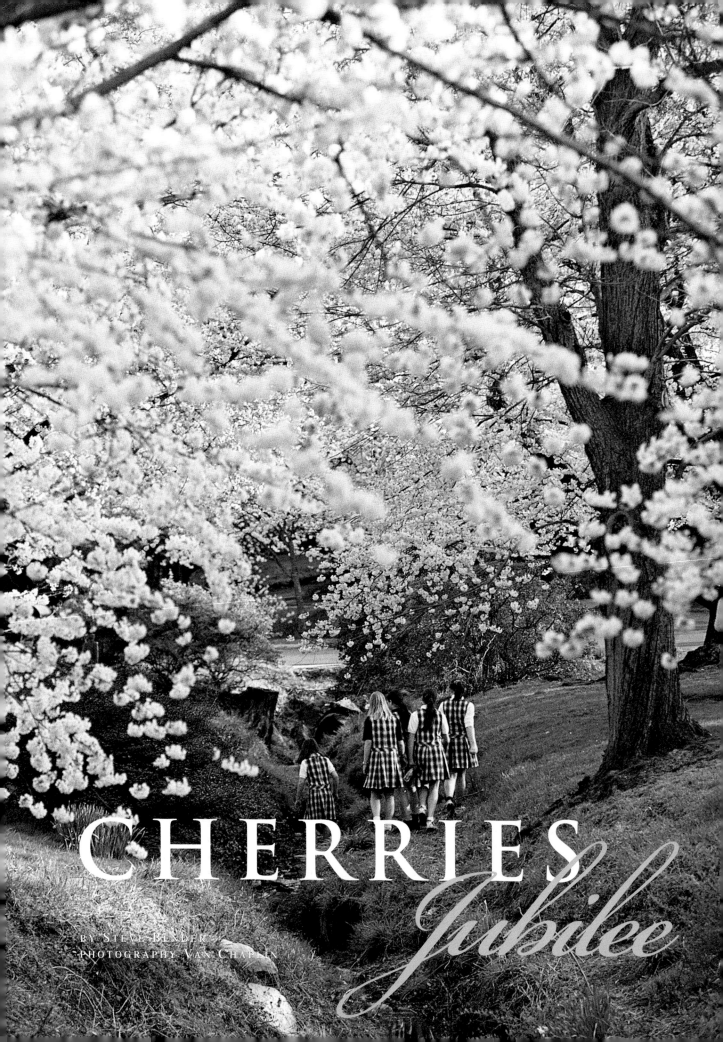

CHERRIES
Jubilee

BY STEVE BENDER
PHOTOGRAPHY VAN CHAPLIN

This Maryland neighborhood's trees not only herald spring, but are also the ties that bind this community together.

Spring is snowing in Kenwood. Along every street in this community northwest of Washington, D.C., white petals flutter down from the gnarled limbs of hundreds of flowering trees planted more than 70 years ago. The scene is breathtaking, and everywhere you look, people are taking it in—residents, schoolchildren, picnickers, painters, and carload after carload of wide-eyed gawkers.

The trees are Yoshino flowering cherries (*Prunus* x *yedoensis*), the same species selected by First Lady Helen Taft for planting around the Washington Tidal Basin in 1912. Flowers appear in early spring before the leaves, opening blush-pink then maturing to white. Native to Japan, these fast-growing trees form a wide, arching canopy about 35 feet high and wide—perfect for lining suburban streets. Kennedy & Chamberlain, the development company that built

left: Inspired by the blooms, schoolchildren romp by a stream that runs through a grassy median. **below:** What were Mom's instructions to elicit a smile? "Say cheese" or "Say cherry."

Kenwood on old dairy farmland in the early 1930s, knew this. They chose Yoshino flowering cherries as the new community's unifying element, planting many of the trees you see on these pages before building the first house or paving the first street. According to resident Ted Libbey, the neighborhood now boasts about 1,250 cherry trees.

Tending the Trees

All of those cherries need a lot of maintenance, but Kenwood is up to the job. Here, community involvement is considered a privilege rather than a burden, and nearly everyone gets into the act. More than 90% of residents belong to the Kenwood Citizens Association. Kenwood has a Welcoming Committee, a Beautification Committee, and a Juniors Committee for families with young children. The Kenwood Garden Club has been active for more than 50 years. In addition to putting on an Easter egg hunt, Halloween haunted house, and Fourth of July barbecue, residents even write, produce, and act in an original play each year.

"I know people who live 7, 8, 10 blocks away," says Barbara Ann Libbey, Ted's wife. "You don't see that in most communities around Washington. I know everybody because we attend all these functions together—dinners, neighborhood walk-arounds, and the lighting of

above: Kenwood's beautiful cherries are some of the most photographed trees in the world; they're also among the most painted.

the big Christmas tree in the circle."

Obviously, Kenwood takes care of its own—and that goes double for the trees. The maintenance program works like this: The county buys, plants, and prunes all cherry trees in public spaces, such as entrances, parks, and traffic circles. But cherries lining streets in front of private homes are the homeowners' responsibility. Each year, the citizens association negotiates with local nurseries and landscaping companies to get the best price for replacing dead trees on

top and right: When Kenwood's cherries bloom, it's hard to stay indoors. Now more than 70 years old, the original trees were planted before the houses were built. **above:** Keeping the spectacle going means planting new trees to replace old ones that die. "Everybody here nurses their trees like children," says Barbara Ann Libbey. "And if something happens to them, it's like a death in the family."

private property; homeowners willingly pick up the tab.

"What would happen if somebody replaced their cherry with a purple-leaf plum?" I ask. Ted makes a slashing motion across his throat and suggests an especially painful surgical procedure. He's probably kidding, but I wouldn't risk it.

To help beginning gardeners, the garden club distributes care sheets for the cherries. A cherry tree chairman inspects the trees periodically to make sure people are following directions. Mary Shue, cochair of the Juniors Committee, found out what happens if you let things slide: "I got a note saying that overmulching had put my tree at risk."

Three Cheers for the Cherries

But when more than 1,000 cherry trees shower petals on every street in Kenwood, all the work is worth it. Residents turn out in a joyous celebration. Thousands of Washingtonians and tourists descend on the neighborhood to walk or drive its streets—people from the U.S. and as far away as China, India, Pakistan, France, and the Middle East—all reveling in the moment.

No group enjoys the spectacle more than the Japanese, who take pictures of themselves in front of the trees to send home to their country. So great is their enthusiasm that they don't always distinguish between public streets and private gardens.

Recalls Kenwood resident Roger Whyte, "One morning, I walked outside, and two Japanese families were having breakfast by our pool."

The influx of visitors provides an ideal springboard for nascent free enterprise; local kids take advantage. At Abby and Joey's Lemonade stand, proprietors Abby and Joey Kathan (ages 12 and 9) earn up to $100 a day selling brownies, bottled water, and lemonade.

Folks say that once people move into Kenwood, they want to stay forever. It's easy to see why. People here know and care about their neighbors and take great pride in their surroundings. Barbara Ann sums up the general attitude this way. "I was out

left: In 1934, Japanese Ambassador Hiroshi Saito and his wife visited Kenwood. **below, left:** Blooms, opening blush-pink and turning white, appear before the leaves.

for a walk," she recalls, "and a woman came up to me and said, 'You know you live in paradise, don't you?' And I said, 'Yes, I do.'"

For more information about the Kenwood garden tour, e-mail the Kenwood Garden Club at kenwoodgardentour@hotmail.com. To find out when the cherry trees are blooming in the area, visit www.nationalcherryblossomfestival.org.

Peonies (See pages 66–68.)

April

garden checklist

Editor's Notebook

PHOTOGRAPH: ALLEN ROKACH

Art Tucker, whose extraordinary garden is profiled this month (turn to page 82), doesn't look like a mean guy. He smiles a lot, pets his cats whenever they demand it, and happily brags on his wife's field of expertise (Sherry's a limnologist—which, as everyone knows, is just a fancy term for a freshwater ecologist). But when it comes to weeds, he's ruthless. Using a long-handled propane torch, he mercilessly incinerates any plant foolhardy enough to sully his walk. To some, this sounds cruel, but it's really a beneficent act. Instead of dousing the walk with herbicides, which might end up in ground water, he reduces weeds to carbon, which then enriches the soil. So the next time you happen to see Art out in his garden wielding his torch, don't cower—unless your last name is Chickweed. —STEVE BENDER

This is the answer to the question posed on page 87: The large white flower in the center is a double roseleaf raspberry *(Rubus rosifolius* 'Coronarius').

Impatiens

These flowers provide reliable color in the shade throughout the growing season. There are many selections available in just about any color or size you would desire. You can also choose from single- or double-flowering forms. If you are in the Upper South, wait until all danger of frost has passed (around the middle of the month) before planting. They look great in hanging baskets, containers, and borders. For an easy combination in your garden, use Southern shield fern in the background, your favorite caladium selection in the middle, and impatiens in front. You will quickly become known as the one with a green thumb in your neighborhood.

TIPS

■ **Mulch**—Apply an extra layer of mulch, such as pine straw or pine bark, to newly planted trees and shrubs. This reduces evaporation, helps keep plants' roots cool, and slows down weed growth.

PLANT

■ **Easter lily**—*(Lilium longiflorum)* can be added to your garden once flowers fade. Remove the plant from its pot, and set it in a sunny, well-drained location in your border. Wait until foliage turns yellow before cutting back to the ground. The bulb will settle back into its normal bloom sequence.

■ **Lawn**—Plant plugs of warm-season grasses, such as Bermuda, St. Augustine, centipede, and Zoysia, in the Middle, Lower, and Coastal South. Water newly planted lawns regularly for healthy roots. Infrequent, deep watering is better because it promotes deeper root growth. Established lawns need about an inch of water a week. In Texas, now is a good time to plant warm-season grasses. Common Bermuda can be planted from seed, covers quickly, resists drought, and thrives in sunny areas. Zoysia and hybrid Bermuda also do well in sun. St. Augustine is good for shade or partial shade. All are available as sod or plugs.

■ **Perennials**—For repeat color, set out agapanthus, butterfly bush, daylily, pentas, shrimp plant, lantana, rudbeckia, and verbena.

dahlia

■ **Summer bulbs and tubers**—Plant cannas, dahlias, gladioli, caladiums, and elephant's ears in the Lower and Coastal South. These great plants will add bright color and bold texture to any garden.

■ **Vegetables**—In the Middle, Lower, and Coastal South, set out tomatoes, beans, squash, peppers, okra, zucchini, eggplant, and corn.

■ **Ferns**—In Florida, add these spring staples to shaded areas of your landscape as a background for other plantings. Some popular choices that can tolerate both acid and alkaline soils include leather fern, Southern sword fern *(Nephrolepis cordifolia)*, autumn fern, whisk fern, wart fern, Australian tree fern, and marsh fern.

■ **Warm-weather annuals**—In Florida, plant flowers that can tolerate the heat of the coming months. A bed planted with globe amaranth *(gomphrena),* in purple, pink, and lavender, makes an impressive mound of color in full sun. Globe amaranth is available in regular and dwarf forms. Melampodium, with its bright gold flowers, also tolerates the heat well and forms nice 2-foot-tall mounds. Torenia, or wishbone flower, is available in purple, blue, or pink and will grow in full sun to light shade.

tomato

■ **Trees**—In Texas, set out live oak, bur oak, Chinese pistache, cedar elm, and bald cypress now. Select healthy container-grown plants, and stake newly set-out trees to protect them from wind damage. Water them every few days. Mulching the root zone with bark, hay, or similar materials helps prevent drying.

■ **Tropical vines**—In Texas, these trailing plants require little space at the ground level but can create spectacular displays of foliage and flowers while providing screening and welcome shade during summer. Choices include bleeding heart vine *(Clerodendrum thomsoniae)*, butterfly vine, hyacinth bean, Rangoon creeper *(Quisqualis indica)*, and air potato vine *(Dioscorea bulbifera)*.

PRUNE

■ **Shrubs**—Cut back early-spring flowering shrubs such as azaleas, forsythias, quince, and spireas once they have finished blooming.

FERTILIZE

■ **Roses**—Feed lightly once a month with a fertilizer such as 15-0-15 or 18-9-18 all-purpose plant food. If black spot becomes a problem, spray with Immunox fungicide according to the package directions. If insects such as aphids and thrips are also causing trouble, use Immunox Plus Insect & Disease Control instead.

■ **Vegetables**—Use a light monthly application of low-nitrogen fertilizer, such as 5-10-15. Set out okra, eggplant, and peppers in full sun. Water new plants daily and established ones several times a week.

■ **Lawns**—For established turf in Florida, apply a fertilizer without phosphorous, such as 15-0-15, at the rate of 6 pounds per 1,000 square feet of grass. On new lawns, use 15-5-15 or 18-9-18 all-purpose plant food.

Cut Flowers

Zinnias, sunflowers, cosmos, gladioli, Mexican sunflowers, celosias, purple coneflowers, and globe amaranth are excellent for indoor bouquets. Plant in a sunny, well-drained site. Begin by working in 3 to 5 inches of organic matter, such as composted pine bark, peat, or compost, along with 3 to 5 pounds of balanced fertilizer per 100 square feet of bed. Choose flowers that will complement the colors inside your home. Garden blooms freshen interiors, and they're economical and fun to share with friends and relatives. Many kinds will produce in greater abundance if cut often. If it isn't practical to have a separate area for cut flowers, set aside a couple of rows in the vegetable garden, or work them into borders and containers. Plant now to enjoy a summer of harvest.

Tip of the Month

To prevent peonies from being broken and destroyed by heavy rains, place a piece of chicken wire over the leaves and stems as soon as they emerge from the ground. The stems and foliage will grow through the wire and be supported against the weather.

RICHARD STONE
AMHERST, VIRGINIA

Classic Beauties

Wish you could grow gorgeous peonies? Follow our tips for success.

BY ELLEN RUOFF RILEY
PHOTOGRAPHY ALLEN ROKACH, JEAN ALLSOPP, RALPH ANDERSON

This rambling peony border in eastern Maryland demonstrates a lovely landscape use for the long-lived perennial shrub.

When the first huge peony unfurls into a flounce of petals, you want to touch it, wear it, and live somewhere inside that magnificent bloom. The perfume, lifted by late-spring air, can't be inhaled deeply enough. You hope it will last forever.

Such giddiness is a springtime ritual in the Upper South. There, peonies become large, shrubby plants festooned with flowers. Divided and passed along for generations, peonies are a long-lived legacy. But move them to the warmer Middle and Lower South, and they're a challenge.

Peonies need cold winter weather to flourish, and without sufficient cooling, few flowerbuds are produced. Greg Jones, with Gilbert H. Wild and Son in Sarcoxie, Missouri, is an expert on their cultivation. "We've found that peonies need about three to four weeks of cold—around 32 degrees. But every variety has a different cooling requirement," he says.

A herbaceous perennial, peony *(Paeonia lactiflora)* has flowers and foliage that emerge from large buds or "eyes" on tuberous roots. In the Upper and Middle South, the eye should be covered by an inch of soil. But in the Lower South, place it barely beneath the surface. "You want the eyes as close to the top of the soil line as you can get, so the plant can benefit from cool winter temperatures," Greg says.

Avoid mulching peonies, because this insulates the roots and prevents sufficient cooling.

Surefire Success

Peonies are considered potentially poor performers in the Middle and Lower South, but there are secrets for helping them thrive. "Location is a big part of how well you'll do with peonies," says Rick Berry with Goodness Grows in Lexington, Georgia. "Here, we recommend partial shade, preferably with protection from afternoon sun." Peonies grown in full sun often suffer leaf scorch by midsummer. The plants go dormant

above: 'Sarah Bernhardt' peonies bloom with volumes of soft-pink petals. **left:** Semidouble selections, such as this rosy pink one, appear to open more easily than some fully double ones.

early, preventing them from building up food reserves. This reduces flowering the next year. In filtered light, however, peony foliage continues growing into late summer or early fall, storing energy for the following year's blooms.

Peonies do not require fertilizer when planted in good soil. "If you consider the beautiful ones you see in cemeteries, plants that have been there 30 years with virtually no attention, you realize they do just fine without supplemental feeding," Greg says. However, in many parts of the South, gardeners are faced with heavy, clay-based soil, which lacks the necessary nutrition. In these areas, apply Holland Bulb Booster after bloom, following the directions to prevent overfeeding.

Soil preparation is important—peonies falter in wet conditions. "They don't want to be in soil that holds moisture," Greg says. So dig a large, wide hole and amend the soil with leaf mold or soil conditioner, which is available at garden shops. To plant, mound the improved soil inside the hole. Then place the roots with the eyes just below the soil surface, facing up. This ensures adequate drainage and aids winter cooling.

What To Buy
The selection you choose may determine how well your peony blooms. "We've found that early-blooming and semidouble ones generally do very well in the South," Greg says.

Don't hesitate to cut peonies and bring them inside for a fragrant bouquet.

"There are also some really beautiful doubles that do well, but they should be the early kinds too." Many Southern gardeners believe the single varieties perform best in warmer regions. Dependable peony selections include 'Festiva Maxima,' 'Paula Fay,' 'Bowl of Beauty,' and 'Kansas.'

When you order by mail, the plant you receive will be bare root. This means it is not actively growing and not planted in soil. "Order your peonies in spring, when you can see what the blooms on plants in your area look like. You shouldn't receive your peony until fall when it is shipped dormant," Greg says. If planted immediately, the peony will resume a normal growth cycle in its new home. If you plant peonies in the spring, avoid bare-root plants. Instead, look to garden centers and nurseries where you will find them already growing in large containers.

The Truth About Moving
"They say you should plant a peony for life," Greg says. "What that means is that a peony will easily live for 50 years. It doesn't mean you can't move it." The time to relocate a plant is late fall, when it's dormant. After the foliage has died down, dig a wide ring around the plant, and carefully lift the roots. Replant it as you would a new peony. "Have patience. It may take several years to become established and bloom well," Rick says.

Peony blossoms tug at heartstrings and perfume the air with an old-fashioned fragrance. Take the challenge, and enjoy the rewards. ◆

This single peony has flourished for more than 20 years. The simple white bloom with a burst of yellow is pure elegance.

above: Don't be afraid to use ground covers under windows. Here a bed of wintercreeper euonymus links a pair of boxwoods. **left:** White 'Flower Carpet' roses form a nearly everblooming skirt beneath these large windows. They won't get much taller than this.

Don't Block the Windows

When plants get too big, you can't see out.

Maybe I'm just dense, but I've always thought that the main reason houses have windows is to let light in and let people see out. However, this principle seems to escape some folks when they plant trees and shrubs next to their houses. What's the perfect spot for a Colorado blue spruce recently used as a living Christmas tree? Why, right in front of a bay window. And what about some nice wax myrtles and thorny elaeagnus? Let's stick them in front of our living room windows.

The problem may not seem apparent at first, especially if you start with small plants. But unlike tables and deck chairs, plants have this disturbing habit of growing. If you don't ascertain their mature sizes before planting, you could quickly find yourself living in the dark. Of course, you might attempt to solve the problem by hacking back the offending plants every weekend. But this makes for ugly plants and irritable plant owners.

Planting the Right Way

The three examples shown here demonstrate the correct way to plant under first-floor windows. Caroline Benson of Easton, Maryland, planted a sweep of white 'Flower Carpet' roses beneath the handsome windows of her sunroom (above, left). These roses were originally marketed as a spreading ground cover reaching no more than 24 inches tall. Caroline discovered, however, that they grow up to 36 inches tall. That's no problem, because they still don't block the windows. And in addition to anchoring this corner of the house, they bloom all summer, don't need spraying, and require very little pruning.

In Arlington, Virginia, garden designer Tom Mannion broke with the notion that foundation plantings must consist of only woody plants. Instead, he combined shrubs, perennials, and ground cover (below, left). Two hollies, one green and one variegated, frame the windows without blocking them. Between the hollies is a mound of bigleaf golden ray *(Ligularia dentata)*, with coarse, burgundy-and-green leaves that are perfect foils for the grassy, light green patch of creeping liriope *(Liriope spicata)* in front.

You can't get much more simple and elegant than our third example (above, right), which comes from a home in Nashville. Here, a pair of boxwoods in a bed of wintercreeper euonymus *(Euonymus fortunei)* frame a window in a classic design. The euonymus forms a graceful sweep that contrasts nicely with the lawn and links the boxwoods. Just remember that some ground covers can climb—wintercreeper euonymus and English ivy are two examples—and you don't want them climbing wooden siding. So keep them low, and let the sunshine in.   STEVE BENDER

This mixed planting of hollies, bigleaf golden ray, and creeping liriope anchors the front of the house without obscuring the windows.

Nothing Shy About Wallflowers

Lovely and easy to grow, these blooms take center stage in spring.

When it comes to early-spring color, wallflowers don't stand on the sidelines. They're front and center in the garden, rolling out a carpet of sweet-smelling blooms that last for weeks. And get this—no flowers are easier to start from seed, so you can grow a magic carpet for the price of a washcloth.

Wallflowers, believe it or not, are close kin to cabbage and broccoli. You can discern the family resemblance in the clusters of four-petaled flowers. (Let your cabbage and broccoli bolt, and you'll see what I mean.) Two species are primarily grown. Siberian wallflower (*Erysimum* x *allionii*) is the hardier and more compact of the two. It forms a mound about 12 inches tall and wide. 'Orange Bedder' features bright orange blooms, while 'Moonlight' sports soft yellow blooms. English wallflower *(E. cheiri)* grows 18 to 24 inches tall and wide. Its somewhat larger, velvety flowers may be yellow, cream, orange, red, pink, purple, apricot, or mahogany.

Though technically perennials, both types often act more like annuals or biennials in the South. Siberian wallflower may persist for two years or so, but that's pushing it for English wallflower. Don't get bent out of shape though—both reseed. And if you want guaranteed wallflowers every spring, do what I do—set out new plants each spring. That way, when old plants kick the bucket, new ones will kick in.

To start plants, simply sow seeds about ¼-inch deep into cell packs filled with moist potting soil in early spring or late summer. Seeds sprout quickly. When roots fill the cell packs, transplant the seedlings to the garden. Plants set out in spring sometimes bloom by fall, but certainly by the following spring. Plants set out in fall bloom the next spring.

For the best effect, plant sweeps of wallflowers in the foreground of flowerbeds. They combine well with pansies, violas, calendulas, candytuft, blue phlox, snapdragons, daffodils, and tulips. For just pennies a plant, they'll put on a show you can't ignore.

STEVE BENDER

WALLFLOWERS
At a Glance

Types: short-lived perennials treated as annuals or biennials
Size: 12 to 24 inches tall and wide
Light: full sun
Soil: moist, fertile, well drained
Sow: early spring or late summer
Degree of difficulty: easy

Sweeps of orange and yellow Siberian wallflowers provide stunning spring color at Boone Hall Plantation in Mount Pleasant, South Carolina.

The Shadow Knows

One of the South's most respected nurserymen, Don Shadow, tells the secrets to growing dogwood.

Flowering dogwood combines just about everything in a tree that a homeowner could want—gorgeous spring blooms, picturesque form, handsome bark, and colorful fall foliage and berries. Many people believe flowering dogwood (*Cornus florida*) does better in shade and, in fact, will croak if planted in full sun. To find out the truth, I asked someone who should know—Don Shadow, considered by many to be the South's foremost nurseryman.

A wholesale grower in Winchester, Tennessee, Don works tirelessly to develop and distribute superior plants to the public. He's totally ruthless when evaluating plants. He'll grow thousands of dogwoods to find the few worth keeping and propagating. His advice about growing these trees, summarized below, may surprise you.

■ Planting in a sunny, open spot is usually okay. You'll get many more flowers and also much less fungus on the leaves. Placing them under dripping trees may result in powdery mildew, leaf spot, or dogwood anthracnose fungus. The latter disease, which causes tan blotches on the leaves and twig dieback, has caused great damage in forests. The native habitat for flowering dogwood is in the light, high shade of tall trees. So light afternoon shade is especially beneficial in the Lower and Coastal South.

■ Don't forget to water. "Dogwood has a shallow root system," he explains. "After planting, it has to be carefully watered for two to three years to get established. I don't mean sprinkle—I mean *water*. Put the soaker hose around it, and leave it on all night. Even large trees need watering when it's dry." Drought-

PHOTOGRAPHS: ALLEN ROKACH

FLOWERING DOGWOOD
At a Glance

Size: 25 to 35 feet tall and wide
Light: full sun or light shade
Soil: moist, acid, well drained, lots of organic matter
Prune: in late spring after flowering
Water: thoroughly while tree is young and also during dry spells
Range: Upper, Middle, Lower, and Coastal South

top: Flowering dogwood likes an open, sunny spot. Don't let it dry out in summer. **above:** White is the most common bloom color, but you can also buy pink- and red-flowering forms.

stressed trees often suffer from leaf scorch—brown edges on leaves—and are more susceptible to pests.

■ Don't use string trimmers and lawnmowers to cut grass around trunks. "That kills more dogwoods than anything," says Don. "A young dogwood is a very thin-barked tree." Accidentally stripping off the bark at the base can be fatal. Instead, mulch around the trunk to keep down grass, or use hand clippers.

■ Choose named selections rather than unnamed seedlings. Though seedlings may be cheaper, named selections bloom better and are more resistant to insects and diseases.

Don's favorite selections include 'Appalachian Spring' (white flowers, attractive foliage, resists dogwood anthracnose), 'Barton' (large white flowers, blooms at a young age), 'Cherokee Brave' (red flowers with white centers, resists mildew), 'Cloud Nine' (similar to 'Barton,' resists mildew), and 'Pygmaea' (white-flowered dwarf, blooms when it's 2 feet tall, reaches 12 feet tall after 20 years). Look for these selections in garden centers this spring.

STEVE BENDER

Little Lawns

You can enjoy all the benefits of lush, green grass without all the hassles.

If spending weekends wrestling a lawnmower isn't your idea of leisure, yet you still love the feel of fresh-cut grass under your toes, here is the perfect solution: Reduce the amount of grass in your yard.

Small Lawns—Big Rewards

The first step is to evaluate what you want. If you have visions of riding horseback across the back 40 or hosting the local Little League championship, perhaps a bordered lawn isn't for you. But if you like clean landscape lines, healthy green grass, and free weekends, consider hemming your lawn in with pavers or a brick patio.

If there are places in your yard where grass just doesn't grow or where mowing is a problem, reshaping your lawn can be the solution. It's often difficult to grow grass under the shade of trees, in spots with poor drainage, or where there is competition from shrubs with shallow roots. Growing grass in places without these challenges reduces the amount of required maintenance.

Another benefit of a bordered lawn is how the other plants in the yard will prosper. Lawnmowers and string trimmers can damage the bark of trees and shrubs. This incidental contact is common and can have disastrous effects. When a string trimmer cuts a tree's bark, the wound immediately becomes a vector for disease and insect damage. Without proper care, this can eventually lead to the death of the plant. A simple solution to this is to reshape your lawn so that all your trees and shrubs are outside its perimeter, thus avoiding accidental contact. This also benefits the turf by

Stone steps and English ivy create the perfect formal border for this turf pathway.

This Dallas front yard combines flat stone pavers with turf to create a formal but functional entrance. For added fun, the circular walkway doubles as a children's racetrack.

reducing water and nutrient competition and providing more sunlight. With less fertilization, less watering, and less mowing to do, you can enjoy your yard more.

Design Advantages

In addition to the many maintenance benefits you'll reap, there are some wonderful design rewards as well. Redbrick or black stone borders around your lawn create a contrast of color that breaks up the monotony of green. Hardscape borders can also provide continuity between the house and lawn. Replicating the brick or stone of a house's foundation in the landscape will pull the eye from the curb to the front door. The shape of a lawn can also play off a house's design. Repeating the straight lines of a front porch or the curved lines of an archway will create a pleasing effect.

Installation

Putting in turf for a smaller lawn is like putting in turf for a regular one, just easier. Instead of truckloads of turf, all you need are the design and the materials for a border. Begin by marking off the area for your new lawn with stakes, powdered lime, or a garden hose. If you're going to replace the existing grass, solarize the area by putting down black plastic for a few weeks, or spray a selective herbicide, such as Roundup. Once the grass is dead, till the area you marked including space for the border. Add an inch of compost to the soil, and rake the area smooth. Put the border material in place using sand or cement filler. The ideal height of the border will be the height of the grass when it's ready to be mowed.

The grass can be seeded, plugged, or laid as sod. This will depend on what kind of grass you're using and how long you're willing to wait for the perfect lawn. Regardless of the method, the final step is to water. Grass needs to be moist for optimal

Fifteen minutes behind the push mower is all it takes to keep this small lawn looking wonderful.

PHOTOGRAPH: KARIM SHAMSI-BASHA

KINDS OF GRASS

There are two important considerations when selecting grass: Where do you live, and do you have sun or shade?

The vast majority of Southerners should use warm-season grasses, such as Bermuda, centipede, or Zoysia. These types thrive in heat and are dormant in winter. For those of you in the Upper and Middle South, try an evergreen type of fescue, such as 'Rebel' or 'Kentucky 31.' However, be aware that evergreen types do not grow when temperatures reach 80 degrees.

The other factor to consider when selecting grass is whether you have sun or shade in your yard. Most grasses naturally grow better in sun. However, there are some types that can get by with much less than others. If your lawn receives less than eight hours of sun a day, you should probably consider either centipede or Zoysia.

growth at this stage. Wait to mow or fertilize until the grass has thoroughly filled in.

Maintenance

Deep, infrequent watering is critical to encourage deep rooting and reduce the risk of the lawn dying during drought. All grass requires a certain amount of supplemental fertilizer; the quantity depends on the type you choose and the region where you live. Mowing can actually provide some nutrient requirements for grass; just leave the cut blades to break down naturally in the soil. Mowing is also the best defense against weeds. By regularly cutting the grass, you don't give weeds a chance to develop seeds and spread across your lawn. If this is not sufficient, try a pre-emergence herbicide to kill weeds before they germinate.

Heavy clay soil is great for holding on to water and nutrients, but a healthy lawn also requires air for proper growth. Many grasses will become compacted, causing a lawn to suffocate. Aerating the soil each spring is a simple solution. A machine called a core aerator lifts a 3-inch plug out of the turf every foot or so and deposits it on the lawn. These holes allow air and nutrients to penetrate to the turf's root zone for healthy new growth. A core aerator can be rented at a garden-supply store, and using it takes about the same amount of time as mowing the lawn.

Liming the soil is another important maintenance job for lawns in the South in which soil is not alkaline. Heavy rains and decomposing organic matter, such as pine straw and pine bark, tend to create acid conditions. Adding lime once a year will bring the pH of the soil closer to neutral and make it more favorable for turf growth. Buy a bag of pelletized lime or gypsum at a garden-supply store, and sprinkle it on the lawn. The application rate ranges from 2 to 6 pounds per 100 square feet, depending on your soil type. EDWIN MARTY

left: These crabapples are an attractive flowering and fruiting screen.
below: A steel cable running between two brick columns supports and guides the graceful trees.
inset: Each spring, clouds of light pink blooms emerge on this living fence.

Crabapple Crossing

Train fruiting or ornamental trees to grow in unique ways, and add a nice design element to your garden.

Trees tend to have a mind of their own, but with coaxing, they can be manipulated to form espaliers, which will beautify any garden. Join hands with nature to create interesting designs and graceful boundaries.

The word "espalier" describes trees that are trained to grow flat against walls or fences. Freestanding espaliers may be supported by a post-and-wire framework. These crabapple trees, planted at a 45-degree angle, crisscross making five neat X shapes. Their gray trunks create an interesting diamond pattern.

A Living Fence

This garden needed a buffer between the parking area and a small formal garden. The homeowner didn't want a wall or solid planting. She envisioned an open screen so you could see the adjoining sunken garden. She came up with the idea to grow and train crabapples in this narrow bed.

X Marks the Spot

Most espaliered trees are flat against a wall, but these freestanding espaliered crabapples create a living fence. A steel cable stretched between two brick columns secures the limbs and holds the trees in place. As the spring flowers fade, green foliage appears and tops the trees through the season. In fall, the trees produce attractive fruit.

The homeowner planted trees at alternating angles and staked them to a wire running from the ground to a 6-foot-high horizontal cable. Once the trees reached the cable, she clipped the tops to force lateral branching and trained side shoots to wrap around the horizontal cable.

It took a few years for the trees to grow and fill out. Suckers from the main trunks must be removed each year during the growing season. The homeowner plucks them by hand.

Fruit Trees and More

Espalier techniques originated in Europe's medieval walled towns, where confined areas left gardeners with little space to grow fruit. They soon discovered that when trees were grown flat, their fruit was bigger and ripened earlier. They were also easier to prune because they were low and within reach.

Other fruiting trees, such as apple, pear, peach, and fig, also work well. But you don't have to use fruit trees; ornamental plants make beautiful espaliers. Evergreens, such as camellia, cotoneaster, pyracantha, and 'Little Gem' magnolia, are good choices. Deciduous plants, such as crepe myrtle, Japanese maple, forsythia, and flowering quince, can also be trained to grow flat. Espaliers are traditionally placed in formal gardens, but a loosely espaliered Japanese maple looks at home in a natural setting.

If you don't know where to start, look for plants that are already growing on flat trellises at nurseries. Some garden centers and nurseries sell plants such as camellia, pyracantha, or privet that have been trained to grow on flat forms. Or look for plants that are growing flat or one-sided and can be placed against a wall.

Train a tree or shrub to grow the way you want, and it will reward you with foliage, flowers, and a decorative garden feature. CHARLIE THIGPEN

Spring Baskets

Hop into gardening by nestling small, plant-filled containers in strategic locations throughout the landscape. To create a fun seasonal look, we gave this display an Easter theme, mixing foliage, flowers, eggs, and a small rabbit statuary.

Classic Wicker

We lined our traditional Easter baskets with burlap and filled them with soil. Then we placed plants inside. To make the wicker last longer, you can leave plants in their plastic pots and arrange them in the basket. Fill in the voids between containers with moss or burlap. Take the pots out when watering, so the baskets won't stay wet.

Durable Metal

A metal basket makes an excellent, long-lasting planter. This one needed drainage holes, so we drilled a few in the bottom before planting golden club moss and hostas. Golden club moss grows flat and covers the soil like a shimmering chartreuse blanket underneath the leafy hostas. This shade-loving mix provides a medley of foliage from spring till summer.

New Life for an Old Basket

A rusted, wire-framed hanging basket makes a great planter. We removed the chains and let it rest on the ground. Then we added a coco-fiber liner and filled it with potting soil.

When choosing plants, be creative and try a shrub. We put a small boxwood in the center and tucked petunias around it. Once the boxwood outgrows the space, plant it in the yard. We used variegated ivy along the outside edge of the container.

Tasty Treats

Two of the baskets contain edible greenery (top photo). One is filled with creeping thyme and topped with a large ornamental egg. The thyme's fine texture makes a nice green nest for the egg. The largest basket contains chartreuse leaf lettuce mixed with chives, which have spiky, hollow foliage. Chives produce beauti-

above, left: Thyme, lettuce, and chives make a tasty and showy mix.
above, center: Ornamental eggs add flair to hosta and golden club moss.
above, right: Variegated ivy and petunias contrast for a nice effect.

ful pink spring blooms. For a decorative touch, use eggshells as pots. Crack open eggs, wash the shells, and fill them with small sprigs of thyme.

This season, let baskets decorate your landscape. It's a great time of year to garden, and plants are plentiful. So what are you waiting for? Plant one for yourself, and give one to a friend for a memorable spring treat.   CHARLIE THIGPEN

Woodland Azalea

Mother Nature douses woods and gardens with perfume and fresh flowers as native azaleas come to life after a long winter's nap.

left: Native azaleas are a great addition to the landscape and can be combined with leatherleaf mahonia berries for a pretty spring arrangement.
top: Alabama azaleas have pure white flowers with blotched yellow centers.
above: This Alabama azalea fills a small patio with fragrance and beauty. Its delicate blooms look like lace.

Each spring, a sweet fragrance dances through forests across the South. Tall, slender shrubs sprinkled under mature hardwoods and pines release this wonderful scent from their clusters of trumpet-like blooms. Native azaleas are one of the most beautiful flowering plants indigenous to our Southern landscape.

Many of us grew up calling this plant wild honeysuckle, because the flowers are very similar to the blooms of the honeysuckle vine, and both are sweet smelling. But this native shrub or small tree is truly a rhododendron. Many gardeners fill their yard with the popular evergreen azaleas that are native to Japan, China, and Korea, but few think about planting native ones, which are naturally suited to our climate. But more and more native azaleas are finding their way into nurseries, and many can be found in mail-order catalogs. Never dig these plants from the woods; wild colonies should be left alone. Container-grown native azaleas purchased from nurseries will go through less shock when planted.

Design Use

Native azaleas make a great addition to any landscape. They're well suited for naturalized areas or wooded lots, but they also can be used effectively in a more formal setting. Use them as a featured specimen for a courtyard, patio, or front entryway. Plant them in front of a wall or fence where their shape is visible and their blooms will stand out. They also look great against a backdrop of large evergreen plants, such as magnolia, holly, or anise tree. Be sure to plant them close to high-traffic areas so you can experience their flowers up close and inhale their sweet scent. Plant ground covers underneath native azaleas. Their long, brownish-gray trunks look great rising from low-growing plants including autumn fern, English ivy, liriope, mondo grass, or pachysandra.

Shrub or Tree?

Most people refer to them as upright free-form shrubs, but with age some selections can grow 8 to 14 feet tall and can make attractive small trees. The graceful upturned branches look

top: This Florida flame azalea has orange-red buds that open pale orange, giving the blooms a two-toned look.
above: The blooms of Piedmont azalea are usually pink, but they can be white.
right: Piedmont azaleas are native from North Carolina to Texas. This grouping shows how effective they can be in a residential landscape.

as if they were made to present their showy blooms. Don't confine them to a tight area, because heavy pruning will ruin their graceful shapes.

Light Requirements

Native azaleas thrive in dappled light as understory plants. It is best to place them under a large, established tree where the plants will receive high shade. They will grow in heavy shade, but blooms will be sparse and plants will be leggy. Grown in full sun, native azaleas will flower heavily but need lots of water. Their roots are shallow, like those of all rhododendrons, and dry out quickly in sunny locations. They'll require mulch, such as pine needles, during dry periods to become established.

Soil and Planting

Native azaleas prefer a well-drained, acid soil that contains lots of organic matter. When planting, add sphagnum peat moss, leaf mold, or finely shredded bark, and mix it into the soil. To give your azaleas an extra boost, add 1 cup of cottonseed meal per plant, mixing it into each hole. Plant them high to improve drainage, leaving the top 2 inches of the root ball above the ground. Add 2 to 3 inches of mulch, such as pine bark or pine straw, to keep the roots from drying out so quickly. If you live in Central or West Texas where the soils are alkaline, you may want to grow a few in large containers placed in a shaded, protected area. Fill pots with a soil mix heavy in peat or shredded pine bark.

Different Colors

The funnel-shaped blooms of native azalea come in a wide range of colors including bright white, pink, yellow, orange, and scarlet red. Alabama azalea *(Rhododendron alabamense)* has highly fragrant white flowers with yellow blotched centers. It will grow 8 to 10 feet tall. Piedmont azalea *(R. canescens)* can have aromatic white, pink, or rose flowers. It grows 10 to 12 feet tall. Florida flame azalea *(R. austrinum)* has pale yellow, cream, pink, or orange-red flowers. It grows 8 to 10 feet tall and tolerates heat, humidity, and drought. The plumleaf azalea *(R. prunifolium)* is a late bloomer that produces orange-red or bright red flowers in July. It grows around 12 feet tall and is a fine specimen in any summer garden.

Native azaleas look great in our Southern forests, and they can make your garden look great too. Once established, they are carefree and self-reliant. Plant this shrub, and you can enjoy one of Mother Nature's miracles in your own yard.

CHARLIE THIGPEN

tiny TOMATOES

For big taste in a small package, try these. They're easy to grow.

Big or small, tomatoes are one of life's simple pleasures. Their reds, yellows, and oranges bring color to the table. Round, oblong, and elliptical shapes are a feast for the eyes. The sweet, tangy flavors can send your taste buds into orbit. And these tiny ones, known as cherry tomatoes, are some of the best and easiest to grow.

More Than A Mouthful

So which one should you choose for your garden? Jason Powell, owner of Petals From the Past nursery in Jemison, Alabama, grows and sells a wide variety of tomato plants. He loves all the different selections of cherry tomatoes. Jason says, "So many flavors are available, from acid to sweet." It all comes down to taste.

So how will you know which one you prefer? If this is your first time, try growing three different types. 'Yellow Pear,' 'Supersweet 100,' and 'Sungold' will give you a nice range of flavors from mild to sweet to tangy. Then, the following year, plant a new selection. Trade with your friends. Just try them, because you will love them. Use the chart to determine which selections are right for you.

With such a wide range of flavors, these tomatoes are great

above: These small tomatoes are dwarfed by the giant 'Beefsteak' selection.
right: Once plants start fruiting, there are hundreds of tomatoes to be picked.

TOMATO	COLOR	FLAVOR
'Sungold'	orange	tangy
'Supersweet 100'	red	sweet
'Sugar Snack'	red	sweet
'Ildi'	yellow	sweet
'Sweet Gold'	yellow gold	sweet
'Jenny'	orange	sweet
'Yellow Pear'	yellow	mild

for snacking, but they are also great in salads and salsas. "Another bonus," declares Jason, "is that kids love eating them; they are not as overwhelming as sliced tomatoes."

Easy To Grow

Jason says it's important to select the right location for planting. Choose a sunny, well-drained, fertile spot. Soil with a pH that is slightly acid is ideal. If you plan to sow seeds, it will be around 65 days before your first harvest. Transplants will shorten that time by several weeks. If you are in the Upper South, wait until the danger of frost has passed before planting (around the middle of this month).

If you are keen on getting the first tomatoes of the season, try covering plants with tomato tepees—plastic, water-filled protectors that reflect warmth back to the plant. Or you can cut the bottom off

BY GENE B. BUSSELL
PHOTOGRAPHY TINA CORNETT

top, left: The tomatoes ripen as you need them, so few are wasted. **above, left:** Cut side shoots off to direct plant energy into fruit production. **above, right:** Nothing beats a bagful of colorful cherry tomatoes.

empty milk jugs and cover plants after transplanting. Either way will help plants transition into the garden and get a jump on the growing season.

When setting out transplants, remove a few of the lower leaves, and set the plant deeply. Roots will then form along the main stem. Then dust with sulfur or Dipel to control powdery mildew, mites, and hornworms. To help prevent early and late blight, don't let leaves touch the ground while plants are getting established.

Cherry tomatoes are great for containers. You can grow them on your deck or near your kitchen door so they will be right at your fingertips. Though any container will do, try using The EarthBox, a self-watering, self-feeding system designed with the weekend gardener in mind.

Train your tomatoes well. All of those mentioned are indeterminate, which means they are vinelike and bear fruit over a longer period of time. They do need a little support. There are lots of ways to stake your tomatoes. Wire tomato cages are the first to come to mind, but cherry tomatoes can really travel. So wooden or spiral metal stakes that are at least 60 inches tall will work best. You can use stretch ties, twine, or nylon ties to attach the vines to the stakes.

It's important to pinch the side shoots of indeterminate tomatoes. With your fingertips or pruning shears, remove any shoots that emerge between the leaf and the main stem from 12 to 18 inches from the ground. This encourages a stronger main stem and helps keep the fruit off the ground and within easy reach.

Incorporating a well-balanced fertilizer prior to planting is very beneficial. A second light application during the middle of the growing season will help. But do not overfeed, as you will see more growth in leaves than in fruit.

Growing cherry tomatoes is almost as much fun as eating them. Though they are tiny, they will find a big place in your heart. ◆

Sweet-Smelling Tuberose

This timeless plant provides months of summer flowers and fragrance.

If you are looking for an easy plant with beautiful blooms and great fragrance, try tuberose *(Polianthes tuberosa)*. This Southern favorite is a breeze to grow, and its flowers can scent your garden or be cut for arrangements. All it really needs is a sunny spot and ordinary, well-drained soil.

It Just Takes a Few

A couple of tubers, planted close together when the soil has warmed in the spring, will quickly fill out into a thick mound of slender, grassy green leaves up to 1½ feet tall. This foliage is crowned with 3- to 4-foot-tall stalks of white tubular flowers in loose clusters in late summer or early fall. There are two basic types. The original 'Mexican Single' is the hardiest and most long-lasting. 'The Pearl' is the most popular double, combining shorter bloom spikes with larger, more generous flowers.

A favorite way to use these grassy plants is to arrange them in beds close to sidewalks or doorways so that their enticing scent can be fully enjoyed. Tuberoses make excellent plants for perfuming the evening garden, especially near porches and patios. The blooms have a ghostly white glow in twilight, while drifts of fragrance surprise the senses. Some people swear that singles have a stronger scent. Edna Toland, who used to keep tuberoses going in the flowerbeds of the Schultze House in San Antonio's historic district, believes there is no difference. She adds, "When the weather is really hot and dry, the single kinds may have an edge over the doubles, which do not always open properly."

Careful planning in the garden will help bloom stalks stay upright. Try planting them next to perennials, such as mealy-cup sage, 'Indigo Spires' salvia, or pink gaura, which grow outward during the season and will help hold the tuberose flower spikes in place.

Give Them a Lift

Tuberoses have been known and loved for many years in Mexico where they are called *nardo*. Edna says, "I let the plants go through the summer season till the foliage yellows in the fall. Then I cut back and dig the tubers, first taking up the largest sets, which will usually be the size of my little finger. I store them for the winter in paper bags of perlite, hanging inside netted grapefruit or onion bags. These can be hung in a dry room out of the way until spring."

The thrifty gardener can also pack them in boxes or flowerpots of sand for safekeeping. Be sure that each of the tubers you keep or plant has a green tip. Smaller offsets can be saved, if there is room, or given away. They will need to grow for another season to get big enough to put on a good display.   WILLIAM C. WELCH

PHOTOGRAPHS: TINA CORNETT

STARTING TUBEROSES EARLY

In areas of the South where they may be nipped by frost or discouraged from early growth due to cold soil, tuberoses may be started indoors in pots. Set out in the garden when the weather is warmer, or keep through the season in containers. Plant them 2 inches deep in good potting soil, carefully setting the tubers 2 inches apart. Feed with an acid-type fertilizer. Dig the tubers, and let them dry out when the leaves start to yellow in the fall. Store in dry peat or perlite away from freezing temperatures until planting time in midspring.

Look for tuberoses at your favorite local nursery in the spring. They may also be purchased through mail-order sources. Expect to pay about $10 for a bag of five tubers.

far left: Tuberoses mix well in a garden border along a picket fence.
left: Dig the tubers for winter storage.

Cottage Garden surprise

Flowers abound and plants crowd
every corner of this fanciful suburban Delaware home site.

When Art Tucker begins talking about plants, it's like a dam has broken. Torrents of facts, maelstroms of science, and tsunamis of obscure foreign phrases rush from his mouth in a deluge of words that's often too quick to follow. The man just knows so much. And the sprawling garden that surrounds his house is a living, blooming library of his gardening knowledge.

One of the country's foremost experts on herbs, Art teaches horticulture at Delaware State University in Dover. There he analyzes the essential oils in herbs and tries to figure out why and how they affect us. His inquisitive nature accounts for many plants, some comely and some weird, that you find in his garden. For example, Art grows greater celandine *(Chelidonium majus)* not because of its lovely yellow flowers, but because he discovered that the juice in its stems cures warts. He also cultivates Paraguayan sweet herb *(Stevia rebaudiana)* because its leaves contain a compound up to 300 times sweeter than sugar without any calories or threat of cavities.

left: A grape- and kiwi-covered arbor and path direct you to a gate decorated with 'Shailer's Provence' and 'Cl. Cécile Brunner' roses. **right:** Yellow-flowering dyer's woad *(Isatis tinctoria)* engulfs the fence in front of the maze garden. Historically cultivated as a source of blue dye, this plant can be invasive, but Art likes the flowers.

BY STEVE BENDER / PHOTOGRAPHY ALLEN ROKACH / STYLING ROSE NGUYEN

Art also teaches a semester course in plant identification. You can't help but feel for his students when his garden becomes their classroom. Not only must they identify dozens of obscure roses, bulbs, and pass-along plants, but also, at any moment, Art might throw them a real stumper. For example: +*Laburnocytisus,* which is a bizarre combination of two different plants whose tissues grow side by side without exchanging genes. Perfect scores in this particular class are scarcer than sincerity in Hollywood.

Birth of a Gardener

Don't be surprised if Art bleeds green, because gardening is in his blood. "I've been interested in plants since I was a kid," he says. "My

> ## "I think I'm reinventing my childhood."
>
> *Art Tucker*

grandparents had big gardens, my father had a huge orchard, and my mother grew lots of flowers." Unfortunately, his childhood fascination with plants left less-gifted friends and classmates wondering if he was a bit loony. "I would take hyacinths I'd grown to show the kids at school and say, 'What's up with your gardens?' " he recalls. "More than once, the teachers screamed at the class, 'Why can't you be more like Arthur?' You can imagine what recess was like."

Neighbors must have had their doubts, too, when Art and his family moved to Camden, Delaware, in 1980. Cape Cod houses lined his street, each with a lawn as neat and orderly as a stamp collection. But the plain lawn the Tuckers inherited

above, left: Beside white-flowering money plant and yellow greater celandine rests Art's "anti-gazing ball," a clay sphere bought at a discount store.
left: Surrounded by Oriental arborvitae, Art and his cat, Chloe, bask in their notoriety.
below: From the path you can glimpse the wild garden in back. "Almost every plant you see was grown from a 3-inch cutting," Art says. "I'm cheap."

In the front yard where lawn once ruled, now a cottage garden reigns. The assembled plants include yucca, old roses, reseeding poppies, lavenders, and a rosy pink mat of caraway thyme (*Thymus herba-barona*).

Art and wife Sherry create little surprises for kids. In the back of the garden lies a huge nest Sherry wove from twigs and filled with large plastic "dinosaur eggs" covered with paper.

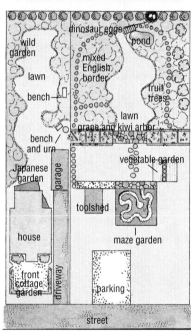

'Miss Kim' lilac, blue Siberian iris, and an urn filled with vetiver grass (*Vetiveria zizanioides*) make a splendid combination in the English mixed border.

was doomed from the start. "I spent part of my college time earning money cutting grass at a golf course," he says. "I know how to do it, but I don't like it." Out went the lawn, and in went a picket fence, gravel paths, wildflowers, herbs, perennials, roses, bulbs, succulents, and conifers. When he ran out of space in his yard, he bought the lot next door so he would have more room to plant. The kids on the street called his garden "the jungle." Before long, though, their parents were requesting tours.

The Cottage Style Defined

Ask Art to describe his landscape, and he replies, "Eclectic. Maniacal." His is the quintessential cottage garden, where exuberance, color, and freedom reign supreme. Formality and regimentation are verboten. Few straight lines, no stairstep plantings, no sheared hedges, no edged lawns. Plants intertwine and jostle for sunlight; seedlings come up where they will.

Yet stroll through the plantings, and you discern a method to the madness. Fences, gates, trees, and shrubs divide the garden into distinct rooms, each with its own personality. A grape- and kiwi-covered arbor frames a view; urns and benches provide focal points, and curving paths hint at surprises just around the bend. Whimsical elements, such as an "anti-gazing ball" (it absorbs light) and "dinosaur eggs" (they're really big) bring a smile. To a first-time visitor, this may look like chaos, but it's very organized chaos.

Connecting With the Past

There's no denying, though, that when it comes to plants, Art's a bit

of a pack rat. He receives strange and wonderful plants from friendly gardeners all over the country. And he scours gardens, cemeteries, and old home sites for heirloom selections of roses, daffodils, iris, and other plants that have all but disappeared from the nursery trade.

"I think I'm reinventing my childhood," he explains. "My grandmother's garden had thousands of different plants. It made such a vivid impression on my mind. I later inherited the property and then sold it to pay for my college education. I wish I could go back and dig up the plants that are probably still there."

Doing so would, of course, require researching all of their complete histories, as Art unfailingly does for nearly every plant in his garden. "I'm a bit anal," he admits. "I want to find out exactly what the dumb thing is, when it was introduced, and how it got here."

No such mysteries plague Art's neighbors. They know exactly when the strange plants arrived. It all started the day Art ripped out his lawn.

above, left: Above a peony, an old rosebush laden with blooms clings to a fence for support.
left: When Art's family moved in, the front yard was mostly lawn. The grass never had a chance. Art wanted flowers.
above: A multitude of colors, sizes, and forms shows just how many different roses Art grows. But one flower here is not a rose. Can you find it? (The answer is in Editor's Notebook on page 68.)

Oakleaf hydrangeas grace the South with their blooms (See pages 108–111.)

May

Editor's Notebook

Houseflies are the dumbest living things on Earth, literally incapable of learning anything, which makes me wonder sometimes if houseflies equipped with pruners have been savaging our neighborhood's crepe myrtles. No matter how many times I tell folks not to chop their crepe myrtles into big, ugly stumps each spring, they do it anyway, maiming the beautiful trunks and ruining the natural treelike form. But perhaps "crepe murder" is a matter of taste, not intelligence. If so, here is a pruning task everyone can agree on. You know how a crepe myrtle typically sprouts a thicket of suckers at the base each spring? Reach down now, and pull them off at ground level. That will keep your crepe myrtle from turning into a thick, unkempt shrub. It will also prove to the world that you're not a housefly. For most of us, that's a good thing. —STEVE BENDER

Plants for Shade

Brighten shaded areas with masses of wax begonias, impatiens, coleus, and caladiums. Prepare the soil by adding 3 to 5 inches of organic material such as composted pine bark, peat, or your own compost. Till this into the existing soil along with an application of slow-release fertilizer, such as 19-6-12, at the rate of 3 tablespoons per 4 square feet of bed. Select 4- or 6-inch pots of plants for a quick effect, and place them 10 to 12 inches apart. The bright flower colors of begonias and impatiens can be blended with fancy-leaf caladiums or coleus that feature chocolate, maroon, or green leaf patterns.

TIPS

■ **Bloom supports**—Stake tall-growing flowers, such as gladioli, dahlias, and lilies, now before they begin to bloom. Bamboo, wire tomato cages, or branches will all work well. Tie branches with strips of cloth or raffia. The bamboo stakes and raffia are available in green if you want to hide the stakes and show off the flowers.

■ **Butterflies**—If you wish to attract them, add plants that will provide lots of nectar, such as butterfly bush, lantana, coneflower, and summer phlox. Also include host plants for caterpillars to feed on. Choices include parsley, dill, and milkweed.

■ **Climbing roses**—They generally flower at the tips of shoots. Train the shoots of your climbing roses to grow horizontally by weaving them through a trellis or lattice. This encourages side shoots to grow from the main shoots and produce flowers. After bloom, trim the side shoots back by 6 inches—or more if the rose is too vigorous. Remove main shoots that are dead or produce little or no lateral growth.

■ **Lawn care**—Continue to sod or sprig Bermuda, St. Augustine, centipede, and Zoysia now if you need to repair or establish a lawn. Zoysia, St. Augustine, and Bermuda prefer a fertilizer high in nitrogen, but centipede needs one low in nitrogen.

■ **Magnolias**—Southern magnolias will drop more leaves than usual this month as they shed their old foliage and sprout new growth. As it is hard to grow grass beneath a magnolia anyway, wait until after the flurry of leaf drop, and then cover the magnolia leaves with mulch such as pine straw.

Annual Vinca

Also called Madagascar periwinkle, annual vinca (*Catharanthus roseus*) has long been a popular drought- and heat-tolerant flower for full sun and well-drained soil. However, vinca is susceptible to a blight caused by a fungus that lives in the soil. If you've had problems growing vinca in the past, don't plant it in the same area again, because the fungus will still be in the soil. Other tips for reducing the chance of disease include buying healthy plants and watering as little as needed once the vincas are established in the landscape. Some of the best selections to plant are in the Little Series, which includes 'Bright Eye,' 'Pinkie,' and 'Linda.'

Daylilies

Perennial color can easily be achieved by adding daylilies (*Hemerocallis* sp.) to your garden this month. Select them now while they are blooming so you can choose the colors, sizes, and flower forms you prefer. Favorites include 'Hyperion,' 'Stella de Oro,' 'Ida Wimberly Munson,' 'Bill Norris,' and 'Happy Returns.' Plant in a location that gets at least six hours of full sun a day. However, these perennials are not too picky about soil, as long as the area has good drainage. Once established, daylilies will provide carefree, reliable color for years. With their easy maintenance and diverse bloom colors, daylilies can become addictive.

■ **Poison ivy**—Use directed sprays of herbicides, such as Roundup or Spectracide Systemic Grass & Weed Killer. Follow label directions carefully. Keep herbicide spray off foliage of desirable plants.

PLANT

■ **Annuals**—If you've not planted them yet, there is still plenty of time to add these blooms to brighten borders and containers. Choose impatiens, begonias, or torenias to cheer up shady locations. For sunny areas, use petunias, marigolds, or salvias for a vivid display.

■ **Caladiums**—Plant them in light to full shade where their leaves can brighten the landscape. Place tubers in moist, well-drained soil, knobby side up, 2 inches deep, and 18 inches apart. For the best show, plant a mass of no more than two selections.

■ **Mexican sunflowers**—*Tithonia rotundifolia* can be sown now to provide cut flowers later in the season. These richly colored bloomers, 4 to 6 feet tall, love the heat and sunshine. Mexican sunflower selections offer a range of beautiful orange hues. A dwarf selection, 'Fiesta del Sol,' grows less than 3 feet—perfect if you don't have much room. Add Mexican tuberose and perilla to your cutting garden too. The fragrant, creamy tuberose blossoms and the purple foliage of perilla will make the Mexican sunflowers shine.

■ **Warm-weather vegetables**—Okra, watermelon, cantaloupe, cucumbers, squash, black-eyed peas, and other Southern peas can be planted from seed at this time. Peppers, tomatoes, and tomatillos can be set out now that the soil has warmed.

■ **Perennials**—In Texas, easy-to-grow plants to enjoy this summer include daylilies, gaura, 'Indigo Spires' salvia, autumn sage, and hardy hibiscus. All of these can be planted now and will rebloom all summer.

PRUNE

■ **Climbing roses**—In Texas, it is safe to prune when the first flush of flowers on everblooming roses is over and when once-bloomers have finished their bloom cycles. Begin by removing any dead or weak canes, and then selectively shorten or remove wood as desired. Keep in mind that when rose canes are trained horizontally, they produce more flowers. Climbing forms of hybrid tea roses may benefit from having some of their older canes cut to the ground to encourage fresh growth to emerge.

■ **Ornamental grasses**—In Texas, cut back when fresh green growth appears. Divide clumps to get more plants. Miscanthus, pennisetum, fescue, and muhlenbergia will all thrive in this area.

May notes:

Tip of the Month

One reason azaleas fail to thrive is that many people simply dig a hole and plop in the plant without first gently spreading out the roots. Years later, you can pull up the plant and see that the root ball is still in the shape of the nursery pot it came in!

STEPHANIE BAUMAN
AVON LAKE, OHIO

make *an* entrance

Boost the value and appeal of your home with a front yard makeover.

This yard's amazing transformation proves it is possible to breathe new life into an older house. Owners Matt and Teresa Lux and their son, Drew, have lived in their cozy neighborhood for nine years. The couple had updated the interior to fit their style and needs, but the tired landscape remained dull and uninviting. They knew it was time to dress up the exterior.

The Luxes needed additional parking and a new entrance. A single strip of concrete driveway was the only off-street parking, and every time one of them needed to leave, they had to jockey cars. The old foundation plantings consisted of a row of tired, over-pruned azaleas. The family wanted colorful plantings that would entice guests to the front door. Matt and Teresa needed a landscape plan that would better utilize their small lot.

Getting Started

The front porch had a dated wooden railing that made the small space seem confining. Teresa removed the old railing, giving the area an open feel. The porch is elevated only about 30 inches above ground level, so there wasn't any need to put up a new railing. (Check codes in your area before removing railings.) The Luxes

enjoy sitting on their front porch, which now has an unobstructed view.

Hardscape First

Walkways, steps, patios, porches, arbors, parking surfaces, or anything else structural in the landscape is called hardscape. Adding these features

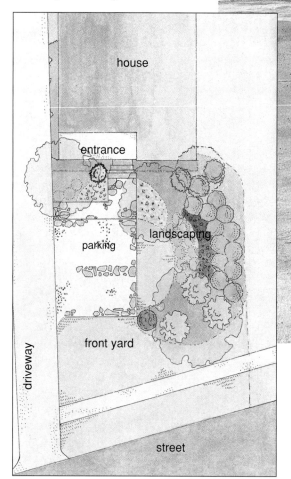

after

above: An updated landscape transforms this front yard. Colorful flowers add seasonal splendor, while a new sidewalk and steps offer a warm welcome to guests.

BY CHARLIE THIGPEN
PHOTOGRAPHY VAN CHAPLIN

should be done first, because it often involves heavy machinery or some type of construction that could damage plants. Using a small front-end loader, a contractor scooped out an area next to the drive for the new parking court. A stonemason built a low wall around the perimeter of the

before

above: By using low-maintenance plants and only a little grass, the Luxes keep yard work to a minimum.

parking area. He also added wide, flaring steps that lead to a gracious flagstone landing and walk.

Seeing the large parking area scared the Luxes at first. At 24 feet wide and 22 feet deep, it was kind of intimidating. But the spacious parking pad easily accommodates two vehicles and makes maneuvering simple. Crushed stone forms an inexpensive, hard-packed surface. It cost around $50, which is a fraction of the cost of concrete or asphalt. Flat stones placed in the gravel help break up the large expanse and also serve as a walkway to the landing.

Prepare Soil Before Planting

With the hardscape complete, it was time to remove the old plantings. The scraggly azaleas were pulled out and thrown away. The new beds' lines were mapped out in the yard with spray paint. (If you prefer not to use spray paint, you can lay a garden hose on the ground to outline planting areas.) Then new topsoil was tilled into the existing soil in the planting areas and raked smooth.

Large Plants First

When installing shrubs, put in the bigger ones first; then work smaller specimens around them. The Luxes chose two 'Natchez' crepe myrtles (*Lagerstroemia indica*) to frame the front porch. These white-flowering trees offer long-lasting color throughout the summer, and their beautiful cinnamon-colored trunks provide

top: Containers filled with colorful foliage and flowers add appeal to this entrance.
above: The new parking area easily accommodates two cars.

year-round interest. Eventually, the trees will grow tall enough to shade the porch and walk. A large 8-foot-tall wax myrtle anchors the right corner of the house. The big evergreen helps to soften the structure so it doesn't look too boxy.

A staggered row of dwarf Burford hollies (*Ilex cornuta* 'Burfordii Nana') creates a hedge between the Luxes' property and their neighbor's. In time, these sturdy evergreens will become a dark green buffer.

Seasonal Shrubs

Forsythia, spirea, and nandina also work well in the landscape. Forsythia *(Forsythia intermedia)* is a wide, sprawling shrub that produces a profusion of yellow blooms in late February and early March. Van Houtte spirea *(Spiraea x vanhouttei)* provides flowers from mid- to late-spring. Its flat clusters of white blooms line long, arching branches. Finally, nandina *(Nandina domestica)* has bunches of tiny pink to white blooms in late spring or early summer. The flowers aren't showy, but nandina produces bundles of radiant red berries in winter that sparkle when most shrubs are dormant. These three old-fashioned plants are easy to grow and help provide color through the seasons.

> Containers in all shapes and sizes can be moved at will to put blooming plants in the spotlight.

Color Where It Counts

Yellow lantana fills a sunny bed along the front walk. Small 4-inch sprigs planted in the spring quickly grew into knee-high mounds of golden blooms. This drought-tolerant, rambling ground cover creates a nice focal point all summer. A few white cleomes, or spider flowers, stand out in front of the dark green holly hedge. The annuals bloom throughout the hot summer and into fall. Planted under a crepe myrtle in partial sun, a small pocket of purple New Guinea hybrid impatiens creates a splash of color next to the steps.

A Little Turf

With the added flowers, shrubs, and parking area, there isn't a lot of room for grass. Two small patches of 'Z-52' Zoysia complete the new landscape. The turf quickly rooted in and shimmers green all summer long. Matt can easily cut the grass in a few minutes.

Finishing Touch

Containers in all shapes and sizes line the porch, steps, and landing. They add seasonal color and can be moved at will to put blooming plants in the spotlight. The larger pots are made of lightweight plastic foam. The containers were bright white when purchased, but brown wood stain was applied with an old cloth to give the exterior a more subtle, aged look. Red-flowering Dragon Wing hybrid begonias and orange Profusion Series zinnias provide colorful blooms in some of the planters. Showy foliage plants, such as chartreuse creeping Jenny, variegated ivy, and sedge, also brighten the entry. The planters catch your attention and guide you to the front door. They contribute plenty of personality to the design and help soften the hardscape.

Matt and Teresa are proud of the new landscape. The added plants seem to embrace the old home and give it new life. Strangers walking down the sidewalk and driving down the street sometimes stop just to tell them how good their yard looks. First impressions mean a lot, and when visitors drive up to the Luxes' house, they feel welcome before they even get to the door. ◆

above, left: Purple New Guinea hybrid impatiens thrive in this lightly shaded spot next to the front steps. **above, center:** Yellow lantana produces thousands of golden blooms from spring until fall. **above, right:** White cleome, sometimes called spider flower, sports airy clusters of blooms atop 3- to 4-foot stalks.

Give Them What They Ask For

Ever wonder why some plants look so great in one place and so bad in another? Well, wonder no more.

Sun-loving black-eyed Susans welcome you into this front yard with a mass of brilliant yellow-and-black blooms.

Ask seasoned gardeners what the key to a low-maintenance, colorful yard is, and they will undoubtedly say it's putting plants where they naturally want to grow. Trying to coax a sun-loving plant to look great in the shade is about as easy as picking the winner at the local racetrack—every time. Don't rely on luck for a fantastic yard. Do your homework, and match a plant's needs with its conditions.

The first step in this process is to observe the patterns of sunlight in your yard. Perhaps this seems elementary, but you'll be surprised how different the light can be from both morning to night as well as from spring to fall. A few hours of direct afternoon light in the height of summer will absolutely torture a shade-loving plant. Keep a notebook in your garden shed, and jot down notes throughout the year on what parts of your yard receive the most and least sunlight. Use this information to plan where to place new plants, and you will instantly increase their beauty and reduce their maintenance needs.

Once you have a good idea where to plug in sun-loving or shade-tolerant plants, find a home that fits the role of your perennials. Annuals and perennials have similar growing needs but different functions in your yard's design. Perennials usually serve as the showy focal points, with different species rotating throughout the season, while annuals are the pawns of your yard and don't make much of an impact on their own.

Now that you know where the sunny and shady parts of the yard are and what role perennials play, choose the right plants for your garden.

Perennials for Sun

■ **Black-eyed Susan** *(Rudbeckia hirta)* is a signature of summer in most parts of the South. With yellow-orange rays and a black center, this is the perfect bold statement for any border or container. It looks best when planted en masse behind a contrasting bed of annuals.

■ **Mealy-cup sage** *(Salvia farinacea)* is a perennial often used as an annual in planting beds or borders. Its spikes of small blue or white flowers are good companions to softer annuals such as dusty millers or begonias.

■ **Fernleaf yarrow** *(Achillea filipendulina)* blooms generously with few problems throughout most of the summer and fall. The deep green, fernlike leaves play host to yellow flower heads on 5-foot stems. Yarrow is excellent for cut flowers and as a splash of color in a drought-tolerant garden.

Perennials for Shade

■ **Common bleeding heart** *(Dicentra spectabilis)* provides a touch of graceful color in the cool, shady part of your garden. If it is given rich, moist, porous soil, bleeding heart will give back dainty flowers in pink, rose, or white. Mix with summer-maturing perennials, such as astilbe, for continuous color throughout the hot days of summer.

■ **Feverfew** *(Chrysanthemum parthenium)* is a compact, leafy perennial with a yellow or white flower head. The leaves are broad, have a strong smell, and are believed to reduce fever. It can be easily grown from seeds or cuttings.

■ **Hardy begonia** *(Begonia grandis)* reaches 3 feet tall with branching red stems and spectacular coppery-red leaves. The flowers set in summer with a drooping cluster of pink or white. It's an excellent choice for adding color to a bed of hostas or ferns. After a frost, the tops will die. Mulch to protect the roots.

EDWIN MARTY

The pink, rose, or white flowers of common bleeding heart will brighten up a shady spot.

An assortment of bold caladiums step up the entry to this house.

Caladiums for Color

The leaves of these plants will brighten your containers and borders from spring till fall.

W ant your garden to have a vibrant, tropical look this summer? Plant some caladiums. The red, pink, green, and white hues of their foliage will make your garden glow.

All Shapes and Sizes

Caladiums *(Caladium bicolor)* may not be the same plants you remember from your parents' garden. No longer hiding in the shade, many new selections like sun and can take heat. Sunlovers include 'Florida Sweetheart' and 'White Queen.' The familiar arrow-shaped leaves of the past now have cohorts with foliage in lance and strap shapes. These also like to bask in sun. Lance-leaf types include 'Pink Symphony' and 'Jackie Suthers.' Strap-leaf forms include 'Red Frill' and 'Pink Gem.' There are also miniature selections such as 'Gingerland.' These new caladiums have varying

degrees of sun tolerance, so read the plant labels, or ask your garden center to determine the best performer for your area of the South.

Warm Enough for You?

Caladiums are some of the easiest plants to grow from tubers. They love heat and prefer rich, moist, organic soil. You can start tubers early indoors in flats or pots. Once nights get above 60 degrees, plant them outside. Place 2 to 3 inches deep, depending on the size of tubers, with the knobby side up. If you are not sure which is the top, turn and look for dried remnants of last year's roots. Don't worry; if you plant them upside down or sideways, the new shoots will reach around the tubers for light and grow fine. They just may take longer to get started. During the season, feed with a slow-release, granular fertilizer,

such as Osmocote (14-14-14) Vegetable & Bedding food or Scotts (10-10-10) Flower & Vegetable Food.

Caladiums can go just about anywhere in the garden. They can be dramatic placed en masse in the border. When planting a large number, choose one selection that you really like, instead of several selections mixed together. They are such strong plants alone that different types compete with each other when combined in the border and make less of a design statement. They work in window boxes too. In the shade, caladiums do well mixed with ferns and impatiens. In the sun, plant in individual groups or use ornamental grasses as a backdrop for a textural contrast. They are also right at home in terra-cotta pots.

What do you do with your caladium tubers in the fall? They can be left in the ground in the warmest parts of Florida and Texas. Otherwise, cut back the foliage, and lift out the tubers. Remove excess dirt, and let them dry in partial shade for a week. Bring inside, and store in dry sphagnum peat moss at temperatures between 50 and 60 degrees. Keep containers indoors through the cold weather, and they will add an extra sparkle to your days.

Remember, you can count on caladiums for a long-lasting display of color. These carefree plants will make you feel as if you've escaped to the Tropics.　　GENE B. BUSSELL

Step 1: Plant tubers, and water well.

Step 2: When leaves start to emerge, top-dress with a little bit of additional soil, and add a slow-release, granular fertilizer such as Osmocote.

Step 3: Enjoy. Once the leaves have fully emerged, 'Aaron' caladium puts on a big show.

A Border on a Budget

It doesn't cost a fortune to turn an eyesore into a garden spot.

W hen my wife, Margaret, and I purchased our home, the garden at the end of our long driveway had all the charm of a train derailment. So this high-profile area was the first one we decided to redo.

We began by shifting a few plants around. The stiff-soldier row of small ornamental 'Bradford' pear trees came out. We dug up the two butterfly bushes (*Buddleia* sp.) and set them aside so we could amend the soil. The 10-foot-tall corkscrew willow tree (*Salix matsudana* 'Tortuosa') in the center of the bed was the only thing that remained untouched.

After pulling weeds, we tilled the hard-packed clay soil and added two pickup loads of clean leaf mold, available from our local landfill at a bargain price. A load of aged "zoo-doo" was free from the zoo. (Many zoos have more manure than they know what to do with, so they offer it to the public at little or no cost. **Note:** Be sure the manure comes from the herbivores; the manure of meat eaters contains harmful bacteria.) All of the materials were then tilled into the existing topsoil and raked smooth.

The two butterfly bushes were replanted close to the front, where their lacy foliage and perfumed flowers could be better appreciated. We splurged a little on 10 new 'Carefree Sunshine' shrub roses and wove a curved row of these low-maintenance beauties around the butterfly bushes.

We placed an inexpensive birdbath among them so the lemon yellow petals would create a floating potpourri as they dropped. A dovecote-style bird feeder, which we purchased at a local home-center store and painted white, makes a stand-out accent. To construct the wattle edging, we used the plentiful supply of privet clippings taken from the back of the property.

Zinnias planted from seeds cover the remaining space. These colorful, drought-tolerant annuals germinate quickly, draw butterflies, and provide cut flowers all summer.

The last of the frugal planting was done by the cardinals and finches that dropped sunflower seeds from the new bird feeder. As the seeds fell into the soft, fertile soil, they quickly sprouted and grew tall enough to peek over the tops of the zinnias. The bright sunflower faces were such a nice finishing touch; it made us wish we had thought of it ourselves.

GLENN R. DINELLA

BARGAIN BLOOMS

For this makeover, our goal was to be speedy as well as thrifty. Here's how we spent (and saved) our money.

- 2 loads of leaf mold $40
- 1 load of zoo-doo ....free
- wattle edging...................................free
- birdbath $80
- bird feeder, post, and brackets.........$85
- 1 (25-pound) bag sunflower seeds ..$10
- 5 packs of common zinnia seeds $10
- 2 flats of *Zinnia angustifolia* $25
- 10 'Carefree Sunshine' roses.........$150
- 4 bales pine straw mulch.................$10

Total **$410**

With a little work and a little cash, we transformed a formerly neglected area into an eye-catching garden. Choosing plants wisely saved money.

PHOTOGRAPHS: CELIA DEATON

left: The shrub form of ivy on the left is named 'Glacier' and has great-looking varicgated foliage. When planted next to green English ivy, it really stands out in the landscape. below, left: Shrub ivy produces inconspicuous flowers and bluish-black fruit.

Worth the Effort

Before you run out to buy this can't-miss shrub ivy from a local nursery, you should know that these plants are tough to propagate, so they're hard to find. (See sources at southernliving. com; AOL Keyword: Southern Living.) Frank Pokorny, president of Oak Bend Nursery, and Warren Davenport, president of Timbercrest Farm, have teamed up to propagate, select, and distribute these ivies, making them more available to the public. Now, they offer five selections in their Vintage Ivy Collection: 'Glacier,' 'Treetop,' 'Prince Avenue,' 'Lexington Gardens,' and 'Green Spice.'

'Glacier' is a variegated shrub with beautiful green-and-cream foliage. The other selections have green leaves that vary in shape and size. 'Prince Avenue' boasts large glossy foliage. In winter, this selection shines when most plants with evergreen foliage look dull or weathered.

A Well-Behaved Ivy

Shrub ivy is a mannerly plant with many landscape uses.

Most people think of ivy as only a rambunctious vine that runs everywhere, gobbling up gardens and climbing trees. But you may not know that once ivy grows into the tops of trees, it undergoes a remarkable change. The pliable youngster becomes a shrubby adult. Its leaves change size and shape, it starts flowering and fruiting, and it no longer climbs. Cuttings rooted from such shrubby ivies are giving us great new ornamental plants.

Not Your Average Ivy

Shrub forms have stiff branches and a mounding or sometimes weeping form. They can grow 6 to 8 feet tall and up to 9 feet wide. The great thing about them is that they are easy to care for. The shrubs are tough and thrive under dry conditions. They grow in coastal settings where salt spray can be a problem. Their only requirement is well-drained soil. This resilient ivy will do well practically anywhere except where the ground stays damp.

They like sun or shade, depending on selection, and have very few problems with pests or diseases. Spider mites and aphids sometimes attack plants, but they are easy to control using an ultrafine dormant oil.

Many Uses

Shrub ivies look great in a large pot surrounded by annual color, where they will become a great centerpiece. Set them by your front door or on a deck or patio where they can be seen. When placed around a fountain or a sculpture, they make interesting specimen plants. Or put them at the corners of your house for a nice addition to your foundation planting.

Once in place, shrub ivies are low maintenance. Little pruning is required because they are slow growing and maintain their compact form. Keep an eye out for juvenile shoots that sometimes sprout from the base of the shrub. Clip them off so plants will maintain their shrubby form.

If you like the look of ivies but don't like the way they grow out of control, try a shrub ivy. It's easy and manageable.   CHARLIE THIGPEN

Mondo grass eliminates weeds and keeps this herb garden looking lush.

Fresh Herbs, No Fuss

When we say you can have fresh herbs from the garden with very little fuss, we're not just blowing smoke—even if the herbs in question are growing in flue liners.

The idea of using flue liners came from Dallas landscape architect Naud Burnett, who designed a garden for Doug and Polly Urquhart. Polly wanted fresh herbs for the kitchen, but she didn't want a lot of upkeep. She also didn't want the barren look typical herb gardens have in winter. So Naud inserted a row of planters made from chimney flue liners into a bed of dark-green mondo grass between a concrete walk and the garage. Polly filled the flue liners with a mixture of topsoil and potting soil and then planted a single herb in each one.

The project proved to be an aes-thetic, practical, and horticultural success. The terra-cotta flue liners repeated the color and texture of the nearby brick wall. Surrounding them with mondo grass eliminated concerns about weeding and gave the space a lush look year-round. Moreover, the 2-foot-tall flue liners, which are open on the bottom, supplied a basic requirement for cultivating herbs—good drainage. (Flue liners come in various lengths and widths and are available from chimney supply or pipe companies.)

Polly grows chives, tarragon, basil, oregano, thyme, rosemary, mint, lemon balm, and Italian parsley. Annual and biennial herbs such as basil and Italian parsley must be replanted each year. So must the tarragon—a short-lived perennial. The other herbs do great, though. As a bonus, the flue liner containing the mint keeps its invasive roots safely confined.

Polly doesn't have to weed, and thanks to an automatic sprinkler placed beside each flue liner, she doesn't even have to water. She can just harvest and enjoy. ◆

WHAT HERBS NEED

Light: full sun

Soil: Slightly acid to slightly alkaline, containing plenty of organic matter. Good drainage is essential. If your soil is mostly clay, consider planting in pots or raised beds.

Water: Get new plants established with plenty of moisture. Then water only enough to keep plants from wilting. Too much moisture causes root rot and weakens the flavor.

Fertilizer: Use sparingly. Too much fertilizer causes rank growth with poor flavor.

Easy Wildflowers

Success in shade requires good soil and the right plants.

Helen Titus begs to differ with those who say you can't have color in shade. Her small backyard is perfect proof. Waves of wildflowers roll down a terraced slope, their blossoms of blue, yellow, purple, and red nearly lapping at her back door. Visitors can't quite believe it. "So many people are amazed at what I have blooming back here," she says.

What Helen has accomplished may look complicated at first. But when you listen to her story, you realize that a garden like this is something almost anyone can do. She began the garden about 10 years ago to beautify a shady, sloping backyard that held little more than moss and fallen leaves. She planted woodland wildflowers, because she'd liked them since her childhood and because they'd thrive with just a few hours of dappled sun each day. But before planting, she knew she'd have to improve her soil.

Start With the Soil

"I'm from Nebraska," Helen explains, "so I love rich, black dirt. When I'm in contact with the soil, I think clearer and feel closer to God." Her community collects and composts leaves raked to the curb each fall, then sells this material to gardeners. Helen figures she brought in 25 to 30 truckloads of leaf compost over several year's time. To this she added her own compost made from fall leaves. "Good soil is the key to my garden," she declares.

Now for the Plants

Helen's first wildflowers were rescued from sites where homes were going to be built. Others, such as purple trillium *(Trillium erectum)* and yellow-flowered golden groundsel *(Senecio aureus)*, apparently came with the new soil. But her garden really started taking shape when she became involved with The Wildflower Society at the Birmingham Botanical Gardens. One year, she brought home eight plants of blue phlox *(Phlox divaricata)*, which is as prolific as it is showy. Those plants spread quickly by seed. Now, she has hundreds.

Other wildflowers also went forth and multiplied. Walk her garden's narrow paths, and you come upon dwarf-eared coreopsis *(Coreopsis auriculata* 'Nana'), Jacob's ladder *(Polemonium caeruleum)*, violets, hybrid columbine, wild columbine *(Aquilegia canadensis)*, and ferns.

No Labor Required

The best thing about a garden like Helen's is that it's not only beautiful, but it also needs little care once established. Wildflowers fill in most bare spots on their own. Sun-loving weeds can't compete. The soil's so good that Helen rarely uses fertilizer. "I'll add some compost around plants as they peep out of the ground in spring," she says. "That's their food."

So don't give up on a garden just because the chosen spot isn't sunny. As Helen's flowers show, its future can be bright. STEVE BENDER

WILDFLOWERS FOR BEGINNERS

The following require only dappled sun and good, rich soil.

bird's-foot violet
(Viola pedata)

bloodroot
(Sanguinaria canadensis)

blue phlox

celandine poppy

dwarf-eared coreopsis

golden groundsel

golden star
(Chrysogonum virginianum)

Jacob's ladder

purple trillium

wild columbine

above: A spectacular sweep of blue phlox smothers the slope each spring. Most are seedlings started from eight original plants. **right:** Blue phlox and golden groundsel make a splendid combination.

PHOTOGRAPHS: VAN CHAPLIN

Just Add Water

Make the most of a damp spot with moisture-loving plants.

Does that low area in your garden look more like a swamp than a flowerbed? Well, creating a bog may be the answer. Flowers and exotic foliage can fill it with beauty. Most perennials prefer well-drained soil, but there are many that will make a splash in a soggy spot. Whether you have a damp area in your yard or just want to build a bog, there are many great-looking plants that will prosper in soil that goes squish. Here are some tips for making a bog.

Select a Site

Choose a slightly sloping area that receives full to partial sun. Water should be able to run in and out of the bog slowly. If your yard is level, you may have to dig your hole so that the bottom has a gradual slope. Bogs are sensitive to chemicals, so avoid putting them in areas that receive fertilizer, herbicide, or pesticide. Also remember to make sure that you have a faucet close by so the bog can be watered as needed during dry periods.

Dig a Hole

This bog was built at the end of a surface drain. The drain was a small ditch cut through the garden to carry away rainwater. We dug a round hole 12 feet wide and about 18 inches deep at the end of the drain. All the runoff water from the ditch flows into the dug-out area.

Roll Out the Liner

We lined the hole with a black butyl pond liner like the ones available at many garden centers. The liner was big enough to cover the bottom and sides of the hole.

Make a Drain

On the low side of the bog, we installed a small sleeved drainpipe to allow excess water to run out. You want your bog to stay damp but not soupy or stagnant. A 1-foot-deep layer of sand was spread over the top of the liner to form a base. Use coarse builder's sand (the kind used for mixing concrete); the type for sandboxes is too fine.

To build this bog, we dug a 12-foot, circular hole 18 inches deep. Then we covered the hole with a pond liner. A pipe was installed for drainage at the low end of the bog. We spread sand over the liner to a depth of 1 foot. A soaker hose, which we put on top of the sand, can be attached to a water source to keep the area moist. An 8-inch-deep layer of leaf mold and sphagnum peat moss was spread over the sand and soaker hose. Plants were set out in this thick layer of organic matter.

Create a Water Source

Every bog needs to have a steady supply of incoming water to give plants the moisture they require. We set a soaker hose on top of the sand. It is hooked up to a regular garden hose, and it acts as a simple irrigation system for the bog to help keep the area damp.

top, left: Japanese iris thrive in this damp garden. **top, center:** Yellow flag iris have swordlike foliage and clear yellow flowers. **top, right:** Common calla lilies' white trumpet-like blooms make excellent cut flowers and give this bog an elegant look. **above, left:** Here, golden ray *(Ligularia dentata)* is surrounded by scarlet cardinal flowers. **above, center:** Black elephant's ears add bold foliage to the bog. **above, right:** Pitcher plants have red veins running through tube-shaped leaves.

Distribute Organic Matter

An 8-inch-deep layer of leaf mold and sphagnum peat moss, mixed, was then spread over the sand and soaker hose. The leaf mold and moss create a rich planting medium. (If leaf mold isn't available in your area, straight sphagnum peat moss will do.)

Water It Well

It took a lot of water to soak the area thoroughly. The peat moss was so dry that it seemed to repel the water at first, but after a while it absorbed the liquid like a sponge. We walked over the bog to pack the fluffy sphagnum peat moss. After that, we added a few large, flat stepping-stones to make a natural-looking walkway across the center of the bog.

Set Out Plants

Plants that like damp to wet soil and have attractive flowers or foliage were the obvious choices to fill the new garden. We selected Japanese iris and yellow flag iris for their beautiful spring blooms and their spiky foliage. Common calla lilies also added a nice touch with their elegant white funnel-shaped blooms and large arrow-shaped leaves. Although they produce no flowers, the black elephant's ears possess bold leaves that look striking against the iris foliage. For the summer, we planted cardinal flower, whose scarlet spikes would reach 3½ to 4 feet tall and tower over the bog.

Finally, no true bog would be complete without a few pitcher plants.

Their tubular foliage is topped with burgundy red veins. These insect eaters are a novelty in any garden. Bugs climb down into the tubes and are trapped. If you want to use these carnivorous plants, never collect them from the wild; only purchase them from a reputable source. The plants you buy should be commercially propagated and not collected from wild colonies.

Building this bog was not difficult, and it's really simple to maintain. Just weed it occasionally, and water it during dry periods. It doesn't require any fertilizer. The plants that grow in this damp soil produce outstanding blooms and eye-catching foliage with little effort.

CHARLIE THIGPEN

Heavenly HYDRANGEAS

With billowing clouds of white flowers, these native shrubs will lift your garden to higher ground.

The creamy-white petals of 'Snowflake' shimmer in the warm sun.

In the woodlands of the Deep South grows one of the finest hydrangeas in the world, one with a truly Southern soul. Beginning in late spring and continuing through early summer, the white blossoms of oakleaf hydrangeas *(Hydrangea quercifolia)* illuminate the forests. Their creamy spires rise up and wave in the wind, welcoming blue skies. Though the blossoms would be enough to satisfy most, these elegant deciduous shrubs offer something special throughout the year and deserve a generous place in your garden.

A Show for Every Season

One of the best things about oakleaf hydrangeas is that they perform in winter, spring, summer, and fall. When the days are blustery and cold, the cinnamon-colored peeling bark adds a bit of warmth. As the light lengthens, richly textured, oak-shaped leaves emerge bright green to greet spring. When the weather warms, cone-shaped blooms appear when few other shrubs are flowering. Its blossoms continue to fill the air with clouds of coolness to lessen the heat of summer as the mercury

soars. Finally, autumn arrives, and the leaves slowly begin to turn brilliant reds, oranges, and maroons. For weeks, they salute the fall with a kaleidoscope of colors.

Hundreds of Hydrangeas

Selections of oakleaf hydrangea have proved more popular than the species itself. Each has its own merits, but all are great in the garden.

'Snowflake' may be the most popular. With its impressive size and large flowers, this shrub certainly makes a strong statement. When the blossoms emerge, they're a pale green, though they gradually turn white. As the flowers mature, they arch over and slowly fade to a rosy pink. New blooms continue to form as the older ones fade, creating a nice multicolored effect that lasts for weeks. The flowers eventually turn a rich, warm brown as the summer wanes.

If you need a little balance in your life, plant a hedge of 'Harmony' hydrangeas. The blooms are often so large and heavy that they cause the branches to teeter to the ground. A well-established planting will stop cars when it's in full bloom.

Joan and Jack Fagan of Homewood, Alabama, love their 'Harmony'

top: All oakleaf hydrangeas make great cut flowers. **right:** The blossoms of these 'Snowflake' hydrangeas seem to float in the air.

BY GENE B. BUSSELL
PHOTOGRAPHY ALLEN ROKACH, VAN CHAPLIN, LACY KERR ROBINSON

OAKLEAF HYDRANGEA SELECTIONS

Name	Size	Flower
'Snowflake'	large, up to 8 feet	large, double, white, matures to rose-pink
'Harmony'	large, up to 10 feet	large, white, matures to green
'Alice'	large, up to 12 feet	large, white, matures to rose-pink, fragrant
'Snow Queen'	medium, 6 to 8 feet	medium, white, matures to rose-pink, fragrant
'Pee Wee'	small, 3 feet	small, white, matures to rose-pink, fragrant

above: This hedge of 'Harmony' hydrangeas creates a stunning effect when in full bloom.

oakleaf hydrangeas. Jack says, "I think they're great and not a lot of work." He has actually rooted a few by placing a brick over a branch lying on the ground. It takes a couple of years, but eventually the plant develops roots under the brick, creating an entirely new plant. Once the branch is rooted, he cuts it from the mother plant and transplants it to a new spot in his yard.

'Pee Wee' is a smaller selection, perfect for the compact spaces of suburban or urban gardens. This plant is perfectly at home in front of a low wall or gracing a large terra-cotta container. Its leaves turn a deep wine color in the fall and often persist till spring.

See the chart above for some of the best selections and to determine which oakleaf hydrangea best fits the conditions of your garden.

What They Need

When planting oakleaf hydrangeas, the most important thing is to make sure that they're planted in well-drained soil. "Good drainage is key," says nurseryman Eddie Aldridge of Hoover, Alabama, who introduced 'Snowflake' and 'Harmony' to the gardening world. He recommends locations with morning sunshine and shade after 2 p.m. "It's very important to give them protection from the late-afternoon sun."

Eddie also says hydrangeas are not too picky about the soil, but they do appreciate a bit of peat moss to retain moisture. It also helps keep the soil acid, which they prefer. Once

established, oakleaf hydrangeas can tolerate drought, though they will definitely appreciate an additional drink during extended periods without rain. Mulches, such as pine straw or leaves, will also help the soil retain valuable moisture.

What's more, you've got to give them lots of room to grow so they can reach their full potential. "I'm a spacer," Eddie admits. "I like to space plants so they can mature." If you crowd hydrangeas, you will end up pruning them and sacrificing their graceful form.

A Hydrangea Here, a Hydrangea There...

So how do you use oakleaf hydrangeas in your own landscape? First, choose a selection that will best fit the space of your garden. The ones listed in the chart give a range of sizes from large to small. The bigger selections such as 'Alice' really need

extra room to grow. These look especially great planted en masse along woodland edges. A medium selection such as 'Snow Queen' can find a home in most any garden. Its best traits are its size and blooms, which are held straight up and do not weigh down branches.

The coarse texture of oakleaf hydrangeas makes them well suited for use near natural stone outcrops. Rustic stone walls and paths and brick structures are also a complement. They look nice planted along fences, especially white ones that repeat the color of the flowers. 'Harmony' does very well when planted near rustic post fences, which provide support for the branches when they are heavy with flowers. Remember, too, when using oakleaf hydrangeas for hedges that they lose their leaves and will not screen out unwanted views during winter.

Excellent companion plants include broad-leaved evergreens, such as Southern magnolias *(Magnolia grandiflora)* or camellias, which have deep green leaves that help highlight hydrangeas' rough-textured foliage and flowers. They also work well with ground covers such as Southern shield fern *(Thelypteris kunthii)*; its fine-textured leaves complement the native shrub. Accentuate their fall color by planting them near red maples or sourwoods *(Oxydendrum arboreum)* for a riotous show.

Revered throughout the South, oakleaf hydrangeas are particularly cherished in Alabama, where they hold the title of official state wildflower. "Hydrangeas are the first plant I remember," says Eddie, a native Alabamian who grew up working in his father's nursery. "I just love them. The appearance is outstanding."

To see these hydrangeas and more, visit Aldridge Gardens in Hoover, Alabama. Aldridge Gardens is a newly opened, 30-acre botanical garden featuring the genus *Hydrangea*. Peak bloom times for oakleaf hydrangeas occur from late May into June. For more information call (205) 682-8019, or visit their Web site at www.aldridgegardens.com.

top: Most oakleaf hydrangea blooms mature to a beautiful pink. **above, left:** These shrubs offer excellent fall color over many weeks. **above, right:** Peeling cinnamon-colored bark will help warm your winter. **above:** Plant oakleaf hydrangeas with broad-leaved evergreen plants such as magnolias.

Freshly picked blackberries warmed by the summer sun (See pages 122–123)

June

Editor's Notebook

PHOTOGRAPH: VAN CHAPLIN

Friends, with this month's commentary, we are about to attempt what few before us have dared try—merging the exciting world of horticulture with that of pyrotechnics. Our subject is the storied gas plant, which despite what you might think, is not a pseudonym for the lima bean. No, gas plant *(Dictamnus albus)* is an old-fashioned perennial that combines handsome compound leaves with showy summer flowers of pink, white, or lavender.

This plant is rather slow to establish, but once it gets going, it can live in the same spot for a century—that is, unless you blow it up, which is theoretically possible given its volatile nature. Legend has it that on warm summer nights, gaseous compounds emitted by its flowers and seedpods briefly ignite if exposed to flame. Sounds like a bunch of hooey to me. So to test this ridiculous notion, I've assembled 300 gas plants before me in a heated closet. Now I'll just strike this match and prove once and...

—STEVE BENDER

Crepe Myrtles

Select these trees while they are in bloom. Remember, they can vary greatly in size and bloom colors. Choose the right size for your landscape to help avoid the ultimate Southern gardening sin, "crepe murder" (severely pruning your tree to just a few sticks and ruining its natural form). Large selections (more than 20 feet tall) include 'Natchez' (white) and 'Miami' (pink). Medium selections (less than 20 feet tall) include 'Near East' (pink) and 'Regal Red' (deep red). Dwarf forms (less than 3 feet tall) include 'Centennial' (purple) and 'Chickasaw' (pink). Select a sunny location, and remember to mulch and water well to ease your tree into the landscape. Container-grown trees are easy to transport and transition into the garden well.

TIPS

■ **Garden journal**—The summer solstice on June 21, the longest day of the year, marks the beginning of the season. If you didn't start a garden journal this spring, there's still time. Keeping a small notebook of your observations throughout the seasons is a great way to learn about gardening.

■ **Lawns**—Water your grass infrequently but thoroughly to encourage a deep root system. Only do so when the lawn has gray, wilted areas. Apply 1 inch of water, as measured by a rain gauge. Don't water again until the next wilt. This program will build a stronger lawn.

■ **Vegetables**—To encourage production, pick tomatoes, squash, okra, beans, and cucumbers regularly. Harvest every other day in early morning or late afternoon.

PLANT

■ **Crepe myrtles**—Choose selections of this flowering tree while they are in bloom. But don't just consider flower color. Growth, form, and ultimate size vary by selection, so there is one for every landscape use.

■ **Cut flowers**—In a sunny, well-drained area, prepare the bed by working 3 to 5 inches of organic material into the top 8 to 10 inches of existing soil. Add 5 pounds of cottonseed or alfalfa meal per 100 square feet of bed or a slow-release chemical fertilizer, such as Osmocote 14-14-14 Vegetable & Bedding fertilizer, according to label instructions. Favorites include zinnias, bachelor's buttons (gomphrenas), cosmos, sunflowers, tithonias, marigolds, and celosias (cockscomb and spike forms). Start with both transplants and seeds for a prolonged season of blooms.

■ **Drought-tolerant annuals**—There is still plenty of time to set out transplants of narrow-leaf zinnias, marigolds, moss roses, celosias, and globe amaranths. These easy annuals will provide dependable color and need minimal watering once established.

■ **Vines**—Accent walls, arbors, and trellises with vines. Hardy ones such as silver lace vine *(Polygonum aubertii)*, coral honeysuckle, wisteria, 'Tangerine Beauty' crossvine *(Bignonia capreolata* 'Tangerine Beauty'), most clematis, and climbing roses such as 'New Dawn' and 'Red Cascade' are all good possibilities.

purple globe amaranth (gomphrena)

- **Flowering trees**—In Florida, plant trees that bloom in summer. Golden shower *(Cassia fistula)*, royal poinciana, yellow poinciana, and queen's crepe myrtle are medium-to-large landscape trees, 30 to 60 feet tall. Pink trumpet tree *(Tabebuia heterophylla)* and frangipani are smaller trees, 20 to 30 feet tall, with 20- to 25-foot spreads.
- **Palms**—In Florida, plant them so the top of the root ball is at the same level in the ground as in the container. Small palms include Florida silver palm *(Coccothrinax argentata)*, lady palm *(Rhapis* sp.), licuala palm *(Licuala grandis)*, saw palmetto *(Serenoa repens)*, pacaya palm *(Chamaedorea tepejilote)*, and pygmy date palm *(Phoenix roebelenii)*.
- **Tropical fruit**—In Flordia, Barbados cherry and guava can be grown as large shrubs or small trees. Avocado, lychee, mango, and sapodilla are bigger trees, so give them plenty of room. Lychee, with its dark green foliage and red fruit, makes a particularly attractive landscape tree.

PRUNE

- **Blackberries**—As soon as they have finished producing, cut canes to ground level, because next year's crop will occur on the new growth. Fertilize the plants, and prepare them for the hot weather ahead by mulching with grass clippings, hay, or another organic material. To learn more about growing this delicious summer fruit, read "Bigger, Better Blackberries" on page 122.

FERTILIZE

- **Lawns**—Fertilize warm-season grasses such as Bermuda, St. Augustine, and Zoysia with a 27-4-6 granular fertilizer, as this is the optimum growing time. For centipede, which is sensitive to too much nitrogen, use a formulation such as 18-0-18. Apply at rates recommended on the labels.
- **Tropical flowers**—Chinese hibiscus *(Hibiscus rosa-sinensis)* offer bright, flashy color all summer. They are available in reds, pinks, oranges, yellows, and whites and are great for beds or containers. Good companion plants include asparagus fern and purple heart *(Setcreasea pallida)*. To encourage a continuous supply of flowers, fertilize regularly, as these plants are heavy feeders. Liquid products work well, but if you are on the go and do not have much time, try using a granular, timed-released one such as Osmocote (14-14-14) or Scotts All-Purpose Flower & Vegetable Food (10-10-10).

Easy Color

Select combinations that grow well together and provide beautiful contrasts. For partially shaded areas, consider wax begonias (shown below), 'Blackie' (dark purple) or 'Margarita' (chartreuse) sweet potato vines, coleus, caladiums, Persian shields *(Strobilanthes dyeranus),* or fanflowers *(Scaevola* sp.). Cream or white variegated English ivies are a good way to further brighten shaded areas. For sunnier locations, possibilities include Profusion Series zinnias in orange, pink, or white; purple heart *(Setcreasea pallida);* purple, striped, or white angelonias; lavender or white trailing lantanas; and pink or white gaura.

Tip of the Month

Instead of buying those clay pot feet to rest a large container on, I get really small (1- to 2-inch) clay pots and invert them. It works great. Three of these cost the same as one pot foot!

PAT BEHRENS
COLUMBIA, TENNESSEE

Colorful Coleus

Want bright, easy foliage? This is the plant for you.

Gardeners want lots of show for not much dough. That's why they should plant coleus. It costs little, grows quickly, and has the gaudiest foliage imaginable. It's equally happy in the ground or in a pot. And from the time it's planted until a hard freeze in fall, it supplies eye-popping color.

A tropical plant usually treated as an annual, coleus owes its appeal to phenomenal genetic variability. There is hardly a leaf color, shape, size, or growth habit that coleus hasn't mastered. Red, orange, yellow, or pink leaves. Huge, scalloped, frilly, or tiny leaves. A plant that creeps, a plant that stands tall, coleus does it all.

Tacky No More

As popular as coleus is now, not long ago people considered it tacky. Hot, cheery, assertive colors were out; cool, tranquil, shy pastels were in. But then folks discovered an unsettling equation: Pink + lavender + white + nothing else = one boring garden. According to Pam Baggett of Singing Springs Nursery in Cedar Grove, North Carolina, Southerners picked up on this quicker than others.

"On a typical summer day in the South, it's so hot and humid and sunny out that the sky's almost gray. Under those conditions, pastels don't look like much," she says. "I also think we've gotten over wanting our gardens to look soft and silver like British ones. People are injecting more personality into their gardens."

Pam is certainly doing her part. Her mail-order catalog lists 58 selections; another 150 or so lurk in her greenhouse, waiting to be liberated.

PHOTOGRAPH: ALLEN ROKACH

above: Planting coleus on each side of the porch is a surefire way to draw attention to the front door. **right:** Several types of sun-loving coleus form a lush, vibrant border. No flowers are needed for continuous color.

She attributes her ardor for coleus to her childhood in Carolina Beach, North Carolina, "back when it had this exquisite boardwalk and enormous carousel. It was like a carnival every night. I fell in love with color."

Tips for Beginners

If the colors of coleus have you smitten, too, now is the time to act. Garden centers are offering more and more named selections. But for better assortments and really wild-looking plants, buy from a mail-order nursery.

Although it's tempting to plant one of each coleus you find, don't mix them all together like toppings on a pizza. You'll get more impact by planting a sweep of one type here and a mass of another type there. Large,

BY STEVE BENDER / PHOTOGRAPHY VAN CHAPLIN

shrubby selections (up to 36 inches tall), such as 'Aurora' and 'Alabama Sunset,' work well in the back of the border. Creepers and spreaders, such as the Ducksfoot Series and 'India Frills,' are great for edging, filling in spaces between other plants, or cascading from hanging baskets and window boxes.

Native to Java (an island of Indonesia), coleus loves the heat. Give it fertile, moist soil, some liquid fertilizer every couple of weeks, and a good Southern summer, and it will grow faster than the national debt.

Most older selections, such as those in the Wizard Series, fade and burn in full sun, but some newer types tolerate both sun and shade. They include the beautiful selections shown on these pages as well as the Florida Sun, Solar, Stained Glassworks, and Sunlover Series. Older types also sprout antenna-like flower spikes all summer, which detract from the foliage. But the new sun coleus bloom very little, keeping all eyes on the prize.

above: Brian Bender shows off a coleus cutting he rooted in water in just four days. (He sold it to his dad for a buck.)

How can you avoid losing your prize when a frost finally threatens in fall? One way is to root a cutting. Though coleus root quickly in water during summer, in fall they do better in potting soil. Dip the cut ends in rooting powder, and stick them into moist soil. Provide the bright light of a windowsill, and they should make it through winter. But even if they perish, don't feel cheated. You got lots of show for a little dough. ◆

top: Coleus is superb in containers. A single plant displayed well becomes a focal point. **above:** (from left) 'Leopold,' 'Christmas Candy,' and 'Tilt a Whirl'

Hydrangeas Cut and Dried

These classic blooms make a simple, elegant display.

Nothing says summer like the bursting of blue and pink flowers from a French hydrangea *(Hydrangea macrophylla)*. Luckily, their colors don't have to stop at the door. By bringing the flowers inside and drying them, you can enjoy the beauty of hydrangeas year-round.

Fresh-Cut Blooms

Penny McHenry, founder of the American Hydrangea Society, says, "These blooms are ideally cut in the spring as fresh flowers and then in the summer as dried ones. Hydrangeas must be mature flowers when harvested to dry properly."

In the spring, gather the flowers when they are in their budding stage and have a deep green color. A few weeks later, the flowers can be cut at full bloom, when they are blue or pink. In another month, the flowers begin to fade to pastel shades.

How To Cut

Hydrangeas will last the longest if cut in the morning and placed immediately in a bucket of water. Next, strip off all the leaves, and slice the stems vertically or slightly crush the stem tips with a hammer or a knife. This allows water to be absorbed more efficiently by the stems and ensures blooms last longer. Penny then suggests totally immersing the stems and flower heads in tepid water to fill the blooms with moisture and give them a longer vase life. After an hour, place the stems in a vase of fresh water, and add 2 tablespoons of Penny's Floral Preservative (see box at right), a commercial product such as Floralife, or a lemon-lime soft drink. Change the water every few days, and recut the stems to remove decaying material.

Hydrangeas for Drying

The joys of these flowers can be extended to last throughout the year. But Penny cautions, "Not all hydrangea

left and below: French hydrangeas are the perfect Southern flowers for inside or out. Commonly called mophead hydrangeas, they thrive throughout the region. Available in blue, pink, red, or white, they add a distinctive touch to any garden.

selections dry the same. Try 'Penny Mac,' 'Preziosa,' or 'Altona' for flowers that hold their color. Regardless of the selection, hydrangeas are best harvested when the flowers are either mature or just beginning to feel papery. It's also important to gather the blooms when they are totally dry. Don't cut immediately after a rain or an overhead watering."

Hanging hydrangea flowers may be the easiest method for preserving them. Cut the stems as long as possible, and strip off all the leaves. Tie six stems together, binding them with twine or a rubber band. In a hot, dry place out of direct sun, hang the bundles upside down. Closets, attics, or garages work great. Provide adequate circulation. Without plenty of air movement, the flowers will rot instead of dry, so don't crowd them. After a week or two, blooms should be dry. Place bundles in an airtight container, and store until ready to use.

Another way to dry hydrangeas is to place stems in a container about a quarter full of water. Add two drops of bleach to prevent bacteria buildup. Put the container in a warm place out of direct sun. After about two weeks, the water will have evaporated, leaving the flowers dry. EDWIN MARTY

PENNY'S FLORAL PRESERVATIVE

1 tablespoon sugar (provides food for flowers)

2 teaspoons lemon juice (citric acid lowers the pH to prevent bacteria)

½ teaspoon bleach (helps keep the water clean)

3 cups water

Combine all ingredients, and use 2 tablespoons of this liquid per each quart of water.

below: Reach down into the shrub, and prune branches that are thicker than a pencil. Cut back to a bud or another branch.

Azalea Summer Care

Keep these beauties in bounds without ruining their looks.

above: June is a good time to prune azaleas so they won't get out of hand.

Now that your azaleas have finished blooming, you can forget them until next spring, right? Wrong. Keeping them healthy and looking great means giving them some attention during the next few weeks. Two things in particular that you shouldn't forget are pruning and insect control.

The Kindest Cut

Azaleas, especially those planted near the house, can get too big eventually. This necessitates pruning. Though the mere thought of this terrifies most homeowners, pruning correctly is really quite simple, as long as you remember these tips.

First, finish your pruning by late June. Once you get into July, most azaleas will start setting flowerbuds. Pruning after that will ruin next spring's floral display. Second, leave your hedge trimmers in the garage. The last thing you want to do is flat-top your azaleas. Your goal is to reduce them in size so that you can hardly tell you've pruned them.

How? Grab a pair of sharp pruning shears. Reach down inside the shrub, and cut only branches thicker than a pencil. Feel free to prune 12 to 18 inches of growth, always cutting back to a bud or another branch. Remove equal amounts of growth from all parts of the shrub—it's like giving someone a haircut. No stubs should be visible when you finish. Your azaleas will be smaller, but still bushy, green, and natural looking.

Now for the Bugs

Lace bugs are among the most common pests of azaleas. Small white flies with clear wings, they perch on the undersides of leaves, sucking sap. They leave hard, black spots on the leaves' lower surfaces, while the tops look speckled and bleached. Lace bugs favor azaleas growing in sun and go through several generations each year. Infested plants will drop leaves prematurely and may not bloom well.

Because lace bugs hide under the leaves, they're hard to hit with conventional insecticides applied with a sprayer. But I have a strategy that works pretty well. As soon as I finish pruning, I spray my azaleas according to label directions with a systemic insecticide called Cygon. I don't have to hit the bugs directly. The foliage absorbs the chemical, which then goes into the lace bugs. About three weeks later, I sprinkle granules of Bayer Advanced Garden 2-in-1 Systemic Azalea, Camellia & Rhododendron Care around the base of the plants and water it in. In addition to fertilizer, this product contains the insecticide disulfoton, which provides a good six weeks of control. If any lace bugs show up after that, I spray with Cygon again.

Now my azaleas bloom well, look nice, and don't block the windows. If only they'd plant themselves!

STEVE BENDER

above: Spraying with a systemic insecticide controls insects for weeks.
inset: Lace bugs suck sap from foliage and leave black spots on the undersides.

The Power of One

A single pretty bloom is all you need to feel good.

At a time when life seems to be increasingly busy, there is infinite pleasure in the presence of a solitary flower. It doesn't have to be a pristine, perfect specimen—just pretty petals on a stem, popped into a tiny vase. Sure, there are times when beautifully styled bouquets are exactly what is needed, and they are even fun to assemble. But for the everyday, just-because kind of attitude, the attraction of one flower is dynamic.

Begin with a collection of small vases, looking first to common household items such as perfume bottles, tiny jars, and glass tubes (the ones fresh vanilla beans come in work great). In your travels, search for unexpected items that might hold just a bit of water and a single stem. Look for those with narrow necks to hold stems upright without additional support.

A larger bloom requires a more substantial vase to keep the flower from toppling. It's a good idea to use a flower-arranging device, called a mechanic, to keep a heavy bloom in place. A tiny needle holder with pinlike prongs is good to have, as is florist clay for anchoring it securely to the container. Push the stem onto the needle holder until it is secure. It's that easy.

right: One elegant calla lily graces an old pottery vase. A pincushion needle holder, anchored to the bottom with florist clay, holds the bloom in place.

left: A peony, with its stem cut short, resides in a heavy glass vase designed for just one bloom.

Simple Pleasure, Minimal Space

Where, you might ask, can a single flower be placed so it doesn't get lost in the daily hustle and bustle? This is the fun part: Look to those locations where you spend the most time. The windowsill over the kitchen sink is a good start. I have a refrigerator magnet that's a small vase, and a petite container on a suction cup resides on the bathroom mirror. Then there's the tiny space next to my computer. If there's something fragrant blooming in the garden, that blossom goes on my nightstand—you get the idea. If you have a large flower, such as a calla, use it as an elegant centerpiece. A beautiful, solitary specimen can be more dynamic than a large, complex arrangement.

Another beauty of the one-bloom approach is that you don't necessarily need a garden to indulge in this practice. Many grocery stores sell flowers by the stem, and flower shops offer the option of something a bit more exotic. Rarely will one stem be very expensive, so you can have a beautiful bloom in your life almost all the time.

In the grand scheme of things, flowers may not change the world. But a single, simple bloom in an everyday place is guaranteed to bring a smile. ELLEN RUOFF RILEY

PHOTOGRAPHS: TINA CORNETT

left: 'Kiowa' blackberries produce jumbo fruit that can grow to 1½ inches long. The plants will yield juicy, ebony-colored fruit for around six weeks.
below, left: The 'Kiowa' blackberries on the left grow much larger than wild berries and are just as flavorful.

summery dessert, but I've learned that blackberry picking doesn't have to be painful. Some of today's selections can grow as big as the end of your thumb. Train these superior berries on a trellis, and you can pick the large fruit with ease. There are even thornless selections such as 'Arapaho' and 'Navaho' that have smooth stems and still produce large, juicy clusters of fruit.

Easy Picking
Last summer I visited Jason Powell in Jemison, Alabama, and picked king-size berries at his Petals From the Past Nursery. Along with selling plants, Jason and his wife, Shelley, have a small you-pick operation. Customers can visit the nursery and gather blackberries, blueberries, apples, figs, muscadines, or persimmons, depending on the season. But Jason says everyone flocks to the nursery when the blackberries ripen. In late May, the red and green fruit begins to swell and glisten purplish black. By mid-June, the berries are peaking. The plants produce ripe fruit for about six weeks, and each one yields 8 to 10 pounds of juicy berries.

The Biggest Berries
Jason planted several rows of 'Kiowa' blackberries four years ago and has trained them to grow on a trellis. The upright plants do have thorny canes, but they produce enormous fruit. In fact, they have the largest of any blackberry. They can grow 8 to 10 times bigger than wild berries. (See photo at left.)

Training on a Trellis
Jason sets plants out 5 feet apart in a sunny location. A post-and-wire trellis supports the vigorous growers. (See illustration on opposite page.) Two wires run horizontally between the

Bigger, Better Blackberries

Plump, freshly picked berries warmed by the summer sun melt in your mouth, tickle your taste buds, and temporarily turn your tongue purple.

W hen I was a child, my grandmother would dust me with sulfur powder before I went out berry picking. The yellow powder helped to ward off the chiggers that could make me itch and be miserable for days. So each summer I was brave and fearlessly waded into enemy territory with only a small bucket in hand.

Battling the chest-high briar thickets always left my arms and legs

scratched. The mission was complete only after I had harvested enough blackberries for a cobbler or two. All my pain and suffering was rewarded, though, by the smell of that summertime treat bubbling in Grandmother's oven. A large scoop of vanilla ice cream placed on top of a bowl full of hot cobbler would melt and meld with the berry filling for an unforgettable flavor.

I still look forward to that

left: Glistening black fruit fills this straw hat. above: Blackberries can be grown on a trellis for easy picking.

posts. The first wire is 24 inches off the ground, and the second is 48 inches high. Once the plants begin to grow, Jason selects the two strongest canes to train and cuts the rest to the ground.

Throughout the summer, he prunes out any new canes that appear so they don't take energy away from berry production. He allows the first cane to grow 2 or 3 inches above the 24-inch-high wire, and then cuts it off an inch below the wire. Two side shoots will branch out below where the stem was cut. These are then trained to run along the wire. The second cane is allowed to grow a couple of inches above the 48-inch wire; then it's cut an inch below that wire. The two side shoots that appear are trained to grow horizontally on the upper wire. As the side shoots lengthen, they are wrapped around the wires and loosely held there using plastic ties or twine. While training the thorny selections, you will definitely need a pair of leather gloves.

'Arapaho' and 'Navaho' are two outstanding thornless selections that can be trained this way and are much easier to work with. You can also get plants to grow on an existing fence or even espalier them against a wall. A family of four will need to grow only five or six plants to have plenty of fresh produce.

Around Fourth of July, after the plants stop producing, Jason cuts all the blackberry canes back to the ground and starts the training process over again. The vines grow back rapidly, and by late August or early September, they will completely cover the trellis.

Planting and Care
It is best to plant blackberries in November or December, but you can do so anytime as long as they are watered during dry periods. Many new, improved selections are available at nurseries and garden centers, but if you can't find them, they can be mail-ordered.

Jason says the plants are really tough. Once established, they need little water and have few problems with pests or diseases. Ripe berries will attract hungry birds, so you might need to throw netting over the plants when berries are present. Jason fertilizes in spring with an all-purpose, slow-release product such as 12-6-6 at a rate of 8 tablespoons per plant. After the Fourth of July cutback, he lightly fertilizes plants with calcium nitrate to force new growth.

Find a sunny spot in your garden, and plant a few of the new, improved selections. Grow them on a fence, wall, or trellis, and you won't have to wade through thorny thickets in search of summer's favorite berry.

CHARLIE THIGPEN

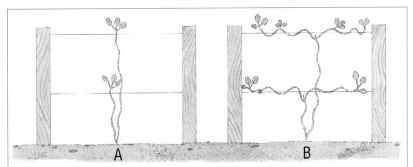

Blackberry Trellis A) Select the two largest canes, and cut the rest to the ground. Allow one cane to grow a few inches above the 24-inch wire and the other to grow a few inches above the 48-inch wire. Then cut each cane 1 inch below the wires. B) Side shoots will sprout at the cutoff point and should be trained to the horizontal wires.

Beyond the Basics

This year, bring a few newcomers into your garden—
add unusual plants to containers just for fun.

STEPS TO SUCCESS

Container gardening is a wonderful way to experiment with new plants. Combine them for stunning results. Here are some GardenSmith ideas.
- Choose plants with compatible light and water requirements.
- Be sure the container has adequate drainage holes.
- Use good-quality potting soil.
- Fertilize regularly (every two weeks) to sustain blooms.
- Design your container with a tall specimen as a focal point and shorter selections surrounding it. Add one with a cascading habit to soften the edge.

I n spring we bound headfirst into the garden, planting the foolproof flowers we depend on. Using trustworthy annuals, such as impatiens, petunias, and zinnias, we are assured a season of reliable color. But according to nursery owner Denise Smith in Jefferson, Georgia, "After you've used the tried-and-true annuals and perennials, it's time to play."

In our enormous universe of plants, there are many slightly different, occasionally odd, and almost always beautiful choices. Through her nursery, GardenSmith, Denise vigorously explores these possibilities. For the curious gardener, investigating new selections is like going to a strange planet, with alien-sounding names such as 'Newellii' cestrum (*Cestrum* 'Newellii') and 'Roseo-picta' snowbush (*Breynia disticha* 'Roseo-picta'). Faced with plants that pique the imagination, it's hard to know where to begin. "Containers are a great

place to start. You can do wild, wonderful combinations with all sorts of bizarre things," Denise says. The pot garden's beauty is the concentration of color in one place, which becomes a showstopping focal point. Use plants with texture, such as Dittany of Crete *(Origanum dictamnus)*, or find an unexpected selection of a garden staple, such salmon-flowered lamb's ear (*Stachys* 'Hidalgo Orange').

above, left: Denise Smith works diligently at her nursery, GardenSmith. **left:** Clockwise from the top: red firespike, 'Gartenmeister Bonstedt' fuchsia, variegated basket grass, caricature plant, and copper leaf.

Guiltless Gardening

It's a gardening truth that occasionally plants just won't survive. "Even professional growers kill things. Get over it," Denise advises. Gather necessary information about your acquisitions, and then relax. "The bottom line is this: The worst that can happen is you might lose a plant or two. If that occurs, just pull them out. It's an excuse to go get something new."

Gardening is an adventure. Plan your landscape based on dependable plants. Then indulge in something new—a flower that steals your heart, a fragrance that makes you swoon, or a leaf you can't help but touch.

ELLEN RUOFF RILEY

left: Cat's whiskers blend beautifully with most other plants in the garden.
below: Perky lavender stamens add a whimsical quality to the plant.

Flowering Felines

It's easy to find a good home for cat's whiskers.

The image of a cat on red alert, with whiskers lifted to filter every possible clue from the passing breeze, comes to mind when faced with a planting of cat's whiskers. Long, delicate stamens extend beyond each dainty flower, curving upward in apparent eagerness to sense the thrilling world around them.

This frisky member of the mint family has been moving into Southern gardens for the last few years, spreading from Florida and Louisiana until it can be found in most nurseries and garden centers. A perennial sub-shrub in its native South Pacific, it is a quick-growing annual in all but the Tropical South. The flowers, either white or lavender, keep their color in full sun or half shade and are produced throughout the growing season.

Whether you grow it in the ground or plant it in a pot, cat's whiskers *(Orthosiphon stamineus)* is an easy keeper. Like other mints, it enjoys moist, fertile soil and appreciates regular feeding and watering, but it will grow just fine in most ordinary garden conditions. Plant it in a 12-inch or larger container, and you can even move it inside and use it as a houseplant by a sunny window. If frost kills the top before you remember to move it indoors for the winter, just store the potted plant in a cool, dark garage until spring, and then set it back out in the garden.

Cat's whiskers has square, purple-green stems that are thickly covered below the flowers with dark green, lance-shaped leaves. The plentiful bloom spikes open from the bottom up in a tidy and efficient fashion. Old flowers drop away cleanly below fresh blossoms, and neat little buds crown the top of each spike. As a result, this plant always looks groomed, even if you don't have the time to deadhead the spent flower stalks.

For gardeners who appreciate the whimsical, it's almost irresistible to group cat's whiskers with feline companions such as tiger lily *(Lilium lancifolium)* or lion's ear *(Leonotis leonurus)*. Just be kind, and keep it away from the dogwoods.

LIZ DRUITT

PLANTING TIP

Put cat's whiskers at the base of taller, leggy plants such as flowering maple (*Abutilon* sp.), angel's trumpet *(Brugmansia* sp.), butterfly bush (*Buddleia* sp.), and certain roses. Its full green foliage and lacy veil of flowers will add color and cover other plants' flaws.

CAT'S WHISKERS
At a Glance

Range: perennial in Tropical South, long-blooming annual elsewhere
Light: full sun to half shade
Soil: It's not choosy but does best in moist, organic soil.
Moisture: Water thoroughly once a week.
Bloom season: late spring until frost
Size: 2 to 3 feet high and wide
Propagate: seeds or cuttings

a **lily** for every garden

These cherished plants will add grace and elegance to any setting.

Lilies are made for gardens. These tall, graceful plants offer beautiful flowers in a multitude of colors. Some possess intoxicating fragrances that will linger in your thoughts for days. All are reliable bulbs, and when you have chosen the right one for your garden, it will become something to treasure for years.

A Field Full

Patrick Snider, gardener at Oxmoor Farm in Louisville, describes lilies as the perfect plant for the garden. They fill in the perennial border nicely, and the flowers are great for cutting. He prefers the Asiatic hybrids that thrive in the Upper South and likes to use complimentary plantings of daylilies (*Hemerocallis* sp.) and yarrow (*Achillea filipendulina*) with them.

Frances Parker, a garden designer in Beaufort, South Carolina, enthusiastically declares, "The Oriental hybrids are the best for the Coastal South." She finds their fragrance "out of this world," especially on a summer evening. Plus, they mix well in the border with montbretias (*Crocosmia crocosmiiflora*) and summer phlox (*Phlox paniculata*).

So which lily should you choose for your garden? Use the chart above to determine the one that works best for your plant-hardiness zone. (Refer to the map on page 240 to determine your zone.) Also, take special notice of tiger lilies (*Lilium lancifolium*). Their beautiful orange, spotted flowers add zest to any garden. They should not be mixed with other lilies, as they can transmit mosaic virus through aphids. Symptoms appear as a yellow mottling in the leaves or stunted growth. Tiger lilies are immune to the mosaic virus.

Lily	Blooms	Zone
Easter lily (*Lilium longiflorum*)	species blooms white, 'Casa Rosa' (pink); very fragrant	AS, but especially good for LS, CS
Asiatic hybrids	'Connecticut King' (yellow), 'Enchantment' (orange)	US, MS, LS
Oriental hybrids	'Stargazer' (rose with white margins), 'Casablanca' (white); very fragrant	US, MS, LS, CS, but especially good for LS, CS
tiger lily (*L. lancifolium*)	typically orange, but also white, yellow, and red	US, MS, LS
Formosa lily (*L. formosanum*)	white flowers; fragrant	AS, but especially good for LS, CS
regal lily (*L. regale*)	yellow, backside of flower petals pink; fragrant	US, MS, LS
Aurelian hybrids	'Black Dragon' (white), 'Thunderbolt' (orange-apricot)	US, MS, LS

AS=All South, US=Upper South, MS=Middle South, LS=Lower South, CS=Coastal South

Love Your Lily

When planting lily bulbs, set them so they are at a depth that is twice the height of the bulb. If you are planting container-grown bulbs, set your plant so the top of the soil in the container will be level with the surrounding dirt. Lilies love rich, moist, well-drained soil. They are very happy if their bulbs can rest on a bed of sand or fine gravel on top of the mix, allowing their roots to grow into the rich soil. Follow this with an additional covering of soil and organic mulch, and they will thrive.

For the best display in the garden, space these tall, narrow plants in groups of threes or fives for more impact. They fit well toward the middle and back portions of a border, depending on the selection. For example, Formosa lily grows 5 to 7 feet tall, and once it begins to bloom, its weight will bring it forward.

Most lilies do, in fact, need a little support, as they are top-heavy when in bloom. Propping them up with readily available bamboo stakes can keep them from toppling. Flowers will last longer if they receive a little protection from afternoon sun too. Remove flowers as they fade, and once the stems have diminished later in the summer, cut the plant back to the ground. GENE B. BUSSELL

right: Lilies mix well with perennials, such as daylilies and yarrow.

TIPS FOR CUT FLOWERS

Lilies, which can be purchased year-round as cut flowers throughout the South, will last for many days in a vase. When buying, choose flowers with a few buds open and others that are about to open. Condition the flowers by placing them in lukewarm water with a floral preservative, such as Floralife Fresh Flower Food. Conditioning will help extend the life of the flower. Recut stems at an angle, and remove any foliage that will be in water. Place recut stems in lukewarm water that also has a floral preservative. Although you will want to put your lilies in a prominent location, avoid placing the flowers in areas with a lot of traffic, as the pollen can stain your clothes.

Jim Long caught a glimpse of his future one
night as he slept. This sparked a passion
for growing and cooking with herbs.

Dream
Garden

by STEVE BENDER / PHOTOGRAPHY VAN CHAPLIN

left: At Long Creek Herb Farm, visitors learn the uses of hundreds of herbs.
top: Dried mugwort, rose petals, lavender blooms, and rosemary are ingredients in Jim's dream pillows.
above: Jim introduces two children to Siberian mint. In this garden, kids are encouraged to touch, smell, and taste.

Twenty-six years ago, Jim Long had a vision. Though it scared him at first, it ultimately set the course for the rest of his life.

"I dreamed I saw my wife in a car falling out of the sky," he recalls. "And below it, I saw some specific plants, one of which was prairie dock.

"Fast-forward a year and a half," he continues. "I'm divorced and living in a little one-room cabin about 40 miles away. A friend says, 'Let me show you where my sister and I live.' So we drive down, and as we come up over the hill, I see the spot that I'd seen in my dream. There was the prairie dock. It gave me cold chills."

The spot was a farm outside Blue Eye, Missouri, a tiny town south of Branson, about a mile from the Arkansas border. When one of the sisters moved away to get married and the second concluded she didn't want to live there alone, they asked Jim if he'd like to rent the farm. "I said, 'Well, this feels more like home than any place I've ever been,' " he

top, left: Hugged by lavenders, this garden art wiggles skyward. **top, right:** 'Pink Wave' petunias bloom at the foot of 'Russian Red' cannas as scarlet runner beans climb a post. **above, center:** Spider flowers (cleome) bloom all summer. **above:** The huge rounded leaves of Indian calabash gourd smother a stick trellis.

remembers. He took such good care of the place that five years later, the family willed him the property.

Putting Down Roots

Jim started a landscaping business to pay the bills, but his heart told him to grow herbs too. He would not plant them merely for show, he resolved, but concentrate instead on those with culinary, medicinal, and historical importance. Today, his collection at Long Creek Herb Farm exceeds 400 kinds, including Ozark natives, herbs gathered from trips to India and Indonesia, as well as those used for Civil War medicines and by pioneers on the Santa Fe Trail. He also grows a wondrous assortment of unusual vegetables, including Malabar climbing spinach and a hibiscus with edible red leaves. And he still has prairie dock *(Silphium terebinthinaceum)*, a member of the daisy family that features showy, yellow blooms atop stalks up to 8 feet tall.

When a serious back injury forced him to quit his landscaping business, Jim began hosting garden clubs at the farm, and a strange thing happened. "People said, 'We love the garden, but what we really want is to buy something,'" he notes. "I realized that they wanted to take home some of the experience of being here—something that smelled or tasted like my garden."

Jim quickly obliged. He opened a gift shop stocked with all sorts of herbs and herbal health products. You can't buy gold here, but you can find frankincense and myrrh. You can get juniper berries, chamomile flowers, hops, and patchouli. You can also buy dreams.

Well, dream pillows, to be exact. Filled with various mixes of herbs and flowers, they are said to interact with brain chemistry to produce specific types of dreams. Jim has one pillow to inspire creativity, one to promote restful sleep, and one to elicit "romantic" dreams. Do they work? "One customer who used the romantic dreams pillow said her dreams were 'way too romantic to put on paper,' but *very* enjoyable," he reports.

Fun and Flavor

Schoolchildren are frequent guests at Long Creek Herb Farm. Jim delights in introducing them to herbs and assuring them that, in this garden, it's okay to touch. "Kids have the idea that gardens aren't for touching or tasting," he explains. "So I encourage them to try dill, fennel, and basil—things with flavors they recognize from spaghetti sauce or dill pickles."

If you're lucky, Jim might cook for you. He's an excellent chef, having dabbled in cooking since he was a child. His enthusiasm for the subject changed the local 4-H club forever. At Jim's insistence, the girls agreed to do a project on electricity if the boys would learn to cook. "We had really interesting meetings," Jim recalls.

Whether pulling weeds in the garden or chopping mint in the kitchen, Jim Long couldn't be happier. In sight of the blooms of the prairie dock, he's living out his dream.

HERBAL HINTS

If you're just getting started with growing herbs, Jim has some advice. First, pick a spot with full sun and well-drained soil. Plant six or seven different herbs you'd like to grow. Try tasting each one mixed into cream cheese or scrambled eggs. This is a good way to become acquainted with the various flavors. His can't-miss list of herbs is right out of a Simon & Garfunkel song—parsley, sage, rosemary, and thyme.

Tours of Long Creek Herb Farm are available by appointment only. A fee of $25 per carload will be credited toward purchases from the gift shop. Call (417) 779-5450. You can find Jim's recipes at www. longcreekherbs.com.

top: A row of Indian guar beans grows next to some zinnias. Wild grapevines shade the gift shop porch. **above:** Jim loves to cook using herbs from his garden. He let us sample lemon balm-blueberry cake, fresh basil sorbet, and fresh ginger tea—all were yummy.

A gazebo adds the finishing touch to an outdoor retreat *(See page 139.)*

July

garden checklist

Editor's Notebook

PHOTOGRAPH: VAN CHAPLIN

It's sunny and hot. You want shade. Wouldn't it be great if there were a MIRACLE TREE that would grow UP TO 10 FEET THE FIRST YEAR? Well, thanks to the marvels of modern science and journalistic hyperbole, there is! It's called the empress tree *(Paulownia tomentosa)*. Featured regularly on the back page of your favorite Sunday tabloid, this AMAZING TREE shoots skyward literally BEFORE YOUR EYES with leaves as big as parasols! But wait! There's more!!! Its wood is SO VALUABLE in Japan that chain saw-wielding thieves will cut it down WHILE YOU SLEEP and leave you with just a stump!! Don't be misled by some *Southern Living* curmudgeon who claims this tree is a weedy, messy, weak-wooded nuisance that's impossible to grow grass beneath and will crack your sidewalk with its roots. After all, who wants reality when we can have SOMETHING BETTER? So call today! Operators with chain saws are standing by!!

—STEVE BENDER

TIPS

- **Fragrance**—Gardenia, tuberose, clethra, and fragrant plantain lily *(Hosta plantaginea)* perfume the summer garden. Enjoy their scents inside by cutting a few stems for simple arrangements or to supplement purchased flowers.
- **Mowing**—Raise your lawnmower's height for the summer. Cutting the grass too short can stress your lawn. Mow centipede at a height of 1½ to 2 inches, Kentucky bluegrass at 2 to 3 inches, Zoysia at 1 to 2 inches, St. Augustine at 2½ to 4 inches, common Bermuda at 1 to 2 inches, and improved Bermuda at ½ to 1 inch.
- **Water conservation**—Using your irrigation system early in the day reduces evaporation. Infrequent, deep watering is better than frequent, shallow watering, as it promotes deeper root growth. Soaker hoses are efficient for newly planted trees and shrubs. Hide the hose with mulch to further reduce moisture loss. Purchase a rain gauge to see how much water your garden receives naturally. Save money by using a rain barrel to collect water for beds and containers.
- **Nematodes**—In Florida, these microscopic worms feed on plant roots, causing them to be stunted or knotted. If you suspect that nematodes are a problem in your garden, try soil solarization. Cover the ground for four to six weeks with clear polyethylene film. Before covering, till the area well, breaking up all clumps of soil, and water moderately. Cover the edges of the polyethylene film with soil to form a tight seal. Leave film in place until time to plant again. The method works because of prolonged increased temperatures beneath the film, so the area must be in full sun for the method to be effective.
- **Ornamental peppers**—In Texas, taller types (up to 4 feet) are useful at the backs of borders and for large pots. Dwarf and medium types such as 'Pretty Purple' pepper are also available. Chile piquin or McMahon's Texas bird pepper can be found growing wild. Edible types include 'Gypsy' (lime green) and 'Tequila Sunrise' (bright gold).

Gardenia

Tropicals

In Texas, add these beauties to borders and containers for bold color and texture. Some of the best are variegated shell ginger *(Alpinia zerumbet* 'Variegata'), bloodleaf or 'Rojo' banana, and 'Pink Sunrise' cannas. Sweet potato vines such as 'Blackie,' 'Margarita' (pictured at right), and 'Tricolor' provide quick foliage color from now until frost. Consider them for use as ground covers. Angel's trumpets *(Brugmansia* sp.) come in gold, cream, pink, and orange and add fragrance as well as tropical color to the garden. They bloom from early summer until late fall and are usually root hardy in the Southern half of the state.

Plants for Hummingbirds

Choose flowers that attract and feed these whirling wonders. There are many blooming now that they love, including cardinal flower *(Lobelia cardinalis)*— pictured at right, firebush *(Hamelia patens)*, coral honeysuckle *(Lonicera sempervirens)*, pineapple sage *(Salvia elegans)*, and bee balm *(Monarda didyma)*. Plant these, and hummingbirds will regularly visit your garden and reward you with their beauty.

PLANT

■ **Perennials**—Purple coneflower *(Echinacea purpurea)*, black-eyed Susan *(Rudbeckia hirta)*, and summer phlox *(Phlox paniculata)* are in full bloom this month and are great to add to your garden. Strong sun, hot weather, and wind can make these introductions tricky. Plant in late afternoon or in early evening when the sunlight is diffused. Loosen the roots of container-grown plants before transplanting them, and set plants into the soil at the original growing level. Water well, and then add mulch to keep roots cool and reduce water loss. To further transition plants into your garden, use a root stimulator such as Miracle-Gro Liquid Quick Start (4-12-4) or Schultz Starter Plus.

■ **Coleus for sun**—In Florida, though coleus has long been regarded as an excellent plant to add color to shaded areas, the many new selections of sun-loving coleus are becoming very popular. Plant 'Gay's Delight,' 'Alabama Sunset,' 'Red Ruffles,' 'Amazon,' or 'Solar Flare' in full sun for a beautiful show until frost. (For more information see "Colorful Coleus" on page 116.)

■ **Grasses**—In Texas, the best choices are Bermuda, Zoysia, St. Augustine, and buffalo grass. Of these, buffalo and Bermuda are the most drought tolerant.

■ **Yuccas, agaves, and red yuccas**—In Texas, plant in containers or borders for easy care and special interest. Red yucca *(Hesperaloe* sp.) has long-lasting spikes of bell-shaped blooms that attract hummingbirds.

PRUNE

■ **Annuals**—Cut leggy annuals such as impatiens, narrow-leaf zinnias, and wax begonias back by about one-third now to encourage a big show in late summer and fall. Water and then add a slow-release, granular fertilizer such as Osmocote Vegetable & Bedding (14-14-14) or Sta-Green 6-month Flower & Vegetable (13-13-13).

FERTILIZE

■ **Iron for the lawn**—In Florida, if your grass looks a little yellow this month, don't fertilize. Instead, apply iron to give the lawn a darker green color. Mix 2 ounces of ferrous sulfate in 3 to 5 gallons of water, and apply to 1,000 square feet of lawn. Or, better yet, use a chelated iron source such as Green-light Iron & Soil Acidifier or Ironite, and follow package directions.

Tip of the Month

A plastic hanging plant basket with a hook and suspension wires makes a great container for harvesting vegetables and fruits that you pick while standing up, such as pole beans, cucumbers, and blackberries. Place the hook in your collar, and let the basket hang at the waist, so both of your hands are free to harvest.

HENRY PITTMAN
SPARTANBURG, SOUTH CAROLINA

Yes, You Canna

Amazingly colorful and easy to grow, these Southern favorites belong in your garden. Here are some new ones to try.

Dear Reader,
We here at Gardening Central have been studying you. Hours of painstaking and perfectly legal research have revealed the following truths about how you choose plants for your garden.

Truth #1: You want color, color, color.
Truth #2: You want it now, now, now.
Truth #3: You want it easy, easy, easy.

Taken together, what do these startling facts mean? That you should be growing cannas.

Native to the Southeast as well as South America, cannas aren't shy. Wherever you plant them, they loudly introduce themselves through audacious blossoms and leaves. Red, orange, salmon, coral, pink, cream, or bicolored flowers bloom on 3- to 7-foot stalks in summer and fall. Huge, banana-like leaves stretch from 1 to 4 feet long. Typical leaves are green or bronze, but many new selections sport foliage so shockingly loud you might want to cover them at night to avoid disturbing your neighbors.

Our Favorite Ones

Two special cannas are illuminating gardens as never before. 'Tropicanna' (also known as 'Phaison') must be seen to be believed. Who could have dreamed up colors like this—deep purple foliage striped with yellow, pink, and red with golden-orange flowers to boot? When backlit by the sun, the leaves glow so brightly you'd swear they're radioactive. On the downside, 'Tropicanna' is quite susceptible to canna leaf roller caterpillars and needs frequent feeding to keep its foliage looking bright. But if you follow our growing tips, you shouldn't have much trouble.

'Bengal Tiger' (also known as 'Pretoria') is just as eye-popping. This selection combines deep orange blossoms with incredibly vivid green-and-yellow striped leaves. It's easier to grow than 'Tropicanna' and doesn't need as much fertilizer. Leaf rollers usually aren't a big deal either.

Other excellent cannas include 'Black Knight' (beautiful, black-bronze foliage and velvety, deep red flowers), 'Durban' (reddish purple leaves with yellow stripes and scarlet flowers), 'Minerva' (green-and-white striped leaves and yellow flowers), and 'Tropicanna Gold' (green-and-gold striped leaves and orange-yellow blooms with dark orange speckles).

Caring for Cannas

Look for potted cannas at home-and-garden centers. Plant them so the top of the root ball is even with the soil surface. Cannas like lots of water. They will even grow with wet roots, but the soil need not be boggy, just moist. They are also heavy feeders and prefer soil containing plenty

top: The foliage of 'Tropicanna' is dazzling. **above:** The striped leaves of 'Bengal Tiger' are as striking as the flowers. **far left:** Like big orange butterflies, blossoms seem to flutter above the foliage of 'Bengal Tiger.'

BY STEVE BENDER / PHOTOGRAPHY VAN CHAPLIN, LACY KERR ROBINSON, AND ALLEN ROKACH

above: 'Tropicanna' adds brilliant color and bold foliage to this mixed flower border.
left: Canna leaf roller caterpillars can make a mess of foliage.

of organic matter such as composted manure and chopped leaves. Ragged and dull foliage tells you that they're hungry, so feed plants weekly with a water-soluble 20-20-20 fertilizer. They will soon perk up.

Cannas grow best in full sun and high heat and form spreading colonies. Cut each flower stalk to the ground after it finishes blooming; new ones will appear and flower into early fall. In the Lower, Coastal, and Tropical South, plants will overwinter. Elsewhere, lift the rootlike rhizomes in fall, and store indoors until spring. Divide clumps every three or four years. Make sure each piece of rhizome has a bud or "eye," or it may not grow.

As mentioned before, canna leaf rollers can be serious pests. These caterpillars roll up canna leaves and then feed and pupate inside, eventually emerging as adult moths. Infested leaves look ratty. To control leaf rollers, promptly cut off and destroy all infested leaves. Spray new foliage according to label directions with a systemic insecticide such as Orthene. Also try applying a fertilizer with disulfoton, such as Bayer Advanced Garden 2-in-1 Systemic Rose & Flower Care.

In the Garden
Give cannas room. Most grow to be big plants, 4 to 7 feet tall and 3 to 4 feet wide. Display them in a mass planting, in a mixed flower border, in a large container, or by the edge of a pond. But be mindful of overdoing the gaudy-leafed kinds, lest you blind your neighbors. We at Gardening Central will be watching. ◆

After a stalk finishes blooming, cut it to the ground. A new one will soon emerge with fresher-looking foliage.

below: Pat and Trish enlisted the artistic talents of their son, Mason, to paint the aquatic-themed canvases that hang from the ceiling of the gazebo.

above: The gazebo is the crowning touch of this backyard makeover, which also includes a goldfish pond and brick steps leading up to the house.

Creating a Garden Getaway

No backyard retreat is complete until there's a spot to sit and enjoy it all.

Located halfway down their sloping backyard, Trish and Pat Poe's new gazebo is the perfect distance away from the home to provide a quiet escape. The structure is just the right size to accommodate a table and four chairs for a casual outdoor dinner. The sounds of the splashing fountain nearby complete the effect of a backyard oasis.

The gazebo has extra creature comforts that allow the couple to get more use out of it; this is especially important with Nashville's long outdoor season. A ceiling fan cools it off during sizzling summer afternoons, and lighting helps extend the hours of use into the cool evenings. To tie the house and garden together, Trish and Pat designed the railing around the gazebo to match a new balcony on the home. The finishing touch was provided by their son, Mason, who painted four triangular canvases and mounted them on the gazebo's ceiling. Playing off the water theme, Mason painted a crane-and-fish motif. The artwork dresses up the structure and also prevents birds from roosting in the rafters.

Trish and Pat can now steal away for a quiet outdoor dinner for two or bring in the extended family for other events. "It seems like now, whenever our relatives want to have a wedding or party, we are voted to be the hosts," Trish says, "because we have the best yard for entertaining—and living!"

GLENN R. DINELLA

EVERYTHING IN ITS PLACE

Deciding on just the right spot to put your gazebo is every bit as important as selecting its style. So before you start construction, take a few minutes to consider the needs of your family and your landscape.

■ **Up close and personal**—Building a gazebo near the home is a nice way to ease the transition between house and garden. Its convenience makes it a popular spot during parties or for family meals. When built on a deck or patio, it is an accessible outdoor place for elderly or disabled homeowners.

■ **In the middle**—When placed in the center of the yard or garden, a gazebo becomes a respite from the summer sun and might even offer a view in every direction. It's far enough away from the home to provide a quick escape and close enough to be convenient.

■ **In the distance**—When placed at the far end of the property, a gazebo makes a peaceful haven from hectic home life. If you have a large lot and don't seem to utilize the back of the property, placing an inviting structure at the far end can draw you out and make your garden live larger.

This circular lawn on the lower level is the garden's centerpiece. Red cedars and wax myrtles screen nearby houses.

Putting the Pieces Together

It sounds contradictory, but breaking this small Dallas, Texas, garden into even smaller parts makes it feel bigger and more inviting. The use of walls, screening, and multiple levels means you can't see everything at once, so your walk slows, and your gaze lingers. You feel sheltered, instead of exposed. And that's just what the owners had in mind.

Big houses don't always have big lots. This home is a good example. The backyard was small (measuring only 60 x 80 feet), sloping, and in full view of nearby neighbors. The owners wanted an attractive spot for relaxing and entertaining without feeling as if they were onstage.

They have it now. Landscape architect Harold Leidner created a very private two-level garden that is easy on the eyes, simple to maintain, and designed as an outdoor room.

You enter the yard from the driveway through an ornate gate crowned with an arch of climbing 'Golden Showers' roses. Once inside, you discover sweeps of flowers and ferns, as well as a spa and terrace shaded by a spreading live oak.

Take a quick right turn, and you descend stone steps to the lower garden. A circular, hybrid Bermuda lawn—edged with a gravel walk, annuals, and a border of clipped dwarf yaupons—immediately grabs your eye. Crisp, clean lines and obvious formality define this area as a gathering space. Wax myrtles and red cedars planted on opposite sides of an iron fence screen the view of adjacent houses.

Wax begonias, yellow shrimp plants, caladiums, and other seasonal annuals supply months of summer color with little fuss. And thanks to the skillful use of evergreens and stonework, this garden appeals even in winter.   STEVE BENDER

above, left: An ornate gate topped with climbing roses marks the entrance to the garden from the driveway. **above, right:** Walls, evergreens, and multiple levels divide this garden into sections, making the overall space seem larger.

Talk of the Town

Plant some tickseed, and start the rumors flying.

Do you have neighbors who are constantly sticking their noses over the fence to see what you're doing in your yard? Well, here is a plant that will keep them talking about you for days.

It's an annual wildflower called tickseed, also known by other colorful names such as beggar-ticks and stick-tights. Actually, many types of tickseed exist, though most are out-and-out weeds. A few forms do offer showy flowers, making them fine additions to the border. But the blooms, pretty as they are, aren't the primary source of neighborhood comment. No, that distinction belongs to the rich green, finely cut foliage, which looks for all the world like marijuana. So be smart—before you plant, hide your lava lamps and David Crosby black light posters, or you might get a visit from the boys in blue.

Of course, once tickseed blooms, your reputation is safe. Two species in particular put on quite a show that begins in midsummer and lasts into the fall. Crowned tickseed *(Bidens coronata)* grows up to 5 feet tall with very finely cut foliage and golden-yellow blossoms up to 3 inches across. Tickseed sunflower *(B. aristosa)* looks very similar, but its leaves are less dissected and its 2-inch blooms are a lighter yellow.

All tickseeds take their name from their barbed seeds, which stick to the clothing or fur of anything that walks by. This is how the plants spread. Seeds planted in spring or summer sprout and grow quickly. Tickseeds prefer full sun and fertile soil that's either boggy or well drained, but not

top: Crowned tickseed quickly grows into a soft, bushy mound about 5 feet high.
above: Showy, golden-yellow flowers appear in summer and fall. Barbed seeds that stick to clothing and fur give this wildflower its name.

arid. Once you plant them, you'll have them forever because they reseed profusely. But then again, seedlings are nice to share, and any you don't want pull up easily.

So if your neighborhood is just a little too quiet, plant some tickseed. But just remember what I said about those David Crosby posters.

STEVE BENDER

TICKSEED
At a Glance

Height: 3 to 5 feet
Light: full sun
Soil: fertile—wet or well drained
Pests: none serious
Propagation: seed
Range: throughout the South

Super Design, Great Ideas

This versatile garden fits comfort and style into a compact space.

When Jim Lommori tackled his backyard, his goal was to use every square inch of the narrow Austin, Texas, lot. A spacious entertaining area was a top priority, as was maintaining a cozy garden atmosphere.

For assistance, he called on local architect Stan Hensley, and together they planned a totally useful, beautifully designed garden. "Our concept was to make outdoor living rooms and use the seasons in Austin to their maximum extent," Stan says.

Simple, Effective Plan

The long, slender space, measuring approximately 20 x 50 feet, is divided into decked sections. A dining pavilion anchors one area, while a potting shed repeats the architectural style at the garden's opposite end. An outdoor sun terrace and sunken garden, including a small water feature, create additional living areas between the two simple buildings. "The whole idea is to make pavilions and spaces that are slightly structured, creating a sense of place relative to the area around the garden," Stan says.

The design has an orderly feel. "As an architect, I am very interested in the post-and-beam structural system. It's very Asian feeling and modular, not unlike a tatami floor mat in a Japanese home," Stan says. "All the posts line up, and all the grids relate. It's just a matter of making subtle connections and layering materials to define the shape," he says.

The House Connection

New French doors in Jim's dining room mirror the already existing door in his living room. Now when Jim entertains, his guests can come and go easily between the indoor and outdoor areas; this practically doubles

top: A view of the sunken garden, sun terrace, and dining pavilion **above, left:** The lava stone fountain brings the cool sound of splashing water to hot summer days and enhances the garden's Asian atmosphere. **above, right:** Containers chosen for their simple lines are filled with tough succulents and houseplants.

the square footage of his residence.

It takes time to make any new landscape your own. "Initially, the decks and garden had a much more contemporary feeling," Stan relates. "But over time, the look has softened tremendously and become more personal." Jim's carefully chosen plants thrive in Austin's hot summer climate and enhance the spacious feeling in the tiny garden. Containers holding single specimens delineate the area with colors and textures carefully chosen to maintain the garden's clean lines and organized appearance.

ELLEN RUOFF RILEY

TERRIFIC TIPS

Stan offers a variety of ideas to employ in your own landscape. He says, "Every person living in a suburban or ranch-style home has the potential to extend the livability of the house into the backyard."
- Build a wall around an area to define space.
- Put a pavilion in the landscape to make a destination.
- Add a deck, and trade the existing windows for French doors to provide easy access to the garden.

PHOTOGRAPHS: VAN CHAPLIN

left: Society garlic is an excellent choice for a mixed border, combining showy blooms with attractive, grasslike foliage.
above: Starlike, pinkish lavender flowers appear repeatedly during warm weather.

Easy Society Garlic

This many blooms for so little trouble will make you so happy you'll almost cry.

SOCIETY GARLIC
At a Glance

Size: about 2 feet tall and wide
Light: full sun
Soil: well drained
Water: Tolerates drought, but blooms better if watered.
Propagation: Divide clumps in fall.
Range: Lower, Coastal, and Tropical South (Can be treated as an annual in the Upper and Middle South.)

It's not hard to say nice things about society garlic. It has pretty flowers, blooms for months, tolerates drought, resists pests, and grows in almost any well-drained soil. But if you bring it home in your car, remember to open the windows.

Society garlic *(Tulbaghia violacea)* smells just like regular garlic. I'll never forget filling the backseat of my car with about eight pots of the stuff destined for a garden in Florida. Within five minutes, my eyes were tearing so profusely you'd have thought I had won the Miss America pageant. For days afterward, people getting in my car kept asking if I delivered pizza.

Where To Plant

Place it out in the yard, away from windows, porches, and sitting areas. It's showy in borders, especially when planted en masse, and does very well in containers. Growing about 2 feet wide and tall (counting the blooms), it forms a fine-textured cluster of long, narrow, grasslike leaves. 'Variegata' features a creamy stripe down the center of each leaf, while 'Silver Lace' has leaves edged in white. Plants spread steadily by underground rhizomes to form large clumps; divide them in fall to get more plants. They can be treated as annuals in the Upper and Middle South.

Society garlic blooms repeatedly in warm weather. In the Coastal or Tropical South, where the plant is quite popular, expect blooms from March to November. Bursts of pinkish lavender, starlike blossoms appear on slender, sturdy stems. The blooms are favorites of butterflies.

As mentioned before, few flowering perennials are as elementary to grow. Its two main requirements are sun and well-drained soil. Society garlic stands up to drought, although it blooms more heavily with regular watering. About the only maintenance you'll need to do is removing the old bloom stalks. Pests don't bother it—indeed, its presence in the garden is said to drive them away.

Polite Society

Now you may be wondering how society garlic got its name. Well, supposedly you can use the leaves just like garlic chives and eat them without getting bad breath. I don't know whether that's true or not, but feel free to test it out. Just remember to open the windows.　STEVE BENDER

Hostas are a favorite shade perennial (See pages 152–153.)

August

garden checklist

Editor's Notebook

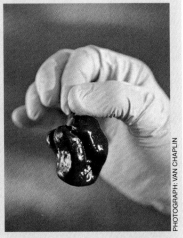

PHOTOGRAPH: VAN CHAPLIN

I love hot food. Nothing brings me greater joy than feeling beads of sweat cascading from my brow as I dine on Thai and Indian foods so caustic they could be used for chemical peels. But nothing could prepare me for the chunks of living napalm I encountered in Mark Viette's garden (see page154). Mark directed me to his row of 'Chocolate Habanero' peppers. "Habanero," he explained, " is a Spanish word that means 'You laugh while my hair is burning.'" This particular pepper is the second hottest in the world, behind only the legendary "Uranium Fuel Rod." Even handling one can burn sensitive skin. So after gloving up, I picked one, admired its beauty, and then gently bit into it to fully appreciate its smoky, piquant flavor. The next morning in the hospital, the doctor explained that the burns on my scalp weren't serious, and my hair should begin growing again soon. Then he fetched me another bowl of that delicious curry ice cream. Yum. STEVE BENDER

Vegetables

Harvest often for an ongoing supply of fresh vegetables. Pick tomatoes, peppers, and tomatillos early in the morning on the day you plan to eat them. Select okra, eggplants, squash, and cucumbers when they're small and tender. Use sharp clippers or a small knife to harvest them to avoid tearing the vines or stalks. Southern peas should also be picked when tender for best flavor.

TIPS

■ **Mosquitoes**—Simple steps can help reduce the number of these insects around your garden. Empty all sources of standing water such as plant saucers, buckets, or old tires. Keep gutters clear so debris does not cause water to collect. Change the water in birdbaths at least once a week. If you have a water garden, add a few goldfish to eat the insect larvae. Mosquito Dunks are another way to get rid of this bug. When placed in ponds, birdbaths, or other standing water, these donut-shaped objects release a bacteria that kills larvae. Insect repellents such as Cutter Skinsations, Off! Skintastic, Cutter Bug Free Backyard, and Cutter or Off! mosquito coils also control these bugs. For more information visit www.mosquito.org.

Mosquito Dunk larvae killer

■ **Mulch**—Shaded annual beds of caladiums, torenias, begonias, and impatiens will benefit from an extra layer of mulch, such as pine straw. This will help conserve moisture and keep roots cool.

■ **Seeds**—Plan your fall garden now. Review mail-order catalogs, and select flower and vegetable seeds for autumn planting.

PLANT

■ **Bulbs**—Plant autumn crocus (*Colchicum* sp.), and you will be rewarded with a multitude of pink blooms. It is available at some garden centers or by mail order.

■ **Tomatoes**—In Florida, plant now for a fall harvest before frost. Choose selections that can set fruit in high temperatures, such as 'Sun Leaper,' 'Florida 91,' 'Sun Chaser,' 'Solar Set,' and 'Heatwave.' Mulch to reduce soil temperature.

■ **Perennial salvias**—In Texas, set out containerized plants now. Choices include Mexican bush sage *(Salvia leucantha)*, 'Indigo Spires' salvia, autumn sage *(S. greggii)*, and mealy-cup sage *(S. farinacea)*.

■ **Sunflowers**—In Texas, seeds or containerized plants should be available now at garden centers. Plant them in a sunny and open location in well-prepared soil.

PRUNE

■ **Basil**—Keep blooms and foliage trimmed to increase production of new leaves.

■ **Fall-blooming perennials**—Early in the month, you still have time to groom and shape perennials such as salvias, asters, and mums. Pinch off loose or unkempt growth with your fingers. This will help maintain the plants' compact habits and produce more flowers for a great fall show.

■ **Roses**—Prune and fertilize your everblooming roses now for a big show of fall flowers. Remove dead stems, and shorten healthy canes by about one-third. Feed with rose fertilizer, and add clean mulch to conserve moisture and reduce disease. Water well once each week if it doesn't rain. To avoid black spot, powdery mildew, and rust, don't use an overhead sprinkler.

PRUNE

■ **Lawn care**—If your centipede grass looks too thin or off color, fertilize it now with a product such as Sta-Green 15-0-15 Centipede Lawn Fertilizer or Pennington Centipede & St. Augustine Lawn Food 18-0-18. Apply according to label directions or using no more than 6 pounds of fertilizer per 1,000 square feet of lawn. Wait until September to feed St. Augustine lawns. Continue to monitor discolored areas for insects.

■ **Palms**—In Florida, fertilize them with a product such as Vigoro 9-4-9 Palm, Ixora & Ornamental Plant Food or Lesco 8-10-10 Palm & Tropical Ornamental fertilizer. Fronds that are already discolored will not regreen. Prune them to give the trees a neater appearance.

■ **Shrubs and trees**—In Florida, if you have not fertilized since early summer, feed young plants now to encourage growth. Use a product such as Sta-Green 15-0-15 or Pennington 18-0-18. Spread it on top of the mulch, and water it in.

Cannas

Set out containerized plants, which are available at garden centers now. Compact types in vibrant colors, such as 'Orange Punch,' 'Princess Di' (pale yellow), 'Louis Cottin' (tangerine with purplish foliage), and 'Pink Sunburst' (striped cream, pink, and green foliage) stay in the 3- to 4-foot-tall range. Older standard selections, such as 'President' and 'Landscape Red,' are also excellent choices but are in the 2- to 3-foot-tall range. To learn more about this plant, read "Yes, You Canna" on page 136.

Tropical Perennials

You can still have color at a time when many annuals are struggling with heat and humidity. Plant angelonia, ginger lily (shown at right), crinum lily, pentas, Brazilian plume flower, coleus, Persian shield, *Calathea* sp., elephant's ear, shrimp plant, or ornamental sweet potato. While some, such as angelonia and ornamental sweet potato, won't survive the winter in North Florida, they'll offer color till the first hard freeze.

August notes:

Tip of the Month

I grind citrus rinds in the blender, add water, and let this mixture soak overnight. Then I strain the water and spray it on my plants to get rid of caterpillars and other insects. This works great!

SUZAN L. WIENER
SPRING HILL, FLORIDA

Angel's Trumpets

BY ELLEN RUOFF RILEY

This easy-to-grow flower will make your heart sing from now until frost.

Everything about an angel's trumpet is dramatic: Pendulous floral bells sway gracefully from sturdy branches, perfuming the sultry evening air with fabulous scent. Its celestial color chart ranges from pristine white to peachy pink and creamy yellow, and mature specimens put on a truly stellar show in full bloom. But the drama stops with appearance—this is one easy plant to grow. And you can find it in bloom at many garden centers now.

An old-fashioned pass-along plant, angel's trumpet has long found favor in the South's coastal and frost-free climates. In these regions, mature plants reach 15 feet tall, with their heaviest flowering time extending from late summer into fall. Gardeners in cooler climates can have the same results by growing one in a container. Before the first frost, move the pot to a heated garage or basement to wait out cold winter months. It will drop leaves, so light is not a concern during this rest period.

The Specifics

Angel's trumpets (*Brugmansia* sp.) are sun-loving, fast-growing plants. In the Lower South, they appreciate light afternoon shade, while in the Middle and Upper South, they welcome all of summer's warmth. Angel's trumpets need well-drained soil; when growing one in a pot, make sure the container has a large hole in the bottom to allow easy water passage. The growth rate is rapid, so plenty of water and fertilizer are necessary to keep these plants vigorous and blooming.

If planted in containers, angel's trumpets require daily watering. But resist the temptation to keep the pot in a saucer of water—although

left: Angel's trumpets are a blooming focal point in this Houston garden. Make them the center of attention to show off their flouncy flowers.

right: This double white selection looks almost like an old-fashioned, ruffled petticoat. **far right and below, right:** 'Insignis Pink' and 'Sunray'

PHOTOGRAPHS: WILLIAM DICKEY

moisture is vital, soggy soil is not what this plant likes. *Brugmansias* are heavy feeders, and a liquid, blossom-boosting fertilizer such as 15-30-15 or 10-50-10 keeps them producing flowers. Water with plant food at least every other week, or more often if you'd like. Remember, you can't feed these plants too much, especially those in containers.

Coarsely textured, large leaves complement the enormous blooms. Wind can cause problems for the broad foliage and elongated flowers, so choose a protected location when possible. The show is spectacular, so be sure to place your plant in a prominent spot on or near a deck, terrace, or entryway.

It's Simple To Share

Angel's trumpets are available in nurseries and through mail-order catalogs. They are also easy to root, making them perfect pass-along gifts for fellow gardeners. Follow these easy steps to grow your own.

■ Cut new stems sprouting from the plant's base, or save older branches when pruning the angel's trumpet.

■ Trim each long stem into pieces that are 6 to 8 inches in length. Make your cuts directly above raised nodes on the stem. The first piece will have leaves, while the others may not.

■ Fill containers with moist potting soil, and gently push the bottom of each stem into the mix, submerging half of its length.

■ Place the pots in a shady place, keeping the soil moist. Within several weeks, roots will form and new leaves will emerge. Keep the plants in these containers until adequate root systems have developed. To test readiness, pull gently on the stems—they should be firmly anchored.

For all the excitement and drama this plant gives to the landscape, angel's trumpet is a must-have for the summer garden. Easy to grow, simple to share, and boasting fabulous flowers and fragrance too—what could be more heavenly? ◆

THE TRUTH ABOUT ANGELS

This plant has a mystique that occasionally confuses fact with fiction. Here are two examples. **Tale:** Some say that angel's trumpet blooms follow a celestial cycle, with the heaviest flower production occurring during full moons. Watch the phases, and see what you think. **Truth:** Angel's trumpets are highly toxic. All parts of the plant are poisonous, so they should not be ingested.

near right: Cut long, new shoots at the plant's base. **center:** One stem yields numerous cuttings. Make each piece 6 to 8 inches long. Note which end is up, and plant bottom end down. **far right:** Put containers in a shady place, keeping soil evenly moist. After several weeks, new leaves will emerge, and the plants will produce well-developed root systems. Transplant into the garden, or move to larger pots.

left: This garden is a great example of basic design principles. The white caladiums and the crepe myrtles provide a sense of unity. The concrete urn filled with ferns and caladiums acts as a focal point.

The choice of plant materials can have a tremendous effect on a garden's sense of unity. Using plants that grow in the same ecological area, such as the desert or the understory of a forest, will usually create a pleasing sense of cohesiveness. Repeating colors or materials used in the architecture of the house, such as red brick or iron, in the hardscape of the garden will also add to this effect. Just remember that the final goal should be to create a feeling of harmony throughout the landscape.

Accent

Provide a garden with a sense of movement or a progression from one point of interest to another by using accents. Without them, a unified and well-balanced landscape can seem somewhat monotonous. Accents can be achieved in a number of ways but should always be done relative to the scale of the garden. Color contrasts provide easy solutions, as do accessories such as sundials, sculptures, or birdbaths.

Another way to achieve an accent in the garden is through the design, by changing either the direction or grade of a visual line. A pathway can have a much bigger impact if it meanders through a garden or changes height, even by a few inches.

Finally, an accent can provide an ending point. It immediately gives the eyes something to focus on and then leads you into the garden. Once you're there, the details become your tour guides, and the plants begin to speak for themselves. Unity ensures that no one element totally dominates the garden, while decorative accents counter any tendency toward monotony and add life and movement to the garden design. Together, these concepts create an overall pleasing effect in which all the parts work together.

EDWIN MARTY

Designed To Succeed

A good landscape plan is a tour guide for the senses, highlighting what's best about your yard and home.

A great garden design doesn't have to be expensive or complicated to be effective. In fact, it requires just a basic understanding of some simple principles. Keeping these ideas in mind can easily lead you to a yard that is pleasing to your eyes as well as your checkbook.

Think of a good landscape plan as a visual road map. As soon as people look at your yard, their eyes should be drawn to a focal point and then should be led through the rest of the garden. Here are a couple of

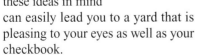

crepe myrtles — urn with ferns and caladiums

pea gravel

caladiums — Southern shield ferns

basic ideas that can help you to achieve this effect.

Unity

This is a concept that involves the overall impression a garden creates. To achieve a sense of unity, there should be no unnecessary components. Everything in the garden should relate to something else in color, texture, and form. If, on paper, one part of the design can be covered up without affecting the overall impression of the garden, that area should be redesigned to relate more strongly to the rest of the space.

PHOTOGRAPHS: VAN CHAPLIN

Help Your Hostas

Some simple care can really make a big difference.

Pretty flowers and big, bold leaves. It's no wonder hostas are favorite perennials for the shade. If yours don't look as fabulous as the ones shown here, the following pointers should help.

■ **Light**—Hostas prefer a few hours of morning sun, but shield them from the hot midday and afternoon sun. Yellow-leaved and variegated hostas need more shade than solid green ones. Light shade from tall trees is fine, but don't plant hostas in the woods. They don't like root competition from trees and shrubs.

■ **Moisture**—Water plants thoroughly once a week throughout the summer. Apply 1 to 1½ inches each time. Brown edges on leaves indicate that plants aren't getting enough water.

■ **Soil**—Hostas like fertile, well-drained soil that contains oodles of organic matter, such as composted manure, sphagnum peat moss, compost, and chopped leaves. If your soil is poor, consider lifting dormant hostas this fall, amending the soil, and then replanting.

■ **Voles**—These mouselike rodents chew off hostas at the base. To foil them, remove all mulch from around the plants—voles like to hide beneath it. When you plant hostas, place a couple of shovelfuls of sharp gravel in the holes around the roots. Voles don't like to dig through gravel.

■ **Slugs and snails**—These pests prefer chewing holes in hostas with thin foliage. They usually don't bother selections with thick leaves, such as 'Elegans' and 'Sum and Substance.'

■ **Coastal South**—Most hostas don't do well in this climate. One that does is fragrant plantain lily *(Hosta plantaginea)*, which bears white flowers in summer. Forget about hostas in the Tropical South. They won't grow there. STEVE BENDER

top: Hostas require afternoon shade and moist, fertile, well-drained soil.
above: All selections sport flowers, some of which are fragrant.

PLANT NOW, SAVE BUCKS

Just because it's hot outside, that doesn't mean you can't plant hostas. Potted hostas can go in the ground anytime, as long as you keep them watered. And because many garden centers are having plant sales now, you can probably pick up good-size plants from 20% to 50% off.

Among our favorite hostas are 'August Moon' (chartreuse leaves; white flowers), 'Frances Williams' (blue-green leaves edged in yellow; lavender flowers), 'Gold Standard' (gold leaves with green edges; lavender flowers), 'Royal Standard' (glossy green leaves; fragrant white flowers), and 'Elegans' (huge, puckered, blue-green leaves; white flowers).

left: The colors in this garden abound in the dry heat of summer. Chaste trees and Mexican bush sage require little maintenance. **below, left:** Roberta McGregor believes soaker hoses answer all of her watering needs.

Water-Wise Garden

Using less moisture can actually mean more flowers, more color, and less expense.

For many gardeners, water is the source of spectacular color, lush foliage, and cooling sounds. However, water can have another side: expensive equipment, ever-increasing utility bills, and time-consuming chores. In San Antonio, Roberta McGregor discovered how to have all the benefits of a lush landscape with only a fraction of the water that her neighbors need. Her approach is simple: Develop a garden design based on the average annual rainfall, select plants suitable for the climate, and have an appropriate maintenance program.

Nine years ago, Roberta's yard was like many others in the San Antonio area—mostly grass. But after a drought killed most of her lawn and shrubs, she decided to experiment with a moisture-conserving garden.

Intelligent Design
Knowing the amount of annual rainfall, as well as when the moisture is naturally available, will help you to select plants that will thrive in your climate. If you live in an area that receives very little rainfall in the summer, growing salvia instead of roses will dramatically reduce the amount of watering you have to do. Your county Extension agent can help identify what plants are appro-

priate for the conditions in your area.

A good garden design also considers the physical reality of your yard. What kind of soil do you have? If it's loose and sandy, the plants selected need to be drought-tolerant ones, such as lantanas or blanket flowers (*Gaillardia* sp.).

All the Right Choices
Self-reliant plants are the ideal solutions for gardens where water is an issue. Every region has choices that are either native to the area or from a similar geographic location. For instance, because of the alkaline soil and dry climate of West Texas, a Shumard red oak (*Quercus shumardii*) makes a much better shade tree than a pin oak (*Q. palustris*). Replacing regular turf grass with drought-tolerant kinds, such as buffalo grass (*Buchloe dactyloides*), will reduce the amount of time and energy you spend maintaining your yard. Selecting the right plants will ensure your investment is around in 10 years and still looking good.

Roberta has another major requirement for the plants that she uses. "I have to really love them. That means they have to do well in a drought, because I don't like to water." With a native plant nursery

within walking distance of her house, she can watch what plants hold up best and provide the most color.

Proper Maintenance
Roberta found that the final key to creating a water-wise garden is maintenance. Installing an irrigation system is a great way to handle most of your plants' needs. Roberta prefers using soaker hoses because of their efficiency and ease of installation. But there are other ways to supply plants with the proper amount of moisture, such as drip systems or misters. Many plants can thrive on a surprisingly small amount of water, especially if it's applied in the early morning to minimize evaporation. Also, providing occasional heavy watering will encourage them to send roots deep into the ground, making them more drought tolerant and hardy.

Mulch is another key ingredient. Not only does a thick layer of mulch protect the plants' roots from drying out, but it also provides nutrients. The trick is to use the proper type. Organic ones, such as pine straw or shredded bark, break down over a season and return nutrients to the soil. Synthetic mulches, such as landscape fabric or plastic, won't provide these nutrients. However, because they don't break down, they don't need to be replaced every year.

Proper maintenance also entails installing plants correctly and at the right time. In most parts of the South, fall is the ideal time to put new plants in the ground because of the cooler temperatures and more consistent moisture. Planting a tree or shrub in the spring forces the new roots to survive a season of hot, dry conditions before they have really grown.

EDWIN MARTY

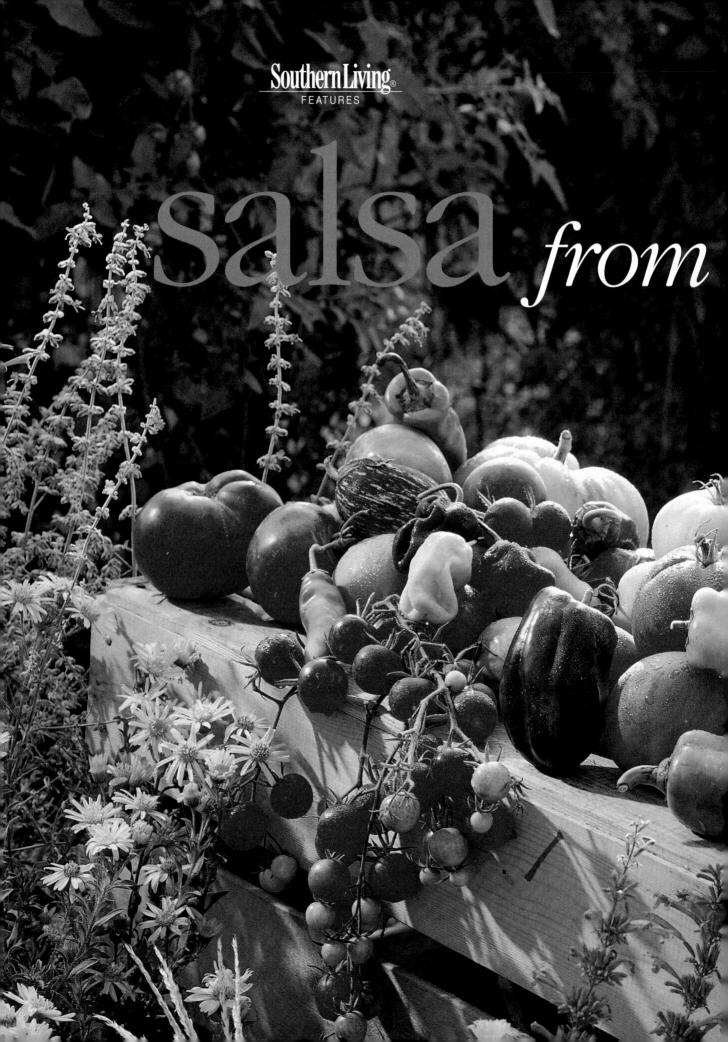

salsa *from*

the garden

Add color to your harvest and flavor to your table with a fiesta of peppers and tomatoes.

BY STEVE BENDER
PHOTOGRAPHY VAN CHAPLIN

george Costanza of the show *Seinfeld* has no doubt what belongs on every dinner table. "Salsa," he states flatly, "is now the number one condiment in America."

Mark Viette agrees. He doesn't live in Manhattan but in the Blue Ridge Mountains of Virginia, outside Fishersville. With his parents, André and Claire, he runs a well-known perennials nursery that bears his father's name. Mark is just as much an artist in the kitchen as he is in the garden. That's where salsa comes in.

At home, he tends a backyard vegetable garden designed for one purpose—to supply the heirloom tomatoes and fiery peppers that flavor his legendary salsa. I asked Claire how a guy who has devoted his life to planting, grooming, and hybridizing flowers finds utter fulfillment dicing tomatoes.

left: Red, orange, yellow, purple, pink and green—vegetables can come in beautiful colors.

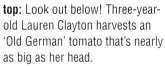

top: Look out below! Three-year-old Lauren Clayton harvests an 'Old German' tomato that's nearly as big as her head.

above: Mark uses a sharp knife to score a tomato in a crisscross pattern and then slices from the top.

above, right: Fresh pineapple, mango, kiwi, and apple are key ingredients in Mark's salsa.

right: Good soil, adequate spacing, and proper weed control yield big results.

far right: Handle with care. These habanero peppers are so hot that Mark recommends wearing gloves while working with them.

Bring together friends, family, pleasant weather, and fresh vegetables, and you have all the ingredients for a salsa party.

"Mark loves to cook. From the time he was little, he was always in the kitchen. Of course," she adds with a laugh, "when he was really young, some of the things he fixed didn't always turn out edible." Obviously, Mark has come a long way. Around Fishersville, his salsa is an event.

Variety—The Spice of Salsa

Mark grows more than 40 selections of both tomatoes and peppers, some rare and some common. To find them, he canvasses local nurseries and scours mail-order catalogs. Such a wide assortment furnishes the rainbow of colors, flavors, and degrees of heat on which a good salsa depends.

"Plant 20 selections of something rather than 3," he urges. "By using one or two plants of each, you can extend the harvest and minimize pest problems. Besides, one big plant can provide all the fruit of a particular kind you'll ever need."

Advice From the Master

Here's Mark's tips for productive plants.
■ Build good soil. Mark's was originally hard clay, but you'd never know it now. Tilling in large amounts of composted pine bark has resulted in soil that's as soft as a baby's tush.

■ Give plants room. Mark puts tomatoes 4 feet apart with rows 5 to 6 feet apart. He spaces peppers at about half these distances. "You're much better off using fewer plants and placing them farther apart," he says. This way, they get better light and air circulation, resulting in bigger yields and fewer pest problems.
■ Control weeds. Mark puts down a weed barrier, such as landscape fabric, between plants. This lets in water and air but inhibits weeds. He hides the barrier under a more attractive layer of pine straw mulch.
■ Grow tomatoes inside sturdy wire cages. "The fruit never gets dirty, and it's easy to pick," he points out.
■ Extend the harvest by planting successive crops. Mark's first plants go in on May 15; the second crop is planted in mid- to late-June. He harvests in both summer and fall.
■ Spread a handful of gypsum around each plant. This provides calcium without changing the soil's pH.

Salsa That Satisfies

Mark's salsa changes each time he makes it, according to what he puts in or decides to leave out. But the essential building blocks remain—onions, tomatoes, and peppers. You

can find his basic recipe along with options at southernliving.com.

A good salsa needs bright color like a surgeon needs insurance. To get it for the salsa shown here, Mark harvests red ('Jersey Devil'), orange ('Persimmon'), purple ('Cherokee Purple'), yellow ('Lemon Boy'), and green ('Green Zebra') tomatoes. He uses only firm fruit. Soft, overripe tomatoes don't slice well.

Now comes the big question: Sweet or hot peppers? Mild salsa calls for sweet peppers, such as 'Sweet Banana.' But Mark likes his salsa spicy enough to take the paint off a car. So he typically employs habanero, Thai, jalapeño, and other sizzling types, which he first grills to add a little smoky flavor.

Not everyone is like Mark, who doesn't mind having his tongue blistered. Adding a cup of brown sugar lets you have your hot salsa and eat it too. "Brown sugar takes the bite away," Mark explains. "It lets you use peppers with more heat and flavor."

This evening, friends and family gather around the table at Mark's house. No eyebrows are singed; people are smiling. America's favorite condiment is a hit once more. The only person missing is George Costanza. George is very upset.

September

Aromatic aster and Mexican bush sage   e an eye-catching combination (See page 167.)

Chrysanthemums

Select plants in bud, and arrange in elongated masses with five plants or more of each color. Sites having at least a half-day of direct sunlight work best. Large plants in 1- to 5-gallon pots have an immediate effect and also do well in containers. Florists' chrysanthemums are less desirable than garden mums, which can be perennials. Prepare the soil by tilling or spading in 3 to 5 inches of organic matter such as composted pine bark, peat, or your own compost.

Editor's Notebook

PHOTOGRAPH: VAN CHAPLIN

Unless you like spray-painting trees or spreading mustard on the lawn, chances are your garden lacks oomph at this time of year. Fall color hasn't arrived yet, and most of the flowers you doted on this summer now resemble crispy fries. But one plant is at its best right now—a vine named sweet autumn clematis (*Clematis terniflora*, formerly *C. paniculata*). In August and September, it explodes into a billowing cloud of sweetly fragrant, creamy white blooms that can perfume an entire yard. It's the easiest of all clematis to grow, needing only sun and good drainage. It's also the most voracious, quickly engulfing arbors, trees, buses, and Ruben Studdard's plate of ribs. Fortunately, it won't crush things the way wisteria will, and regular pruning can restrain it. Watch out for seedlings, though—they come up everywhere, and I mean *everywhere*. So if somebody has wronged you, give them this vine. Revenge is sweet autumn clematis.　　—STEVE BENDER

TIPS

■ **Autumn equinox**—September 23 marks the end of summer and the beginning of fall. Now is the time for setting out this season's annuals, grooming flowerbeds, digging holes for bulbs, and planting trees and shrubs. But the most important thing is getting outside to enjoy your garden.

■ **Daylilies and iris**—Dig and divide mature clumps every two to four years, depending upon the vigor of the plants. After digging each clump, separate individual fans of iris, saving the younger, healthier divisions. Replant in well-prepared soil, and water well. Keep Louisiana iris and daylilies moist during the dividing process. Cut back leaves to make fans about one-third of the original height.

■ **Houseplants**—If you gave your plants a summer vacation outside, get ready to bring them back indoors as the first frost approaches. Reduce watering, and allow the containers to dry out a bit. Examine them carefully to remove any hitchhikers (such as lizards and bugs), and then bring the plants inside.

■ **Citrus**—In Florida, late September usually brings drier weather, which means you may need to begin watering your citrus trees again. Don't overdo it, though, or you may cause fruit splitting. Water only when the surface of the soil feels dry, but then soak well. Once or twice a week is probably adequate even when there is no rain.

■ **Seeds**—Dry the flower heads of zinnias, cosmos, marigolds, and Mexican sunflowers (*Tithonia rotundifolia*), and store the seeds in a cool, dry place.

■ **Hurricanes**—In Florida, prune trees to make them more resistant to the force of hurricanes, which are most common between the months of August and October. Cut off dead, weakly attached, crowded, and potentially hazardous limbs. Remove any dead fronds from palms, and harvest coconuts.

Cassias

Two types of this shrub produce brilliant, deep yellow flowers from now until the first hard freeze. Candlestick senna (*Cassia alata*) has erect flower spikes that resemble candles. Butterfly cassia (*C. bicapsularis*) has yellow flowers resembling its namesake. Plant these large shrubs in full sun from late spring through early fall. In North Florida, these plants will freeze to the ground in winter but should come back in spring.

■ **Pecans**—In Texas, provide deep irrigation during dry periods to ensure that nutmeats develop fully in the shells. Drought may also cause pecans to drop prematurely. Provide water just beyond the dripline (the area on the outer edge of the branches where the rain runs off) on a weekly basis until rains occur.

PLANT

■ **Fall vegetables**—Sow turnips, mustard greens, beets, radishes, collards, and spinach now in the Middle and Lower South. Set out transplants of lettuce, broccoli, and cabbage. To learn more information about planting and harvesting vegetables, see "Secrets From a Homegrown Garden" on page 164.

■ **Fall-blooming perennials**—In Florida, plant tropicals such as firespike *(Odontonema strictum)*, lion's ear *(Leonotis leonurus)*, Philippine violet *(Barleria cristata)*, and cigar flower *(Cuphea micropetala)* for blooms this fall. Brazilian sage *(Salvia guaranitica)*, Mexican bush sage *(S. leucantha)*, autumn sage *(S. greggii)*, forsythia sage *(S. madrensis)*, Mexican sage *(S. mexicana)*, Van Houtte's sage *(S. splendens* 'Van Houttei'), and mountain sage *(S. regla)* also flower heavily in the fall and can be planted now.

■ **Ornamental grasses**—In Florida, plant gulf muhly *(Muhlenbergia filipes* or *M. capillaris)* in sunny, well-drained areas for beautiful purplish pink flower plumes that glisten when backlit by the autumn sun. Maiden grass *(Miscanthus sinensis)* has less colorful yet very attractive seedheads in the fall.

PRUNE

■ **Everblooming roses**—Prune now to encourage flowering. Cut off dead wood; then shorten existing canes by about one-third. Fertilize lightly, and water thoroughly.

FERTILIZE

■ **Cool-season lawns**—Now is an excellent time to establish fescue, perennial ryegrass, and bluegrass. If you are sowing the seeds for a new lawn, use a lower nitrogen, higher phosphorus fertilizer such as 18-24-10. If you have an established lawn, go with a higher nitrogen formula such as 31-2-4.

Fall Flowers

Some of the best autumn perennials are at their peaks this month. Plant old-fashioned mums such as 'Sheffield Pink' and 'Single Apricot Korean' along the front of your flowerbed; their blooms will mound and spill over the edges. Use asters, including 'Purple Dome,' 'September Ruby,' and 'Harrington's Pink,' along with Japanese anemones, such as 'Honorine Jobert' (pictured at right), 'Queen Charlotte,' and 'September Charm,' for the middle and back of the border. They reach between 2 and 6 feet. Swamp sunflowers *(Helianthus angustifolius)* should be put in the very back of the border, as they can grow to heights of 4 to 8 feet. When planting, place them at the same depth that they were in the container, and water them well. Perennials are an affordable way to add dependable color to your landscape.

September notes:

Tip of the Month

Fill a yellow dishpan halfway with water, and set it in the garden. Aphids are attracted to yellow. They will land in the water and drown.

ANNA VICTORIA REICH
ALBUQUERQUE, NEW MEXICO

dazzling
Dahlias

BY ELLEN RUOFF RILEY / PHOTOGRAPHY JEAN ALLSOPP

GARDENING
PLANTS AND DESIGN

These colorful flowers are easy to enjoy in arrangements.

Imagine a blossom with colors that roll the warmth of an Indian summer day into the fire of an early-autumn sunset. This is a dahlia. Its sturdy, late-season flowers show their stamina against summer's slowly dissipating heat while producing a palette of petals vividly reminding us of fall's imminent arrival.

There was a time when cut dahlias were only available to gardeners with the foresight to plant its large, gnarly tubers in the spring. These days, you can purchase smaller, more user-friendly bouquets in flower shops, farmers markets, and grocery stores. A bunch of blooms is affordable and easy to arrange.

Conditions of Survival
All cut flowers require care—called conditioning—to maximize their vase lives. Dahlias that come from your garden require extra help. The cut stems need to be seared. Harvest your bouquet in early morning. Then make a fresh, straight snip on each stem, and pass it over an open flame.

Soak stems thoroughly before arranging. First, remove foliage that's below the water level. Then, put the stems in a bucket of warm water and place in a cool, dark place overnight. (Dahlias from flower shops have been treated already. While the stems don't require searing, they do appreciate the rest of the conditioning process.)

Making the Bouquet
Look to the garden and roadside for materials to fill out your arrangement, and accent it with late-season produce to extend a free and easy attitude. Choose containers that echo the colors of the plants used. A needle-holder frog or chicken wire frame will offer support and allow water to move easily up the stems.

Once your bouquet is complete, extend its life with proper care. Add cut-flower food (available from florists) to the water. Or make your own by adding a drop of bleach and ¼ cup lemon-lime flavored soda to a quart of water. Keep the bouquet in a cool place out of direct sunlight. Change the water and recut the stems every other day to keep blooms fresh.

Dahlias are a floral bridge between seasons; their vivid shades combine summer's vibrant sunshine and autumn's warm hues. Treat yourself to a September delight.   ◆

left: Dahlias reflect the shades of the changing season. **above:** With stems cut short and blooms clustered in copper cups, dahlias make a quick and easy arrangement.

left: These brilliant yellow and scarlet 'Sweet Banana' peppers are traffic stoppers. With color like this, who needs flowers?

PHOTOGRAPHS: VAN CHAPLIN

left: Want to increase production, reduce maintenance, and improve your garden's looks? Try raised beds. **above:** In the fall, Mike and Glenda Western harvest tomatoes, cucumbers, peppers, and squash. What they don't eat raw, they cook, can, or give away.

Secrets From a Homegrown Garden

Growing your own delicious vegetables is easy once you know a few tricks. Now is a great time to get started.

Mike Western is talking, and I should be paying rapt attention. After all, Mike's a really interesting guy. He's a fantastic gardener, he writes country music, and he has a workshop filled with every power tool known to man. But right now, the only things I'm contemplating are the huge black vultures that keep landing on the trees in his Mount Sidney, Virginia, backyard.

"Oh, don't worry about them," Mike says confidently. "They show up here every afternoon." Not yet convinced they aren't some kind of omen, I march warily with Mike into his vegetable garden.

And what a garden it is. Here in the beautiful Blue Ridge Mountains, tidy planting boxes give birth to lettuce, beans, and broccoli. Tomato and pepper plants flex vegetative muscles to hold up an amazing crop of yellow, red, and orange fruit. Cut flowers and produce decorate a potting bench. Weeds are scarcer than culottes at a senior prom.

Mike was introduced to gardening at a young age. "At our house, we always had a vegetable garden," he recalls. "Like any other kid, I hated working in it, but I learned a lot." That knowledge lay dormant for decades until a gardening class inspired him to start one of his own.

From the first, Mike and his wife, Glenda, decided that it would be organic. "We just feel it's so much better for you," he explains. "All the nutrients we put into the ground come back to us in the vegetables." Every year, Mike amends the soil with huge amounts of leaves that he collects from the yard, chops, and composts. To this he adds natural fertilizers—rock phosphate for phosphorus, green sand for potassium, cottonseed meal and blood meal for nitrogen, and gypsum for calcium and improved soil structure. Natural

far, left: Mike and Glenda love fresh lettuce for salads and grow four different kinds—'Oak Leaf,' 'Red Sails,' 'Black-seeded Simpson,' and butterhead. **above, left:** Planting successive crops a few weeks apart extends the harvest. Mike thins two-week-old lettuce seedlings.
left: Here's the secret to his magic soil: chopped leaves gathered from the yard. After they compost for six months, they turn into dark brown, crumbly humus—the gardener's gold.

products don't work as fast as manufactured fertilizers, but they last a lot longer. "I fertilize just once a year," he states. "If I used 10-10-10, it'd be gone in 30 days." To control insects, he uses natural pesticides, such as pyrethrin and rotenone. To head off disease, he sprays with copper.

Raising Them Right

Meticulous to a T, Mike likes for everything in his yard to be just so. After he and Glenda visited the gardens at Colonial Williamsburg, he hit upon an idea to improve plant growth, reduce maintenance, and enhance aesthetics—raised beds. He built planting boxes out of 2- x 6-foot tongue-and-groove, pressure-treated lumber. Glenda designed the layout of 4- x 16-foot raised beds. The narrow width allows easy reach for planting and harvesting. He filled them with his custom soil mix. A layer of mulch between the boxes discourages weeds.

Sections of metal lattice laid on the boxes are an eye-catching twist. Mike uses it like a grid to evenly space his plants. Around planting time, he can stretch floating row covers atop it to keep insects off seedlings. "It also

supports crops such as broccoli against the wind," he adds.

Mike starts most of his plants from seeds sown in pots and then transplanted to the beds. His garden is in production at least nine months a year. Crops for fall or spring include lettuce, spinach, chard, broccoli, cabbage, and radishes. Tomatoes, corn, peppers, squash, carrots, cucumbers, and beans are summer mainstays.

Keys to Success

People often think that vegetable gardens are too much work, but Mike says that everything is so much easier once you take care of the basics. First, and most important, build good soil using lots of organic matter. Second, water regularly. "If you want a successful vegetable garden, you've got to have lots of water," he states flatly. Mike uses sprinklers on his raised beds for an hour almost daily. The rest of the garden gets an inch of water a week. Third, plant disease-resistant selections when possible. (This is easy for tomatoes—just look for the letters V, F, T, and N after the name. These indicate resistance to common maladies.) Finally, harvest

regularly. If you let crops mature and set seed, they'll stop producing.

Mike claims his garden is so productive he can easily feed his family, neighbors, and friends. That sounds great, but one question lingers in my mind. Who's feeding the vultures?

STEVE BENDER

Please note: Scientific studies have shown that pressure-treated lumber preserved with CCA (chromated copper arsenate) poses no significant or unreasonable risk to humans or the environment when used properly. However, due to changing market perceptions, manufacturers are making a voluntary transition to newer types of wood preservatives for consumer use. Although you can find lumber treated with new-generation preservatives now, retailers will not officially phase out their current inventories until the end of 2003. In the meantime, if you are still concerned about using pressure-treated lumber, consider coating your treated wood project with paint, stain, or water sealer. Or use other rot- and insect-resistant lumber, such as heartwood cedar, redwood, and cypress. ◆

PHOTOGRAPHS: VAN CHAPLIN

Color in the Courtyard

This tropical retreat is easy to maintain and full of interesting details.

Don't want to spend your evenings mowing the grass? Landscape architect Jeff Thompson of Orlando didn't want to either. By taking advantage of existing features in his backyard and adding some new ones, he transformed it into a quiet, low-maintenance hideaway.

Begin Here

The trees behind the house presented an opportunity for the new design. They offer shade and help create an instant ceiling for this outdoor room, while an existing fence encloses the sides. Jeff chose pavers for a floor because he could install them without hiring a contractor. He added a bench and hung glass candleholders to provide light so guests can gather in the evenings.

Well Placed

Once the space was in order, it was time to add plants. Jeff wanted an exotic, tropical look, so he chose palms and bird of paradise for their

top: A beautiful bench takes center stage in this shady sanctuary.
above: Brightly colored bromeliads are radiant accents to a quiet oasis.

lacy and lush foliage. Bromeliads became important to his design because they provide exotic leaves in an array of colors. Most of these were then planted in pots. "The containers allow me to locate the bromeliads at focal points in the garden," Jeff says. "They elevate the plants as well, making them easier to enjoy. Also, I can bring the pots into the garage when there's a threat of a freeze."

The heights of the palms and bird of paradise provide a transition between the patio and the overhead tree branches. Jeff used a low-growing ground cover, dwarf mondo grass (*Ophiopogon japonicus* 'Nana'), between the pavers to soften their lines.

A subtle touch in the plan was using a pineapple cutout in the bench. A symbol of welcome, pineapples are in fact bromeliads. By repeating their form in the design, Jeff relates the bench back to the shapes of the bromeliads used throughout the garden, bringing it all together.

GENE B. BUSSELL

Aromatic Asters

Got a passion for purple in the autumn garden? This plant is the answer.

"That is about as purple as you can get and still be legal," says my friend and fellow gardener Libbie Winston-Mize as we admire an aromatic aster smothered in starry flowers. Because we both love purple, Libbie and I decide to add aromatic aster to each of our gardens immediately. For three solid weeks every fall, usually in October, this aster is showstoppingly, heartbreakingly, smack-you-upside-the-head purple.

Mixed with the yellows of rudbeckia or Mexican mint marigold *(Tagetes lucida),* it'll wake you up better than coffee. Partnered with the cool lavender blues of 'Indigo Spires' salvia or purple coneflower *(Echinacea purpurea),* the richness of aromatic aster can set your spirit purring like a kitten with a bottomless bowl of cream. There is absolutely no way that you can garden without an aromatic aster once you've seen it bloom.

Fortunately, this purple flower is both widely available and very easy to grow. As a native of the American prairies, aromatic aster *(Aster oblongifolius)* is tolerant of heat, drought, and overcrowding. In an ordinary garden bed, it's in heaven. It'll go along with whatever

above: Great in containers, aromatic asters mix well with other fall perennials such as Mexican bush sage *(Salvia leucantha).* **left:** Tiny crowns of stamens highlight the royal quality of the purple petals.

care you choose to provide—without any complaints.

Libbie and I did discover that aromatic asters slowly multiply, sending up new little plants from various points along the spreading roots. At the same time, the aboveground branches elongate until they flop about 3 feet in every direction. Even Libbie, who likes robust, enthusiastic plants, feels this is a little too much aster to deal with in the prebloom season. We now dig up the seedlings to spread around our gardens and prune the big plants back halfway in midsummer. Because the aromatic part of this aster is the foliage, we can enjoy the rich scent of the leaves while doing this grooming. The result

is plump, shapely mounds, about 2 feet high x 3 feet wide, that give us major purple right where we want it in fall.

Is that much purple legal? Yes, but just barely.   LIZ DRUITT

AROMATIC ASTER
At a Glance

Bloom season: three weeks or more in mid-fall
Range: all South
Soil: any well drained
Water: drought tolerant once established
Fertilizer: minimal
Sun: full sun to partial shade

BUYING TIP

Aromatic aster may be sold under several names, including 'Fanny's Aster,' autumn aster, or even Frikart aster. Only true aromatic aster has fragrant foliage, so test to be sure you have the right plant. Just rub or crush a leaf to enjoy the sweet, resinous scent.

Ginkgo trees shine like the sun in fall (See page 175.)

October

garden checklist

Editor's Notebook

PHOTOGRAPH: VAN CHAPLIN

Benjamin Franklin was a lucky guy. He could have stewed his brain while trying to discover electricity but instead had a legendary tree named after him. In 1770, the famed botanist John Bartram discovered the tree growing along the banks of Georgia's Altamaha River. Reaching 10 to 20 feet tall, it combines beautiful white flowers in summer and fall with leaves that turn orange and red in autumn. Bartram named it *Franklinia alatamaha* after his friend Gentle Ben. He also collected seeds, from which all of today's Franklin trees are descended. To be honest, they're not the easiest plants to grow, requiring moist, acid, perfectly drained soil containing oodles of organic matter. But a sizable specimen is a testimony to your genius. Most Franklin tree fans are puzzled as to why it totally disappeared from the wild shortly after Bartram chanced upon it. I think the reason is obvious—Ben tied his kite to the tree during a thunderstorm. —STEVE BENDER

Japanese Maples

These beautiful trees will add color and texture to your garden with minimal care. Now is an excellent time to plant them, as the cooler weather allows their roots to become established. In the Upper and Middle South, plant in full sun. Partial shade is better in the Lower and Coastal South. The species *Acer palmatum* has green leaves during the year and brilliant fall color. Selections include 'Bloodgood,' with burgundy leaves; 'Sango-Kaku,' with coral-colored stems; and 'Crimson Queen,' with fine, red leaves. These selections are in the *Southern Living* Plant Collection from Monrovia. To find a nursery near you that carries these plants call 1-888-752-6848, or visit www.monrovia.com.

TIPS

- **Dahlias**—In the Upper and Middle South, lift and divide dahlia tubers before the first frost. Cut stalks about 1 inch above the tuber, shake off any loose soil, and let the clump dry. Store in a cool, dry place that does not freeze. In the Lower and Coastal South, tubers can stay in the ground. Provide a little extra mulch, such as pine straw, to help them overwinter.
- **Mulch**—As leaves begin to fall, they create an ample supply of organic mulch for the garden. Decomposing leaves enrich the soil, nourishing your plants. Rake them up, and add them to flowerbeds. The extra layer of leaves keeps roots cool, retains moisture, and slows weed growth.
- **Seasonal decorations**—Either harvested or purchased, these will brighten your spirits for the fall holidays. Pumpkins, gourds, and Indian corn are available in multiple colors at grocery stores and roadside stands. Mix with dried flowers such as celosia, sunflowers, and gomphrenas to make simple arrangements for your table.
- **Water**—As the weather cools, reduce your watering frequency accordingly. Container plantings that need moisture every day in the summer may now only need it every second or third day. Water your lawn only when grass blades begin to roll inward and portions of the lawn take on a grayish color.

PLANT

- **Cool-weather flowers**—Plant annuals such as pansies, dianthus, alyssum, lobelia, snapdragon, calendula, and flowering cabbage or kale now. In Central and South Florida, you can also add annuals such as ageratum, baby's breath, cleome, dusty miller, gazania, globe amaranth, marigold, flowering tobacco, ornamental pepper, salvia, sunflower, torenia, verbena, and zinnia.
- **Shrubs for fall color**—Add some deciduous shrubs beneath trees in order to brighten your autumn. Good choices include witch hazel, oakleaf hydrangea, fothergilla, sumac, and Virginia sweetspire.
- **Seeds**—Sow poppies, bachelor's buttons, and larkspur now for flowers next spring. Select a sunny location, and scatter seeds on a prepared bed. Rake and water gently.

- **Sasanqua camellias**—These graceful evergreens are blooming now, so choose the flower colors you prefer for your landscape. Excellent selections include 'Mine-No-Yuki' (white), 'Cleopatra' (pink), and 'Bonanza' (red). They can take full sun to light shade.
- **Vegetables**—In Florida, seed beets, carrots, mustard greens, English peas, spinach, and turnips now. Set out plants of broccoli, cabbage, cauliflower, celery, collards, lettuce, and Swiss chard for quicker results.

Camellias or trees

- **Citrus**—In Texas, kumquats are compact shrubs that flower and fruit almost year-round. Plant them in large containers or directly in the landscape. Satsumas are among the most cold-hardy citrus for the area. 'Meyer' lemons are also fairly cold hardy and produce flowers and large lemons much of the year.
- **Grasses**—In Texas, cool-season grasses can be planted now to provide quick cover for bare areas and to overseed permanent lawns such as Bermuda or St. Augustine. Annual or perennial ryegrass should be planted at rates suggested on the label, raked into bare soils, and watered thoroughly. Do not rake when overseeding. Perennial ryegrass is not actually perennial in most of Texas but has a finer texture than annual types. Fescues are permanent only in North Texas and the Panhandle. Use a slow-release fertilizer when seeds sprout.
- **Trees**—In Texas, good small trees to plant now include Mexican plum, crepe myrtle, chaste tree, desert willow, pomegranate, and redbud. All can be set as close as 6 to 8 feet from the foundation of a house, and all lose their leaves during winter, allowing the sun to warm the house.

FERTILIZE

- **Palms**—In Florida, fertilize with a product such as RiteGreen Palm Fertilizer 7-3-7 with Manganese. Follow package directions, and apply at the proper rate.

CONTROL

- **Lawn weeds**—In Florida, a pre-emergence herbicide, such as Sta-Green Crab-Ex Crabgrass Preventer or Scotts Halts Crabgrass Preventer, applied late this month, can greatly reduce the number of weeds that grow in your lawn during the winter and early spring. Follow the directions and precautions on the container carefully.

Bulbs

Select now for pots and flowerbeds. Narcissus, daffodils, ranunculus, anemones, and snowflakes *(Leucojum* sp.) can be set out immediately. Purchase tulips and hyacinths now, and store them in the lower part of your refrigerator for six to eight weeks prior to planting. Combine spring-flowering bulbs with Iceland poppies, larkspur, snapdragons, candytuft, stock, and sweet alyssum. Larkspur is best started from seed, while the others can be set out from transplants.

Tip of the Month

In fall when the temperature drops, I put my pepper plants in pots and bring them indoors to a sunny window. They keep producing, although slowly. The following spring, I put them back outdoors and get a head start on my next pepper crop.

SUZANNE BROWN
GOOSE CREEK, SOUTH CAROLINA

Salvia
Puts On a Show

Crisp autumn breezes make these spiked flowers dance
a happy goodbye to warm weather as fall rolls in.

For a dazzling display in your garden, try fall salvias. They're easy to grow and will create an impressive autumn show. Salvias are topped with hundreds of brightly colored flowers that attract butterflies and hummingbirds. Also known as sages, these large, impressive plants will pump up your landscape till frost.

Fall salvias come in a variety of colors and sizes, and their availability continues to increase in garden centers across the South. These big, rangy bloomers stand out in the landscape and make great cut flowers.

Many gardeners already enjoy summer-flowering salvias, but lesser-known kinds, such as Mexican bush sage *(Salvia leucantha)*, pineapple sage *(S. elegans)*, forsythia sage *(S. madrensis)*, and 'Van Houttei' scarlet sage *(S. splendens* 'Van Houttei'), start to bloom in late summer and thrive as temperatures dip in September and October. Hybrids such as 'Anthony Parker' and 'Indigo Spires' have purple-blue flowers.

Late-Season Blooms
Many annuals and perennials that perform well in the spring and summer look tattered after a long hot season, but fall salvias are just beginning to flourish. Barring a hard frost, they can fill your garden with color until November or December. When a freeze is expected, you can clip the colorful blooms and use them in autumn arrangements. If dried, the velvety, purple blooms of Mexican bush sage will retain their color and can be used to make long-lasting wreaths.

Lots of Bang for Your Buck
The great thing about fall salvias is that you get plenty of impact in your garden for very little money. Often, you can buy them in small 4-inch pots for a few dollars. While gallon pots may cost around $8, these plants will grow 3 to 4 feet tall and wide in a season. Forsythia sage will get even bigger, reaching 5 to 6 feet tall.

Start Small, Think Big
In the Lower, Coastal, and Tropical South, plant fall salvias now. In these warmer regions, they may be perennials. In the Middle and Upper South, plant them in the spring or early summer. Depending on selections, they

right: Autumn leaves sprinkled around Mexican bush sage and pineapple sage create a colorful display.
left: 'Van Houttei' scarlet sage has burgundy, whorled flowers that mix well with yellow swamp sunflowers.
top: Forsythia sage sports yellow, 12-inch blooms and can grow up to 6 feet tall.

BY CHARLIE THIGPEN / PHOTOGRAPHY ROGER FOLEY

LOCATION: REYNOLDA GARDENS, WINSTON-SALEM, NORTH CAROLINA

left: Fall salvias mingle with chrysanthemums and foliage plants to form this lush border.

can be borderline hardy in the Lower and Middle South and should be treated as annuals in the Upper South.

Fall salvias grow quickly; sprinkle 2 tablespoons of slow-release, all-purpose fertilizer, such as 12-6-6, around the bases of plants for a little boost. The more sun they receive, the better they will perform. Salvias need room to sprawl. They also require well-drained soil, and once established, they are drought tolerant.

Salvias may become leggy in midsummer and will benefit from a hard cutback. With a sharp pair of clippers, you can cut them back halfway to the ground. They will quickly flush out, growing full and bushy.

Many Uses

Fall salvias have a loose, mounding habit suitable for the back of a border. In the summer, while they aren't in bloom, they create a nice green backdrop. In fall, their flowers pair well with chrysanthemums, goldenrod, and asters. Consider mixing salvias with ornamental grasses too.

They're also great in containers with low-growing plants such as petunias, creeping Jenny, and 'Margarita' or 'Blackie' sweet potato vines planted around them. Make sure the pot is large enough. It should be at least 21 inches in diameter and deep enough for good root growth.

Cut for Color

Fall salvias work well as cut flowers. Because of their large, bushy shapes, long stems can be clipped and placed in a tall vase. Mix them with colorful maple, sweet gum, and dogwood leaves for a showy arrangement. The blooms also look great with plumes of ornamental grasses and with red berries clipped from shrubs and trees.

If you like summer salvias, you'll love the fall ones, which extend the bloom time of your garden. As the temperatures cool and the humidity decreases, you'll spend more time outside enjoying these colorful plants. ◆

SALVIAS FOR FALL

■ 'Anthony Parker' sage (*Salvia* 'Anthony Parker')—3 to 4 feet tall and wide; dark purple flowers from late summer till frost; hardy in Lower, Coastal, and Tropical South

■ pineapple sage (*S. elegans*)—3 to 4 feet tall and wide; red flowers from late summer till frost; hardy in Coastal and Tropical South

■ 'Indigo Spires' sage (*S.* 'Indigo Spires')—4 feet tall and wide; violet blooms from midsummer till frost; hardy in Coastal and Tropical South—and in Lower South, if protected

■ Mexican bush sage (*S. leucantha*)—40 inches tall and wide; purple or purple-and-white flowers from late summer till frost; hardy in Coastal and Tropical South—and in Lower South, if protected

■ forsythia sage (*S. madrensis*)—6 feet tall and 5 feet wide; large, yellow, spiked flowers in fall; hardy in Middle, Lower, Coastal, and Tropical South

■ 'Van Houttei' scarlet sage (*S. splendens* 'Van Houttei')—4 feet tall and 3 feet wide; burgundy flowers from midsummer till frost; hardy in Coastal and Tropical South

Golden Yellow Tree

Brilliant in color and easy to grow, ginkgo is hard to forget.

Do you have trouble remembering names? Can't find your shoes? Have a hard time with birthdays, anniversaries, and little details such as which house on the street is yours? Have I got the answer for you!

It's ginkgo *(Ginkgo biloba)*, which is also called maidenhair tree. An extract from its leaves is a popular herbal supplement used to increase blood flow to the brain and improve cognitive function. But if you think ginkgo looks great in your medicine cabinet, you should see it in your yard.

A Golden Oldie

Native to China, the ginkgo is slow growing and rather gawky while young, but it eventually becomes a beautiful tree, 50 to 60 feet tall, with a rounded or vase shape. An established tree is tough and undemanding, tolerating drought, pollution, and almost any well-drained soil. Insects and diseases simply avoid it. Ginkgo makes a superior shade, lawn, and street tree if you have sufficient room.

It gets its nickname, maidenhair tree, from its fan-shaped leaves,

GINKGO
At a Glance

Size: 50 to 60 feet tall, 25 to 30 feet wide
Light: full sun
Soil: almost any well-drained soil, not wet
Pests: none
Prune: late winter
Range: Upper, Middle, Lower, and Coastal South

which resemble the leaflets of a maidenhair fern. Bright green in summer, they change to a glorious butter yellow in fall; a fully colored tree shines like the sun. Leaves drop in a shower that completely denudes

the tree in a day or two. If you like to get raking done in one fell swoop, you'll appreciate this courtesy.

Male Call

But before you rush out to buy one, heed this warning—buy only male trees. Females bear a lot of orange-yellow, persimmon-like fruit. The fruit isn't all bad—indeed, it contains edible nuts that are sold in Asian markets. But when the pulp of fallen fruit rots, it releases a stomach-churning stench reminiscent of any number of disgusting organic substances.

Unfortunately, there's no way to tell the sex of a seedling-grown tree until it starts fruiting at 10 to 15 years of age. So, if you value your olfactory nerves, buy only named selections that are guaranteed males. They include 'Autumn Gold,' 'Fairmount,' 'Princeton Sentry,' 'Saratoga,' and 'Shangri-La.'

Well, I'm off to buy a ginkgo, just as soon as I remember where I left the shovel, the car, and my shoes. And, while I'm at it, what the heck is a ginkgo? STEVE BENDER

PHOTOGRAPHS: KARIM SHAMSI-BASHA / HOMEOWNERS: BILLY AND GLORY ANGELL, MOUNTAIN BROOK, ALABAMA

left: The flowerpots you plant for fall will provide a spring surprise if you add daffodil bulbs now.

Colorful Fall Containers

It's easy to put together pots of radiant flowers and foliage. Just follow our directions for beauty from now through spring.

Pansies and violas are "little bundles of joy," says Carol Guedalia, a horticulturist at The Greenery in Bluffton, South Carolina. She's convinced that no matter how cold the weather is, their bright faces will warm your day. Still, everyone wants to know one thing: What do you plant with them?

Keep It Simple

It's easy to create a bright welcome to your home with flowerpots. The important thing to remember is that the less complicated they are, the better. Place three to five pots of various sizes together for a bigger impact of color. Another benefit of grouping your pots is that they are convenient to groom, water, and fertilize.

When visiting the nursery, you will see many beautiful things, and you may want to take all of them home.

The impulse is to buy one of each—don't. Pick a color scheme, and stick to it. The terra-cotta pots shown here relate to the warm colors of the brick steps. The selection of pots is varied but simple. The flower colors are in a warm range of yellows.

The Other Plants

So what else can you use in your pots? Think about what you would like the plants to do.

To soften the edges of containers, use trailing plants, such as periwinkles. Try selections with leaves that are multicolored, such as 'Variegata' periwinkle (*Vinca major* 'Variegata') and 'Illumination' periwinkle (*V. minor* 'Illumination'). For chartreuse leaves, use some creeping Jenny (*Lysimachia nummularia*). Ivy is also a great choice with many selections. **Tip:** When buying ivy, be sure to get

plants that have been conditioned to the cool fall temperatures, and avoid ones straight from a heated greenhouse.

To fill in between the flowers, there are lots of options. Try using lettuce, thyme, parsley, coral bells (*Heuchera sanguinea*), chard, radishes, bronze fennel, red mustard, or kale. All provide a nice contrast to the blooms.

For height, add an old favorite such as variegated monkey grass, or use leather leaf sedge (*Carex buchananii*) or 'Ogon' golden sweet flag (*Acorus gramineus* 'Ogon'). Autumn fern (*Dryopteris erythrosora*) also works well.

You can use pansies, chard, and periwinkles to create a fall container that's sure to succeed; see the diagram on facing page.

Additional Flowers

Want more blooms to go with your pansies and violas? Consider using bulbs. Plant them in fall containers now, and you'll have beautiful blooms in spring. Smaller selections of daffodils, such as 'Jetfire,' 'Tête á Tête,' and 'Topolino,' will not take up too much root room in your pot. Crocus, hyacinths, snowflakes and tulip selections (such as 'Pink Impression,' 'Apricot Beauty,' and 'Golden Oxford') will be welcome spring accents to the containers. Once they have finished blooming, just transfer them to the flowerbed when you change out your pots for summer. This is one of the easiest ways for you to add bulbs to your garden.

Still want more flowers? You can try snapdragons, sweet Williams (*Dianthus barbatus*), calendulas,

above: 'Tête á Tête' daffodils rise from a bed of parsley planted in the center of a pot of yellow pansies and violas.

pansies and violas

ivy

daffodil bulbs

Swiss chard

'Ogon' golden sweet flag

parsley

FALL PANSY POT
16-inch planter

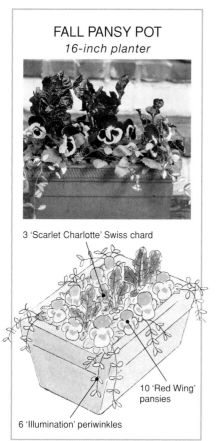

3 'Scarlet Charlotte' Swiss chard

10 'Red Wing' pansies

6 'Illumination' periwinkles

nemesias, and sweet alyssums. Just remember not to stray from your planned color scheme.

Loves the Sun

Carol says that light is the most critical factor when placing your pots. Choose a location that receives at least four to six hours of sunshine every day. Groom pansies regularly, removing spent blossoms to encourage new growth. Violas will not need to have flowers removed, as they bloom freely.

When planting in pots, good drainage is important. Use blood meal or Osmocote as a slow-release fertilizer, or feed with a balanced liquid 20-20-20.

On cold, gray winter days, your pansies and violas may rest a bit. When the weather begins to warm, they will again explode in glorious color to brighten the season. They will also provide another great gift— fragrance—a nice surprise at any time of the year. GENE B. BUSSELL

The Season's Best Flower

The pink blooms of this classic perennial will brighten your garden.

above, left: 'Ryan's Pink' mums grow fast, so save money by buying smaller plants and letting them spread. **above:** It never seems to want to stop blooming.

Fall is simply one of the best times of the year. The cooler weather brings welcome relief from the heat of summer. Plants also love autumn, and many put on a brilliant show right now. One of the best performers is 'Ryan's Pink' chrysanthemum.

Easy, Easy, Easy

"Whether you are just learning to garden or have been gardening for years, this is the plant for you," says Jason Powell of Petals From the Past nursery in Jemison, Alabama. It provides long-lasting color late in the season and offers excellent resistance to disease and insects. As a bonus, it makes a terrific cut flower for fall arrangements.

With its soft pink flowers and yellow centers, this mum takes center stage in the fall border. Its loose, mounding habit blends beautifully with other plants. However, if you would like a more upright, sturdy mum, simply pinch the tips of the branches off 2 to 3 inches in early May and then again in early July. The stronger side branches that develop will help to keep the flowers aloft.

'Ryan's Pink' requires little care, and when adding them to your garden, less is more. Use mulch when planting in the fall to help protect the roots as they become established. "A 4-inch pot is all that is necessary to get started," Jason says. "It is a vigorous grower. You actually don't want to encourage it too much, so apply a slow-release fertilizer once in the spring and again in the summer. You will still be able to share it with your friends the following year."

Good Company

So what else can you plant with this mum? A host of autumn favorites works well: asters, joe-pye weed *(Eupatorium purpureum)*, Japanese anemones, goldenrods *(Solidago* sp.), and swamp sunflowers *(Helianthus angustifolius)*. Salvias are an excellent choice, and there are lots of kinds. Try forsythia sage *(Salvia madrensis)*, with yellow flowers that echo the center of 'Ryan's Pink' mum. The purple blooms of Mexican bush sage *(S. leucantha)* mix beautifully, as does blue sage *(S. azurea grandiflora)*. For more choices, see "Salvia Puts On a Show" on page 172.

Once you've gathered all these brilliant blooms together in your garden, don't be surprised if you find a few welcome visitors this fall—butterflies! GENE B. BUSSELL

'RYAN'S PINK' MUM
At a Glance

Size: 18 to 24 inches with a mounding habit
Bloom time: late August till frost
Light: full sun to partial shade
Soil: average, well drained
Water: drought tolerant once established
Propagation: Divide clumps in early spring.
Range: all South

Abundant Basil

Is it possible to have too much of this flavorful herb?
We asked two Southern gardeners for their thoughts.

above: The botanical name of basil, *Ocimum basilicum,* is derived from Greek words meaning "the king of smell." This gardener is finding out why.

It's the end of summer. The kids head back to school, the nights get the first hint of autumn, and the basil keeps arriving by the truckload. How do you handle the inevitable surplus?

Pete Madsen, owner of Pete's Herbs in Charleston, South Carolina, feels the answer is simple. "Think pesto for Christmas. Think pesto for Valentine's Day. It's the summer's abundance that makes winter bearable."

Besides squirreling away jars of pesto in every nook and cranny of the kitchen, Pete suggests trading fresh basil for meals at local Italian restaurants. "Chefs are always looking for a source of good fresh herbs. It's a win-win situation for everyone."

Pete goes on to describe the importance of proper post-harvesting techniques. "Basil really needs to be cool and dry to last long. Its leaves bruise easily, so it has to be treated carefully. I like the miniature kinds, because their stems are tender and it's easy to use the whole plant. When basil gets too big, the stems can get woody and less useful." Pete has also found that plants usually grow best if he mows them down in late summer, waters and fertilizes them heavily, and then sits back to watch. "A late flush of basil is wonderful," he says. "It will provide enough of a harvest to really stock up for winter."

Randy Harelson, from The Gourd Garden in Seagrove Beach, Florida, has a similar sentiment. "It's really hard to imagine having too much basil. If you get tired of the typical 'Genovese' basil, try a different type such as Thai or 'Cinnamon Basil.' I usually plant about six different kinds so there is always one that's grabbing my attention." Mixing the different selections in a border can also create a striking accent. 'African Blue' and holy basil are two excellent kinds that work well as ornamentals.

The only real question for Randy is what to do when frost threatens the plants. Because the herb is so cold sensitive, it's important to pay attention to the weather forecast and pick all of the basil before it gets burned by the frost. You'll need to have a plan for dealing with this sudden abundance. "I'm not a fan of drying basil, because it quickly loses its vigor," he says.

However, if processed properly, basil can retain all of its flavor. Randy's preferred method is to cut and grind the basil with some olive oil and then pour the mixture into ice-cube trays. He adds a dash of oil to the top of the trays before freezing the harvest. "The extra bit of oil on top really seals in the flavor and prevents any of the basil from getting freezer burn." Once the cubes are solid, Randy stores them in a freezer bag, and adds them to the savory dishes he cooks over the winter.

"There's really nothing that won't benefit from a little dash of home-grown basil," he says, "especially when the winter days seem so short and dark. I can make pesto from the cubes simply by adding crushed garlic and toasted pine nuts."

Regardless of what you do with all your basil, the answer is clear: You can never have too much.

EDWIN MARTY

below: Interplant purple and green basil to carry the colors and flavors of summer into fall.

above: Flower fields surrounding Buffalo Springs Herb Farm produce a bountiful harvest of blooms suitable for drying. **left:** Globe amaranth hangs in neat bundles under the barn's roof.

Everlasting
These Virginia gardeners show you how dried flowers can capture the beauty of the season.
Color

By October, we think of the garden in past tense. The imminent arrival of frosty weather leads us to believe that this year's blooming endeavors will soon be nothing more than memories. But everlasting (or dried) flowers can capture summer's warmth and radiance in each preserved bloom.

In Raphine, Virginia, a lofty barn nestled into the Shenandoah Valley's rolling hills harbors a vibrant tapestry of dried flowers, harvested throughout the summer from the surrounding gardens. Don Haynie and Tom Hamlin, business partners and owners of Buffalo Springs Herb Farm, practice the simple technique of air-drying flowers to create stunning wreaths, door swags, and baskets of blooms. "With everlastings, your garden is alive year-round. In the winter when the garden is asleep, you still have the flowers you've preserved," Don says.

Certain Success

Plan next year's garden around flowers that dry well. Take a look at Don's list on page 183—you might recognize a few plants that you've already established that are perfect for drying. The choices include annuals, perennials, and even a few roadside finds that make good filler.

The drying technique is easy and requires

BY ELLEN RUOFF RILEY / PHOTOGRAPHY RALPH ANDERSON

above: A basket of fresh flowers greets visitors at the old barn's entrance, letting them know what's in bloom each day. **right:** Layering bunches of dried flowers in a shallow basket is an easy way to put together a beautiful display. From bottom to top: silver king artemisia, golden fernleaf yarrow, red cockscomb, hot pink and white globe amaranth, and blue mealy-cup sage. **far right:** Don Haynie (left) and Tom Hamlin grow fields of gorgeous flowers for their magnificent arrangements.

left: An everlasting wreath is a beautiful patchwork of autumn colors.

minimal space or materials. "Cut your flowers when they're in full bloom," Don recommends. "You want to pick them on a dry day, after 10 a.m. so the blossoms aren't holding excess moisture."

Remove foliage from the stems, and gather the flowers loosely. Fasten them with a rubber band, and then hang them upside-down out of direct sunlight. "We dry ours in a well-ventilated barn, but a guestroom is also an ideal place, particularly if it's air-conditioned," Don says. Humidity and excessive heat are not kind to drying blooms. "Air-conditioning draws the moisture out of the blossoms slowly. A hot attic dries flowers too quickly. Slow drying is much better," he says.

Colorful Arrangements

Wreaths are a superb way to use everlasting flowers. They can be large, elegant rings packed with innumerable blossoms or simple vine circles adorned with only one kind. Put a wreath on an interior door, place it above a mantel, or lay it flat on a dining table for a seasonal centerpiece. Hang a small version in a window, on a chair back, or even around a doorknob. This timeless shape adapts effortlessly to a range of sizes, blooms, and styles.

Layering bunches of blooms in a basket is a simple, no-fail way to enjoy everlastings. Find a long, shallow basket, such as those used to harvest vegetables. Choose bunches of assorted flowers, varying blossom sizes, shapes, and colors for an interesting grouping. Include a bundle of dried foliage, such as silver king artemisia, to complete the collection. In arranging lingo, this is called filler. Its neutral shade helps the vibrant and varied floral patchwork look like each bloom was destined to be with the others. Use the filler as the bottom layer, add the largest flowers next, and then place smaller ones

PICK OR PURCHASE

While growing everlastings is lots of fun, it may not be your cup of tea. Many florists and crafts shops sell bunches of dried flowers, so you can decorate your home even if you don't have the greenest of thumbs. Here we've listed some of Don's favorites— grouped in three categories to make arranging easy.

FILLER

silver king artemisia
(Artemisia ludoviciana albula)

boxwood

goldenrod

curly dock
(roadside weed)

mountain mint

German statice

MAIN FLOWERS

wheat celosia or cockscomb

golden fernleaf yarrow
(Achillea filipendulina)

strawflowers
(Helichrysum bracteatum)

globe amaranth
(Gomphrena globosa)

lavender

hydrangeas
(Pick at end of season.)

blue mealy-cup sage
(Salvia farinacea)

FINISHING TOUCHES

lady's-mantle
(Alchemilla mollis)

feverfew
(Chrysanthemum parthenium)

silver sage
(S. argentea)

on top.

Whether you grow your own or purchase a few bunches, everlasting flowers deliver rich, natural color. Use them in simple decorative ways throughout your home, and consider their great gift potential. Best of all, dried flowers keep your garden from becoming merely a memory.

A fall evening by an outdoor fireplace (See pages 202–203.)

November

Editor's Notebook

PHOTOGRAPH: ROGER FOLEY

It's autumn once more, which means big trouble for my parents. You see, their next-door neighbors have this uncanny ability to determine the origin of every single leaf that flutters to the ground. And have mercy on us all if a leaf from my parents' oak tree falls on the wrong side of the property line. "Your tree is dropping leaves again this year," the neighbors mutter. "We don't see why we should have to rake up *your* leaves." Sound like any of your neighbors? Then do three things. First, remind them that raking is great exercise. It gets them outside in the crisp, fresh air to enjoy the sounds, smells, and beauty of nature. Second, tell them that chopped-up leaves turn into great compost and mulch, and show them "A Wealth of Leaves" on page 196. But most importantly, make sure that whenever you plant a tree, you take into account the prevailing winds. That way, with a little luck, all of your leaves will blow into your neighbor's yard. I call this spreading the joy. —STEVE BENDER

Fall-Blooming Perennials

Plant them now to add autumn color. Mexican bush sage *(Salvia leucantha)* has spikes of purple-and-white flowers that will wave in the wind. Pineapple sage *(S. elegans)* has brilliant red blooms (shown at right) and leaves that smell of pineapple when you brush against them. Firespike *(Odontonema strictum)* with its red bloom spikes is great for partial shade. Philippine violet *(Barleria cristata)* brightens fall days with its pretty coat of lavender flowers. The brilliant yellow blooms of swamp sunflower *(Helianthus angustifolius)* will stop traffic a block away. Cigar flower *(Cuphea micropetala)* has an abundant display of small orange-and-yellow, tubular blooms.

TIPS

- **Grass**—For a green lawn through the winter months, overseed warm-season lawns, such as centipede, with annual ryegrass or a blend formulated for overseeding.
- **Harvest decorations**—Gather cockscombs, bachelor's buttons (gomphrenas), gourds, and grassy seedheads for seasonal accents. Combine these with colored corn, dried red peppers, and pumpkins.
- **Perennials**—In the Lower and Coastal South, you can share perennials now. Use a garden fork to lift and divide summer phlox, iris, hostas, and daylilies. When lifted, some will fall apart easily, while others may need to be coaxed. Set divided plants back into the soil at the original growing depth, water well, and mulch with leaves, pine straw, or finely ground pine bark. Give the extras to family and friends.
- **Small trees**—Dogwood, fringe tree *(Chionanthus virginicus)*, hawthorn, and serviceberry all have luminous foliage in fall. Most folks are surprised to learn that crepe myrtles have great color too. To learn more, read "Fall for Crepe Myrtles" on page 191.
- **Tulips**—Buy bulbs now for bright blossoms next spring. Reliable selections include 'Apricot Beauty' (salmon) and 'Monte Carlo' (yellow), which bloom early in the season. 'Ivory Floradale' (white) and 'Golden Oxford' (yellow) are good midseason selections. 'Maureen' (white) and 'Temple of Beauty' (salmon) bloom later. In the Middle and Upper South, go ahead and plant your bulbs. In the Lower and Coastal South, refrigerate them for 8 to 10 weeks before planting.

PLANT

- **Amaryllis**—Pot at least six weeks in advance for blooms before the holidays. Larger bulbs usually have bigger flowers and multiple bloom spikes. They prefer to be crowded, so select a pot that is a bit larger than the bulb. Plant in potting mix that is rich in organic matter, such as peat moss. Water well, and place in a warm, sunny room.
- **Peonies**—Plant peonies *(Paeonia lactiflora)* now. The most reliable one for the South is the white-flowering 'Festiva Maxima,' which is an especially good selection for the Lower South. 'Sarah Bernhardt' (pink) and 'Philippe Rivoire' (red) do well in the Upper and Middle South. Incorporate organic matter into a bed that has well-drained soil and gets at least four hours of sun a day. Set the "eyes" of new plants just below soil level, and water well. Peonies don't

like the heat and humidity of the Coastal South, but you can buy them as cut flowers.

■ **Flowers**—In Florida, sow seeds of larkspur, bachelor's buttons, sweet peas, and California poppies in full sun now to have a colorful spring show. Set out winter-hardy plants such as sweet alyssum, petunia, dianthus, and snapdragon.

■ **Pansies**—In Florida, plant in full sun, 10 inches apart. Select a fertilizer such as Osmocote Outdoor & Indoor Slow Release Plant Food 19-6-12 or Pursell Pansy Booster 19-6-12. Fertilize lightly once a month or according to package directions. Water every other day until the pansies are established and then twice a week during dry periods.

■ **Winter-blooming trees**—In Florida, add trees to provide color in colder months. Hong Kong orchid tree *(Bauhinia blakeana)* blooms during the summer, fall, and early winter. Its flowers do not set seed and drop long pods like other orchid trees. Other desirable options include sweet acacia *(Acacia farnesiana)*, yellow geiger tree *(Cordia lutea)*, and shaving-brush tree *(Pseudobombax ellipticum)*.

■ **Sweet peas**—In Texas, sow seeds of early-flowering, climbing types for best results. An ideal location gets at least a half-day of direct sun and protection from cold north winds. Work soil 8 to 10 inches deep, leaving a trench to protect against frost. Soak seeds overnight in water, and plant about 1 inch deep and 2 inches apart in the bottom of the trench.

CONTROL

■ **Grass**—In Texas, now is the time to use a broadleaf herbicide, such as Weed Stop or Weed-B-Gone, for severe weed infestations.

Fall Flowerbeds

The purple pansies and pink snapdragons shown here are a great combination to add to your garden now. Alyssum, stock, calendulas, violas, and sweet Williams also provide welcome blossoms. Mustard, kale, collards, and chard offer color from their leaves and create vertical accents.

Pansies

Cooler temperatures are perfect for planting pansies. Spade in 4 to 6 inches of composted pine bark, peat, or your own compost into the top 10 to 12 inches of soil. Also work in 4 to 6 pounds of cottonseed meal, alfalfa meal, or slow-release fertilizer such as Osmocote Outdoor & Indoor Slow Release Plant Food 19-6-12 or Pursell Pansy Booster 19-6-12. Finished beds should be 4 to 6 inches above the surrounding ground level for good drainage.

_____
_____
_____
_____
_____
_____
_____
_____
_____
_____
_____
_____
_____
_____
_____
_____
_____
_____
_____
_____
_____

Tip of the Month

To keep squirrels off the tops of those dome baffles that protect bird feeders, smear the baffles with a mixture of petroleum jelly and a few drops of hot sauce. It lasts for months.

KAY MCKEMIE
PALMYRA, VIRGINIA

These fragrant flowers are the easiest and most affordable bulbs you'll ever grow—all they want to do is bloom.

Paperwhites
a holiday favorite

GARDENING
PLANTS AND DESIGN

For this busy season, you want simple arrangements—blossoms so carefree that they can grow in pebbles, water, or soil. And if you don't have time to grow them, you can just buy them ready to go. Whether you are a beginning gardener or an expert, there is one truth to know about paperwhites—they are the perfect holiday flowers.

A Paperwhite Primer
Though these special days are a time to enjoy family and friends, they can sometimes become hectic and even stressful. Flowers are a quick cure for any seasonal troubles. Watching things grow will calm you, help you to slow down and relax. Here's all you need to know to get started.

Paperwhites *(Narcissus tazetta)* can be purchased individually for about a dollar each; in bags of many bulbs; or in prepackaged box sets that come with a pot, soil, and bulbs ready to plant. They are available anywhere fall bulbs are sold.

Growing in Pebbles
These plants are easy and fun to watch emerge, especially for kids. You can see the roots and the stalks growing in clear containers. Shallow bowls or jars work well if you steady the bulbs in pebbles. When using stones in a glass container, pour them in gently so as not to crack or break the glass. Always keep the water level up to the bottom of the bulb.

Growing in Water
Forcing vases work well and are available in many colors. A single vase with one bulb can create a lot of impact. Use multiple vases for a stronger statement.

They fit well on windowsills and other small spaces. Forcing vases will hold bulbs up high, but the water should still be even with the bottom of the bulb.

Growing in Soil
When planting your pot, you can use about four to five bulbs per 6-inch container. Make sure that it has holes for drainage. Fill with soil, and then gently add the bulbs. Don't plant them too deeply; a third of the bulb should be *above* the level of the soil. Place in a cool (around 60 degrees), dark area for seven days to encourage root development. Then move to a warm (around 70 degrees) and bright area to encourage topgrowth.

As the leaves emerge, rotate the pot every few days to keep stalks straight. The cooler the temperature, the sturdier the stalk and the less likely it will be to topple over. Once the flowerbuds swell and begin to open, move the pot to a cooler location out of direct light to extend the life of the flowers. Keep soil moist but not wet.

Blooms
Paperwhites are very fragrant flowers. Most people describe their aroma as perfume, although others feel it is

left: Arranged on a simple table near a window, 'Ziva' paperwhites thrive. Flea market finds make perfect containers. **above:** Flowers can be cut and used in a stem vase.

BY GENE B. BUSSELL
PHOTOGRAPHY LACY KERR ROBINSON

above: Paperwhites grow easily in pebbles. **top, right:** Bulbs begin growing in potting pebbles soon after they're planted. **center, right:** Use bamboo stakes and raffia to keep stems standing upright. **above, right:** Flowers are held high.

closer to being just plain fumes. And here lies a testament to their versatility. If you find their scent too strong, you can use these bulbs outside as long as the temperature does not fall below freezing.

They work well alone or mixed with violas and pansies. Use in containers near doorways and garden entries to welcome guests. In the Lower and Coastal South, you can even plant the bulbs in your garden, where they'll provide blooms year after year.

Staking

Bamboo stakes will keep paperwhite stalks standing tall, but you can use almost anything for support. Try cut branches from your garden. Sweet gum *(Liquidambar styraciflua)* works well for a rustic look at Thanksgiving. The red stems of burning bush *(Euonymus alata)* look great at Christmas. Use willow *(Salix* sp.) after New Year's, as the yellow-green stems brighten the winter months. Tie raffia or twine to stems, if necessary.

Great Gifts

Paperwhites are beautiful through the holidays and beyond, which makes them excellent presents. 'Ziva' is the most popular selection, blooming early. It is the one you'll find before the holidays and the one most often used in prepackaged boxes.

Making Them Last

You can have waves of brilliant blooms from now through winter by planting 'Ziva' every few weeks to stagger the bloom times. Other selections come in different colors, heights, and fragrances. 'Galilee' has white flowers and a mild scent. 'Omri' blooms later, likes cooler temperatures, and offers cream flowers with yellow centers. 'Grand Soleil d'Or' performs well into winter and sports bright yellow flowers.

Design

When using paperwhites for the holidays, just match the colors of the containers to the season. Use warm browns and oranges for Thanksgiving. Reds, greens, golds, and silvers look best at Christmas. Whites and yellows will greet the New Year and warm the later winter months. ◆

left: Rising above this brick wall, a row of crepe myrtles puts on a brilliant display of autumn colors.

Fall for Crepe Myrtles

Blaze into autumn with summer's favorite tree.

When people think of crepe myrtles, they envision warm summer days and pink, red, lavender, and white flower clusters sagging in the sun. But look at these classic trees in fall, and you might be surprised. Brilliant blooms will be replaced by orange, red, and yellow foliage for an outstanding autumn show.

Color Through the Seasons

Crepe myrtles have rounded, light green leaves that emerge in the spring. As the weather warms, the foliage hardens off and turns dark green. Then, when the temperatures drop in the fall, leaves gradually transform from green to sparkling fall hues. Many gardeners select crepe myrtles by bloom colors, but you can also choose a plant by its fall foliage (see chart at right).

Now is the perfect time to plant these beautiful trees, which come in many colors and sizes to fit your needs and space. 'Chickasaw' and 'Victor' are dwarf trees that grow 3 to 5 feet tall, making them perfect for small gardens. 'Acoma,' 'Hopi,' and 'Zuni' are small trees and will grow 7 to 10 feet high. These can be planted in tight areas where you want a tree but have little space. Medium ones, such as 'Centennial Spirit,' 'Tuskegee,' and 'Yuma,' grow 15 to 20 feet tall and work well around sidewalks and terraces but can still be planted close to the house. Big crepe myrtles, such as 'Dynamite,' 'Natchez,' and 'Tuscarora,' will grow 20 feet or more. They make excellent street trees and can be used in large yards. If you live in the Upper South, choose cold-hardy selections, such as 'Acoma,' 'Centennial Spirit,' or 'Hopi.'

Growing Conditions

Crepe myrtles need full sun to perform well. They will grow in shade, but blooms will be sparse, and plants will get leggy. These hardy trees have few pest or disease problems, and they require little water and fertilizer.

Also, crepe myrtles need minimal pruning. Some gardeners top them annually, but this ruins their natural shape and beauty. Remove the sucker growth that sometimes appears around the base. Only prune to shape trees or to take out any cross branching. In the winter, you can remove old seedpods by clipping the tips of branches.

Summer blooms and fall colors make crepe myrtles a garden favorite. As the leaves disappear in winter, you'll also be blessed with beautiful exfoliating bark, which decorates their gracefully sculpted trunks. For year-round interest, remember this Southern classic. Plant one now, and watch your tree change with the seasons.   CHARLIE THIGPEN

CREPE MYRTLES

SELECTION	SIZE	FALL COLOR	BLOOM
'Acoma'	10 feet	purple-red	white
'Centennial Spirit'	20 feet	red-orange	dark red
'Chickasaw'	3 to 5 feet	bronze-red	pink-lavender
'Dynamite'	20 or more feet	red-orange	cherry red
'Hopi'	7 feet	orange-red to dark red	pink
'Natchez'	30 feet	orange-red	pure white
'Tuscarora'	25 feet	red-orange	dark pink
'Tuskegee'	20 feet	bright orange-red	deep pink to red
'Victor'	3 feet	reddish yellow	dark red
'Yuma'	15 feet	yellowish to brownish red	medium lavender
'Zuni'	9 feet	orange-red to dark red	medium lavender

Fashionably Late Mums

As the season advances, fall color beats a retreat. Despairing gardeners across the South now have a new, improved tool to fight brown in the garden: late-blooming mums. They are genetically hardwired to come into full bloom when the rest of the garden palette is getting tired.

These perennials are also bred for a wide range of colors and for good behavior. The new mums are uniform in size and have sturdy cross branching, which keeps them from falling apart in storms. And because they bloom late, they bloom longer; cool temperatures are kind to the flowers.

These mums are easy to grow. In garden centers, they are often labeled as "season-extending" mums. Shop in nurseries that have knowledgeable staffs; they can point the way to the late bloomers and tell you what color each selection will be. Plant these mums when the flowers are just hard, green buds. This takes a little faith,

but it gives them enough time to root into the soil before blooming. Well-rooted plants will dry out less quickly, which means the flowers will last days and weeks longer. Finding them in the tight-bud stage may require a search, as most nurseries stock mums that are starting to show color or are in full bloom. That's because these are the ones that tend to sell best.

To have extra long-lasting color, select hues that blend easily with light brown. When the first hard frost settles on the flowers in late fall, the petals darken along their edges. Pastel, yellow, and white blooms look brown and withered. Darker colors don't show the frost damage at all. Red, bronze, and gold mums look just fine after a little cold.

What Happens Next Fall?

Garden mums—late or otherwise—come back year after year. The key to keeping them looking good is cutting them back. If you're too softhearted to prune, your mums will bloom twice—in spring and autumn.

However, they'll have long, floppy stems with pitiful little flowers.

In late winter, cut dead stems to the ground. New leaves will sprout from underground roots. In midspring, when mums fill out with leaves and flowerbuds, shear plants down to 8 inches tall. Around the Fourth of July, prune and shape them by pinching off soft green stem tips. Test to make sure you're tipping only soft tissue by pinching the stems with your fingernails, and take off only that pliable part of the stem. Then, let the mums grow. They'll develop flowerbuds for brilliant bloom when you want it—in late autumn.   LUCINDA MAYS

MORE MUMS

Some late-blooming favorites include 'Crown Jewel' (plum), 'Emily' (lavender), 'Autumn Denise' (red-bronze), 'Heather' (plum-lavender), 'Raquel' (wine red), 'Grace' (orange-bronze), and 'Sunny Denise' (pastel yellow).

above: Unlike the earlier mums that are gone in a flash, late-flowering selections bloom for weeks during autumn.
above, left: Fill in gaps in borders with bronze or gold mums that blend with other fall bloomers. This one is called 'Grace.'

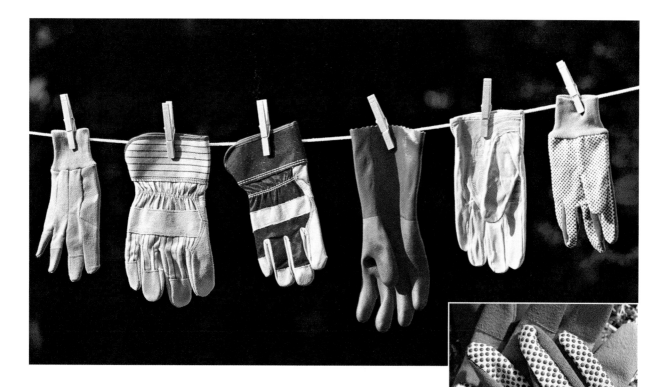

A Handy Guide to Gloves

Choosing the right ones will save your skin.

top: Cowhide, goatskin, canvas, rubber—there are gloves for every garden task. **above:** Reinforced fingertips last longer, and PVC dots on the palms help provide a sure grip.

If you want to garden, the toughest things about you had better be your hands. After all, you're going to be digging, pruning, weeding, and spraying. But this doesn't mean you have to put up with hands that look like country hams. Just buy a good pair of garden gloves.

Pick a Pair

Spraying chemicals or handling liquids? You need some rubber gloves. Rubber is impermeable, so liquids can't reach your skin. It's also flexible, allowing you to pick up small objects. On the downside, it doesn't breathe, so your hands get clammy. I use rubber gloves whenever I'm mixing up those water-soluble fertilizers the manufacturers insist on dyeing blue.

For heavy-duty jobs, such as pruning rosebushes or moving stones, cowhide leather gloves are great. Good ones have protective cuffs to cover your wrists. Thorns won't penetrate them, and they last forever, no matter the abuse. On the other hand, these thick gloves are stiff and not very nimble.

Less demanding tasks, such as using a hoe, trowel, or rake, call for medium-weight gloves with palms made of goatskin leather or cotton canvas. Most have cotton backs, making them lighter, cooler, and quite flexible.

Now for those who pretend to garden while everyone else does the work, I recommend lightweight polyester-cotton gloves. They'll keep your hands from getting dirty or tanned, yet they're flexible enough to pick up your demitasse.

Keeping Them Clean

The best way to wash your gloves depends on the type you have. Some can be machine-washed; others will shrink and bleed. Fine leather gloves demand special treatment. To clean them, gently scrub with a pumice-based soap, such as Lava. Rinse, apply a leather protector, and then hang the gloves on the line to dry. Before they dry completely, put them on to restore their shape. Questions? Read the directions! Almost all gloves come with them.

One more thing. Gloves don't cost much, so every gardener in the house should have his or her own pair. That way, guys won't have to squeeze their mitts into flowered things that their friends make fun of, and ladies won't have to wonder what disgusting goo their husbands were handling before they put on gloves.   STEVE BENDER

Quick Combinations

For great-looking flower arrangements, you don't necessarily need lots of blooms. Take chrysanthemums, for example. A few of these inexpensive, long-stemmed beauties will go a long way. They're available in all the reds and russets, yellows and oranges that speak of the harvest season. You can build an easy display around a bunch of these cut blooms or a potted mum from a garden center. Add a few other elements, and you're all set for creative arranging that will flaunt your seasonal flair.

Fabulous arrangements begin with a unique container, a few flowers, and some freshly cut foliage.

Harvest Touches

Miniature pumpkins and gourds provide a rainbow of hues. Add a few to a glass vase before inserting flower stems; cluster others around the base of the container. Let a wooden box hold a variety of knobby gourds.

Unique Solutions

Collect vases, urns, and other complementary items of all shapes and sizes. Use a grapevine wreath at the base of a large sculptural urn (see photograph on opposite page). For a rustic look, adorn a table with a piece of burlap. Place an iron trivet over the mouth of an urn to hold branches and stems stationary as you arrange them.

Adding Color

Use evergreen foliage as filler when arranging flowers. Look to your garden for a variety of leaf shapes and seasonal colors. The large, lustrous leaves from magnolia trees are the ideal foil for vivid flowers, such as

deep red daisy chrysanthemums or bright and sunny yellow button mums. For a loose and linear effect, arrange the long, needle-like leaves of 'Big Blue' liriope around your flowers so they spill over the edge of the container. Also, utilize the lacy foliage of smilax and the waxy leaves of 'Gold Dust' aucuba. Deciduous plant materials, such as oakleaf hydrangea, maple, beech, and crepe myrtle are easy to find and will also add wonderful color as their deep greens gradually turn to majestic rusts, reds, and golds to match the bold colors of fall.

Keep a few of these favorite things at your fingertips, and colorful everyday arrangements will become even easier.

JULIA HAMILTON

above: Set an urn into a grapevine wreath; then place a potted mum in the urn. Add magnolia cuttings, and flank the wreath with pumpkins.

left: Fall brings a carpet of gold across the South and a chance to enjoy cool weekends outside.

A Wealth of Leaves

With three simple methods, you can turn fantastic foliage into fabulous fertilizer.

If money began falling from the sky, your neighbors would probably think you quite odd if you raked the bills off your lawn and put them in bags for the trash collectors to haul away. But each fall, legions of homeowners charge into their yards with rakes in hand to do just that, throwing away the most valuable resource their yards produce—leaves.

Besides providing trees with the energy they need to grow in the summer, leaves also supply an entire forest with what it requires to thrive in the winter—fresh nutrients. Without a constant supply, most plants can't reach their full potentials and the soil will eventually become exhausted. Luckily you can take advantage of fallen leaves to keep your soil fertile and make your plants happy.

TIPS FOR MULCHING LEAVES ON A LAWN

- A sharp rotary blade mower will pulverize leaves best.
- Chop foliage enough so that grass still receives full sun. Three or four passes with a mulching mower may be needed.
- Mulched leaves don't increase the thatch layer enough to harm the grass.

Let 'Em Lie

Using foliage as a mulch is probably the easiest way to fertilize your yard. Simply letting the leaves of oaks or maples decompose where they've fallen or raking them into specific planting beds ensures a replenishing supply of nitrogen and potassium to the soil. While the leaves themselves may not meet all your plants' nutrient requirements, they will decrease the need to add soil conditioners and organic mulches. Don't let the leaves build up too high around a tree's base, as this can cause rotting or insect damage. A good mulch doesn't need to be more than 3 inches thick. Also, prevent leaves from covering up grass for more than a few days, because the blades require sunlight for photosynthesis and growth.

Break 'Em Down

Another option is to rake up the leaves and put them on a compost pile, where they can mix with other decaying plant materials and provide next year's fertilizer. There are a number of advantages to composting leaves, such as creating a balanced supply of fertilizer and encouraging beneficial soil bacteria. Once leaves are properly composted, they can be reapplied to beds to ensure your plants have all necessary nutrients, as well as moisture-conserving mulch.

Cut 'Em Up

The final option is to use a mulching mower or leaf blower to help foliage break down on its own. On turf lawns, a few passes with a mulching mower will make leaves small enough so they don't affect the grass blades and will return nutrients to the soil.

A blower with a vacuum option can be a great help in getting leaves out of a bed or off a lawn. Most vacuum blowers will also chop the leaves, making it simple to add them to a compost pile or spread them as mulch. While leaf blowers can be helpful when clearing large areas, they tend to stir up dust in the air and can lower the air quality. Limit their use to days without smog problems.

Use these easy, inexpensive ways to get nutrients back into the soil and keep your yard looking great throughout the year.   EDWIN MARTY

PHOTOGRAPHS: VAN CHAPLIN

left: With the front walk divided into a series of steps and landings, the ascent to the door seems less steep.
below: Pots of mums and a sweep of New Guinea hybrid impatiens welcome visitors.

New Walk Is a Step Up

Getting to the house is easy now—no climbing gear required.

Here's the problem: Your front door looks out on a nice side street where you'd like guests to park. But between the street and the door lies a rather steep slope. Now, you could build a walk directly down the slope to the street, but the unbroken series of steps might make folks feel as if they're climbing the Washington Monument. Or you could run the walk to the driveway on the side of the house and have everyone enter from the drive. Or maybe, just maybe, there's another, better solution.

Homeowners John and Gerry York of Washington, D.C., knew there had to be. Jim Sines of Garden Gate Landscaping in Silver Spring, Maryland, took one look at the situation and agreed. He designed an attractive and functional flagstone walk that helps visitors get to the door without losing their breath.

Happy Landings

Here's how it works. As guests arrive on the street, they disembark on a nice wide curbside landing. They take four steps up and arrive at a second landing. Four more steps bring them to a third landing, at which point the walk turns right. A stroll of about 20 feet takes them to the final set of four steps. Turning left, they ascend those, turn right again, and amble about another 20 feet to the front door.

The beauty of the setup is this: Even though the zigzag walk is probably twice as long as one that would zoom straight down the slope, you never climb more than four steps at any one time, so the ascent is always comfortable. Adding turns to the walk carries you through the garden and takes your mind off the fact that you're going uphill. And because the walk is a generous 5 feet wide, two people can stroll side by side.

No Raking, No Mowing

When the Yorks first contacted Jim, they were also unhappy with the plantings on the slope—a hodgepodge of perennials, roses, and scruffy-looking liriope. Jim removed it all and planted easy-to-maintain boxwoods and spreading English yews up by the house. Then he added shade-loving Japanese pachysandra on the slope, after first amending the soil with lots of organic matter. The pachysandra filled in beautifully. Unlike grass, it never needs mowing; it doesn't require raking in the fall either. Small leaves falling from the trees simply filter through it and make their way to the ground. A leaf blower quickly removes larger leaves that gather on top.

As this example proves, good design can turn a minus into a plus. What once seemed insurmountable is now a walk in the park. STEVE BENDER

OTHER GROUND COVERS

Japanese pachysandra is elegant but hard to grow outside of the Upper and Middle South. Shade-tolerant options for the Lower and Coastal South include Asiatic jasmine, wintercreeper euonymus, common periwinkle, mondo grass, and English ivy. In the Tropical South, try mondo grass, Asiatic jasmine, wedelia, or artillery plant.

Citrus for the South

Want something to take the chill off winter days? Try a Satsuma mandarin, and enjoy its unparalleled sweetness and beautiful orange glow.

Satsumas are easily grown on a patio in containers, which can be moved inside during winter. With sufficient sunlight, they'll produce beautiful fruit.

Thoughts of citrus inevitably lead most Southerners down to the Sunshine State with its endless rows of shiny green leaves and glowing orange fruit. Then our thoughts jump to a refrigerator full of slick containers of frozen juice concentrate. But Arlie Powell, former professor of horticulture at Auburn University, believes citrus belongs somewhere else—namely your yard. "Citrus makes a great addition to most landscapes, and, in particular, the Satsuma mandarin is well suited for many parts of the South."

In the Tropical and Coastal South, Satsuma (*Citrus unshiu* formerly *C. reticulata*) is easily grown outdoors year-round, while in the Lower and Middle South, this hardy citrus should be moved inside in winter or grown with frost protection. Regardless of where you live, the fruit can always be enjoyed whether purchased locally or mail-ordered.

A Fashionable Fruit

The Satsuma is desirable for its impressive sweet flavor, lack of seeds, and loose, easy-to-peel skin. In addition, the Satsuma tree is amazingly cold tolerant, often able to withstand freezing temperatures that would kill most other citrus. Because of these attributes, this tree was heavily planted all over the Coastal South. Unfortunately, a series of hard freezes in the early 20th century killed back a number of the trees, discouraging most growers from planting again. Recently, however, the growing demand for the incomparable sweetness of the fruit, coupled with new frost-protection systems, has brought the Satsuma back in favor with commercial growers and homeowners alike.

The Key to Cold Hardiness

Arlie and his wife, Gwen, have been growing Satsumas in their yard for years, and they've learned a thing or two about how to keep them producing great-tasting fruit year after year. "The first step to growing Satsumas is planting them in a sheltered part of your yard. You'd be surprised how much warmer a south-facing slope is in winter," Arlie says. Protecting the trees from wind is another way to ensure their survival. Plant them next to a wall or behind a row of trees. Just make sure the Satsumas get plenty of sun wherever they are—at least 8 to 10 hours a day. They can tolerate some shade, but less sun means less fruit.

Once the tree is in a protected part of your yard, the next important thing to watch is the nighttime temperatures in winter. "Satsumas can handle a freeze down to 17 degrees," Arlie says, "but if they're protected, they'll produce a whole lot more fruit." He builds a PVC frame around his trees every winter and simply slips a cover over the frame if the temperature is going below 28 degrees. If a severe freeze is predicted, Arlie

above: Gwen and Arlie Powell harvest several bushels of fruit from each of their trees. **above, right:** Satsuma fruit ripens in fall, just in time for the holiday season. The kid-glove skin peels back easily, revealing a sweet, seedless fruit.

puts a propane heater under the frame. "The trick is to remember to take the cover off once the temperature climbs back above freezing. A tree can quickly lose its cold-hardiness and begin breaking for spring if the temperatures are kept too warm."

The final key to keeping Satsumas alive in winter is to keep them happy year-round. A healthy, well-watered, properly fertilized tree can handle much colder temperatures than a weak one. Just remember that all citrus trees require plenty of water but also need good drainage. Water is especially important during the flowering and fruit-setting period, which usually occurs in April. If the roots sit in water, they will rot and kill the tree before too long, so only water when nearby lawn grass begins to show stress.

Northern Exposure

While Satsumas can be grown in all tropical and semitropical regions, the farther north they are, the better the fruit is. "What makes the Satsuma's flavor so unique is that it's grown so far north," Arlie says. "The flavor isn't diluted at all, and the shelf life is impressive. When a Satsuma is grown in South Florida, the peak fruit quality won't last a week on the tree or on the shelf, but grow the same fruit in Alabama, and it will be delicious for weeks." Satsumas flower in spring, set their fruit shortly thereafter, and ripen in fall. To ensure a good crop the following year, harvest all fruit by Christmas. Colder temperatures give it a unique sweet flavor that's very juicy and low in acid. According to Arlie, the Satsuma is unmatched by any other citrus for providing fruit in this season.   EDWIN MARTY

Colorful Autumn Houseplants

Enjoy the shades of the season with easy plants.

In fall, brilliant yellows, reds, and oranges dot the landscape, enticing us to bring that same look indoors. While branches of autumn leaves make wonderful short-lived arrangements, you can have sensational long-lasting color with a host of houseplants. Put together a great-looking assortment—it's simple.

Cast of Players

Peruse the garden shop's houseplant selection with a seasonal eye, and you'll be surprised by how many options exist. Here are a few plant choices and tips for their care.

■ **Crotons** contain the full spectrum of fall color within each leaf. This heat-loving plant requires bright light and flourishes with a few hours of direct sun in early morning. Keep the soil moist—dryness causes leaves to drop. There are numerous pot and plant sizes available; petite 4-inch containers combine easily with other houseplants in a basket, while 6- or 8-inch pots can stand alone as colorful specimens. A reminder: Small pots dry out quickly and require more attention than larger ones.

■ **Bromeliads** are easy to arrange and grow. Their long-lasting, sculptural blooms range from brilliant yellows to sunset shades of orange, red, and burgundy. Numerous selections are available, so choose an assortment of flowers along with different pot sizes. These plants require bright light but not direct sun. Keep the soil moist, and avoid the popular practice of filling the plants' cups, or centers, with water.

■ **Dracaenas** bring slender, pointy foliage to the mix, with leaves ranging from colorful stripes to deep-

above: In this long-lasting arrangement, bromeliads, croton, broad-leaved philodendron, and spiky dracaena weave together.

hued burgundy. Bright light is sufficient; moisten the soil when it is dry. Add dracaenas to an arrangement for loose, light texture. Choose 2- or 3-inch pots to fill in between broad-leaved plants, or use a large, brightly colored specimen as a focal point.

The Latest Great Plant

It's always fun to find a new introduction, and **'Fire Flash'** (*Chloro-phytum amaniense* 'Fire Flash') sports color in a surprising way. This plant produces brilliant orange stems virtually glowing with sensational fall color. It is a distant relative of spider plant, which offers clues to its easy care. Provide bright light, and keep the soil slightly damp, although it can adapt to very dry conditions if you forget to water. It's pretty enough to enjoy in a container all by itself.

top: Chrysanthemum's dynamic colors bring fall to the front door. Use small pots inside for that same autumn palette. **above, left:** A small bowl holds a low-maintenance assortment of plants that snuggle together for an attractive arrangement. **above, right:** This new introduction, 'Fire Flash,' boasts beautiful orange stems that deliver fall color in a unique way.

Put It Together

Resist the temptation to buy one of every neat plant you see. Choose no more than three different types, and purchase multiples of these. Vary pot size, leaf shape, and color for an artful balance of scale and texture.

In a large container, place one or two 6-inch pots and numerous 4-inch ones. Center the big pots as a focal point, and surround them with the smaller ones, clustering plants of like kinds. Angle a few pots toward the outer edge, so leaves extend beyond the container. Add green sphagnum moss or silvery Spanish moss to cover edges and soil. Arrange small bowls and baskets in the same manner using 2-, 3-, and 4-inch potted plants.

The plants mentioned here don't need frequent care—a weekly watering should be sufficient. Remove pots from their decorative container, place them in the sink, and water them well. When they have drained, reconstruct the arrangement as it was, or experiment and give it a slightly different look. ELLEN RUOFF RILEY

OTHER AUTUMN BEAUTIES

Besides the plants mentioned, here are a few more choices for fall color—including a few that offer flowers.

- peperomia
- 'Black Cardinal' philodendron
- 'Prince of Orange' philodendron
- chrysanthemum
- kalanchoe

enjoy
fall's first fire

An outdoor fireplace turns your patio into a cozy year-round getaway.

Randy and Sally Royse have it figured out. Their patio—centered around a fireplace made of eastern Oklahoma moss rock—is a carefully planned extension of their living room. It's their chosen destination for everyday relaxation and entertaining. "I love being outside, and this is an outdoor room in every sense of the word," Randy says. "It's just like being indoors, but the sky is your ceiling."

The South is favored with delightful autumn weather that's conducive to outdoor living, and Oklahoma City, where the Royses reside, is no exception. Their fireplace adds to that livability with warmth and comfort, even on the season's chilliest days. "We use it every chance we get—in the dead of winter and even during summer cool spells," Sally says.

Collaboration

When Randy and Sally remodeled their backyard, they engaged interior designer Fanny Bolen and landscape designer John Fluitt in the process. "The idea was to add 1,500 square feet to the house, with no roof on it," Randy says. From the front entrance, you can gaze through the living room's French doors out to the patio. The fireplace terminates the view, and the effect is of one long room.

"The hearth anchors the patio and becomes the focal point of the living room as well," John says. The view from the patio back into the house is equally inviting. The patio's ample size offers room for dining close to the fire on cool evenings and space to admire it from afar. Candles strung across the mantel enhance the personal warmth of this open-air room.

The space feels cozy and intimate, but it's large enough to accommodate guests. The wide stone hearth provides gracious extra seating.

Considerations

John's suggestions for fireplace design balance aesthetics and function. First, do a realistic assessment of your area. "It's easy to get a fireplace too large for your space. Keep the profile low, but make sure the smokestack is tall enough to draw," he advises. This is where professional help is invaluable. Proportions must be correct to have the chimney draw properly and prevent excess smoke.

Choose a building material that is compatible with your home. "Repeat already existing stone or brick to tie the fireplace and architecture together," John recommends. Allow plenty of space for easy movement and seating, and align the fireplace to be viewed from indoors as well.

An outdoor fireplace turns a patio into a sociable gathering place and extends the area's use through the seasons. A crisp autumn evening becomes a magical time when you're warming your toes by the fire and relaxing with family and friends.

right: The fireplace is the patio's focal point. **left:** Stoking the fire is an enjoyable task for Randy and best buddy Pounder. **top:** The design incorporates a stone ledge and mantel for seasonal decorations such as candles, leaves, pumpkins, and berries.

Winter Rose Poinsettia
(See page 213.)

December

Editor's Notebook

PHOTOGRAPH: VAN CHAPLIN

I know what you must be thinking: "Steve, during this festive holiday season, why don't you tell us about a plant with leaves that are used to make hula skirts, so we can dance to Don Ho music on Christmas morning?" Well, meet Hawaiian ti *(Cordyline fruticosa)*, a tropical plant sold at garden centers. Some forms have red leaves; some have purple ones; and some have copper, red, and pink ones. Leaves grow up to 30 inches long and 6 inches wide. When dried, they're perfect for making skirts—especially for folks who wouldn't know a sewing machine from an ATM. In winter, ti needs a sunny window and warm indoor temperatures. To meet its requirement for humid air, you should place it atop a gravel-lined saucer filled with water. From spring until fall, keep it outdoors in a lightly shaded spot so it can grow all the leaves that you'll need to outfit the entire family for a holiday hula. By next December, the whole gang will be shimmying away to the mellow sounds of *A Don Ho Christmas.*

— STEVE BENDER

Christmas Cactus

A favorite for beginning and experienced gardeners, it has blooms in cheerful shades of yellow, red, pink, fuchsia, white, and orange that will brighten your holidays. Long-lived and easy to care for, it prefers bright light and temperatures between 60 and 75 degrees. While blooming, it needs moist (not soggy) soil and a weekly feeding with a liquid fertilizer (15-30-15). Avoid placing Christmas cactus near heating vents. Create a memory this season, and share a few of these plants with your friends and family.

TIPS

■ **Berries**—Looking for plants to add to your garden that will provide lots of color for decorating? Good choices include nandina and deciduous hollies such as winterberry *(Ilex verticillata)* and possumhaw *(I. decidua)*. Other great options are evergreens such as American holly *(I. opaca)*; yaupon *(I. vomitoria)*; and selections of Chinese holly *(I. cornuta)*, including 'Burfordii,' 'Dazzler,' and 'Berries Jubilee.'

■ **Garden gifts**—Tools are welcomed presents for gardeners. Good choices include watering cans, hand cultivators, gloves, spades, bypass pruners, hats, and retractable rakes.

■ **Landscape renovations**—Expand planting beds to incorporate trees and shrubs that are presently elsewhere in your yard or to include areas of the lawn that are too shady to grow grass successfully. Lay out the bed lines with garden hoses, and experiment until you find the shape you want.

■ **Living Christmas trees**—If you can't bear the thought of cutting down a tree for Christmas, then a living tree may be for you. Pick a spruce, hemlock, white pine, or fir in the Upper and Middle South. Virginia pine, red cedar, and Japanese cedar *(Cryptomeria japonica)* work well in the Lower and Coastal South. Keep well watered, and leave them inside no more than 10 days. You can then plant as long as the ground is not frozen.

■ **Mulch**—Azaleas, hollies, boxwoods, and camellias will appreciate extra protection during winter. After the first frost, add a 2-inch layer of pine straw or finely shredded pine bark mulch around the bases of shrubs.

■ **Winter solstice**—December 22 marks the official end of fall and the start of winter. It's a great time to look and learn the "bones" of your landscape. Think of your yard as a room. Where are the walls, ceiling, and floor? Do you need to add a hedge, shade tree, or path? Plan now for additions and renovations.

PLANT

■ **Winter greens**—In the Lower and Coastal South, sow seeds of radishes, turnips, mustard, kale, and lettuce.

■ **Bulbs**—In Florida, finish planting spring-flowering bulbs, such as summer snowflakes *(Leucojum aestivum)*, narcissus, anemones, ranunculus, and Dutch iris now. Tulips and hyacinths must be refrigerated for six to eight weeks before planting to ensure a good bloom.

■ **Flowers**—In Florida, plant petunias, pansies, dianthus, snapdragons, sweet alyssums, calendulas, and gaillardias. In South Florida, add impatiens, nasturtiums, torenias, verbenas, and begonias in protected areas on the south side of your house.

- **Vegetables and herbs**—In Florida, sow seeds of beets, carrots, mustard, kale, kohlrabi, and radishes. Sow seeds or set out plants of broccoli, cabbage, collards, and onions. Plant herbs such as chives, coriander, dill, garlic, and sage.
- **Petunias**—In Texas, plant now for a long season of color. Single-flowering types, such as Wave and Madness Series, are more prolific and tend to last longer than double and ruffled types. Petunias prefer sunny locations with well-drained soil.

FERTILIZE

- **Cool-season lawns**—Now is an excellent time to establish fescue, perennial ryegrass, and bluegrass. If you are sowing the seeds for a new lawn, use a lower nitrogen, higher phosphorus fertilizer such as 18-24-10. If you have an established lawn, go with a higher nitrogen formula such as 31-2-4.
- **Larkspur and poppies**—In Texas, volunteer seedlings tend to be too thick in some areas and too sparse in others. You can carefully dig and replant where needed. Space them 4 to 6 inches apart; then thin the rest. Water in with a weak solution of balanced, water-soluble fertilizer, such as Rapid Gro.

Poinsettias

After the holidays, poinsettias can be planted outdoors. In Central and South Florida, place in the ground in sunny spots sheltered from north winds. In North Florida, replant in larger pots, and bring them indoors during freezing weather. If poinsettias have dropped lower leaves and become leggy, cut them back to 4 to 6 inches to induce new growth. Water as needed, and fertilize with a product such as Osmocote Outdoor & Indoor Slow Release Plant Food. Keep tips of new growth pinched until Labor Day so plants stay bushy and compact. Colorful bracts should develop by the following Thanksgiving. To learn about a distinctive poinsettia with an unusual form, read "Take a Look at Winter Rose" on page 213.

Amaryllis

Amaryllis bulbs can be potted now for holiday blooms. Scarlet, white, and striped flowers, such as 'Charisma' (shown here), in single or double forms will highlight festive displays. 'Apple Blossom,' a pink-and-white blend, is one of the few scented amaryllis. Select large, firm bulbs, and place them in containers of potting soil amended with one-third fine gravel or coarse sand to facilitate drainage and support the heavy bloom stalk. Single bulbs fill 6-inch-diameter containers, while three bulbs work well in 10- to 12-inch sizes. Place pots in bright, indirect light; keep them moderately moist; and turn every few days to keep stalks upright. Small bamboo stakes tied with raffia provide support for the heavy stalks and buds. After they have finished flowering, remove stalks, and water sparingly until leaves appear.

December notes:

Tip of the Month

Those plastic stakes that are used for holding Christmas lights are great for supporting floppy annuals and perennials. The light stakes come in several different sizes and heights. Buying them after Christmas Day means that you can usually get them at half price, just in time for planning your spring garden.

CHERIE F. COLBURN
THE WOODLANDS, TEXAS

simply stunning ORCHIDS

Overcome the fear factor, and enjoy this
gorgeous flower throughout the holidays.

below: An old mandolin makes an unexpected holiday accessory on a mantel with lady-slippers (*Paphiopedilum* sp.) and moth orchids (*Phalaenopsis* sp.).
right: Set a table or sideboard with white moth orchids in silver containers that vary in height for visual interest.

Christmas abounds with blooms—poinsettias, paperwhites, and amaryllis are all traditional staples. However, another flower waiting in the wings to become a holiday favorite may come as a surprise. Orchids are the new seasonal darling. Affordable, easy to care for, and long-lasting, these plants adapt to a number of styles. You can dress one up in supreme elegance or take it in a more casual direction.

What was once an exclusive, exotic, hard-to-find plant now has a new image. Notice these changes, and before you know it, you'll be hooked.

Orchids are abundant. Look for them at mass-market retailers, garden shops, florists, and grocery stores. Choose from many selections with myriad flower shapes, sizes, and colors.

Orchids are inexpensive. You can find small 4-inch pots for as little as $12, and 6-inch containers begin at around $18. While this may seem like more than pocket change, remember that they will bloom for at least two months. Few other flowers perform so beautifully for so long.

Easy Care

Orchids are some of the best blooming houseplants a novice can try—delicate, dainty flowers belie this plant's tough-as-nails nature. Follow these steps, and discover how simple they are.

■ Place orchids in bright light—not direct sun, but somewhere you can comfortably read during

BY ELLEN RUOFF-RILEY
PHOTOGRAPHY ALLAN MANDELL

the day without extra illumination.

■ Avoid cold drafts. A brisk breeze doesn't readily damage open flowers but does cause unopened buds to drop.

■ Give the plants a thorough drink once a week with room-temperature water. Place the pots in the sink, and drench the soil. Mist the leaves, and shake the plants to shed excess moisture. When the orchids have completely drained, put them back in their decorative containers.

Holiday Decor

Personal Christmas styles tap into family traditions, memories, regional attitudes, and budgets. Orchids adapt to a wide range of fashions, depending on the preferred look.

They make wonderful companions to silver. Line your bowl or compote with plastic for moisture protection, put the orchid's pot in place, and fill in around the top with Spanish moss. Wind sparkling glass-bead garland around the top for another decorative layer, draping it over the edge.

For a different approach, group an orchid assortment on your mantel. When a casual look is appropriate, cover the potting medium with lush green moss. Attach some around the pot's rim with a glue gun, and add a few glass ornaments around the leaves. Remove the plant stake supporting the bloom, and introduce a pine or fir branch in its place. Additional cut greenery, potted ferns such as maidenhair, and ornaments on the mantel pull this easygoing yet lush look together.

Guilt-Free Goodbye

After the holidays, we're accustomed to disposing of poinsettias and some forced bulbs when they've given their all. The only difference with orchids is that the flowers last well into January and February. But once they're through, if you cannot imagine hanging on to your plants until next year, pass them along to a friend who might enjoy making them rebloom.

Give yourself a treat, and try this genial, glorious plant. It offers a great holiday look with no fuss and blooms right into the New Year.   ◆

Petite conifers in 4-inch pots, a cyclamen, and an orchid come together in a wide, shallow terra-cotta dish for casual holiday style. The evergreens are coated with spray-on snow for a frosty look.

MORE EASY IDEAS

Here are a few additional tips to make orchids look seasonally special.

■ Bloom stalks are usually supported with bamboo plant stakes. Gently remove the stake from the pot. Then spray-paint it silver or gold to match your container, wrap it in ribbon, or cover it with moss using a glue gun. Replace the stake in the pot.

■ If you like silver's shimmer but don't have a suitable container, spray terra-cotta pots with metallic paint. Copper, pewter, and gold produce dazzling finishes; while you're at it, paint the saucer too.

■ After Christmas, change containers to give your orchid a different look for a New Year's celebration. Place the pot in a crystal bowl filled with sparkling glass jewels (available at crafts stores) or silver beads.

PHOTOGRAPHS: J. SAVAGE GIBSON

Christmas Camellia

'Yuletide' will help you welcome the holidays with its warm red flowers and elegant dark green leaves.

Garden designer Frances Parker of Beaufort, South Carolina, loves 'Yuletide' camellias. She says, "If you want red flowers in your garden for Christmas, plant this lustrous evergreen. It's carefree."

A Beautiful Solution

Truth be told, camellias are easy plants for any landscape. 'Yuletide' (*Camellia* x *vernalis* 'Yuletide') is an especially versatile sasanqua hybrid.

Would you like to define a space in your garden? Its small leaves and upright form make it a fine choice for formal and informal hedges. This plant grows slowly and can be easily clipped, so it's simple to maintain.

Do you have a blank wall? It is also excellent when used as an espalier. Camellias can be purchased already trained on frames and ready to plant. Do you need an evergreen as a backdrop in a flowerbed? It makes a lush screen for the back of the border. How about an accent in your garden? This plant can also be pruned into a lollipop-shaped topiary.

If you have poor, rocky soil, plant it in a large terra-cotta pot, and it will live happily on your patio for years. No room? Keep it trained and clipped as a bonsai on your deck. What more could you ask from a camellia?

'YULETIDE' CAMELLIA
At a Glance

Light: partial shade to full sun
Soil: well drained, rich in organic matter
Water: likes moisture but can be very drought tolerant once established
Size: 8 feet tall and 6 feet wide
Growth: slow to moderate
Range: Middle, Lower, Coastal, and Tropical South. If growing them in the Upper South, provide protection from drying winds, or keep in a cool greenhouse.
Comments: Mulch so roots stay cool, but keep it away from the base of the trunk.

Plays Well With Others

When used in foundation plantings, this beauty's smaller leaves help it to both blend and contrast with other plants. The fine-textured leaves and red berries of nandina *(Nandina domestica)* complement the foliage and flowers of 'Yuletide.' Evergreens such as 'Little Gem' magnolias, boxwoods, monkey grass, Asian star jasmine *(Trachelospermum asiaticum)*, and autumn fern also make good companions.

For contrast, try using selections of oakleaf hydrangea *(Hydrangea quercifolia)* such as 'Snowflake,' 'Pee Wee,' and 'Snow Queen.' The late-fall color of the foliage and their chocolate brown, exfoliating bark go well with the blooms and leaves of 'Yuletide.' Other coarse-textured evergreens to use include fatsia *(Fatsia japonica)* and cast-iron plant *(Aspidistra elatior)*.

With its red and green holiday colors, 'Yuletide' mingles well with just about everything in the garden. So if your yard needs some Christmas cheer, consider this camellia.

GENE B. BUSSELL

A Tree for The Birds

Here's a great way to decorate for Christmas while encouraging more winged visitors.

Looking to add a little spice to your landscape for the holidays? Why not help your feathered friends by adorning a tree with tasty birdseed? This is a great activity for you and your children, and it brings more seasonal cheer to your yard.

The Feeding Tree

Use an existing outdoor tree, or buy one to put on your deck or patio. Pines work great and can be easily planted in the yard after the holidays if bought with the root ball intact. Make sure your tree gets plenty of water while it's a decoration so that it will adjust well when transplanted to your landscape. You can also use cedars, spruces, firs, or other young evergreens.

Adorning a tree with birdseed mimics how songbirds naturally eat; most prefer to feed above the ground while keeping an eye out for predators. So a decorated Christmas tree is an ideal feeding spot that will bring lots of life to your winter landscape. Use different types of seed to attract the greatest variety of birds.

Entertain the Kids

Making edible ornaments for birds is great fun for children who are home for the holidays. There are a number of easy projects that don't take much time or money.

Popcorn garlands: String popped kernels of unsalted popcorn together using heavy thread and a needle, and drape them over the branches. Add dabs of peanut butter to them for an even tastier treat. Or make a garland using inexpensive stiff ribbon threaded through O-shaped toasted cereal. Multicolored cereal makes even brighter decorations.

above: This Leyland cypress, decked with tasty treats for colorful songbirds, also makes a perfect holiday accent. Because food for birds is least abundant during winter, a decorative feeding tree is ideal at this time.

Goody baskets: Carefully cut orange or tangerine peels in half, and dry them until stiff. Punch three evenly spaced holes in the sides, and attach 8-inch-long ribbons to the holes. Hang the baskets from branches, and fill them with dried fruit, such as raisins, apples, or prunes.

Peanut butter pinecones: Heat peanut butter in the microwave or on the stovetop, and pour it into the crevices of a large pinecone. Tie thread to the tip of the cone, and hang it from a branch. Roll pinecone in raisins or nuts for an extra treat.

Creating these ornaments is a great way to encourage kids to learn about nature. Take some time to help children identify and appreciate the birdlife around them; it could begin a lifelong passion for bird watching.

EDWIN MARTY

FOODS BIRDS LOVE

Millet: ground-feeding birds such as doves or quail
Niger (thistle): finches
Sunflower seeds: cardinals, chickadees, and woodpeckers
Peanut butter: great for insect eaters such as bluebirds and Carolina wrens

left: The Winter Rose Series may cause a second glance. This poinsettia's apple-size bloom is a cluster of curly bracts with the yellow center inside. **below:** This selection is a deep rose color, befitting its name.

including rich crimson, deep rose, pink, white, and marbled.

Traditional Care

Despite its differences, Winter Rose's requirements are the same as those for other poinsettias. Keep your plant at its peak with a minimum of six hours of bright light. Avoid direct sun—place the plant where the sun's impact is slightly diffused. Poinsettias are tropical by nature; they prefer a warm room, protected from cold drafts and heat vents.

Dryness is the most likely culprit if leaves yellow and drop. Poinsettias prefer a moist environment, and soil will dry quickly in a warm home. If allowed to dehydrate, foliage will fall. To water this poinsettia properly, place the pot in a sink, and thoroughly wet the potting medium. Allow the plant to drain completely before you display it in a decorative container. Never let your plant sit in water.

Take a Look at Winter Rose

If you think poinsettias are ho-hum, check out this fresh introduction.

Poinsettias are synonymous with the season. Over the years, various colors have been introduced, offering an artist's palette of shades. Now the holiday icon comes in a different style. "For something really unusual in a poinsettia, the Winter Rose Series is a great choice," says Scot Thompson, owner of Southern Gardens, in Vestavia Hills, Alabama.

Developed by poinsettia specialists at the Paul Ecke Ranch in California, it has a very individual form. "The bloom has several layers of curly petals, with the center tucked down inside. The flower is small, about the size of a baseball," Scot says.

Special Qualities

As a grower, Scot has become familiar with this plant's personality. Dark green leaves are a handsome foil for the almost double flowers that are held erect on thick stems. "With Winter Rose, each plant may produce only three or four blooms, whereas other selections may give you up to a dozen," he says. "Because we don't get a large number of flowers, we have to put more plants in the pot to get a big bouquet. That means Winter Rose is going to be a little more expensive."

You'll find this fabulous hybrid available in a variety of colors,

Transportation Tips

We've all been there: You pick out the perfect poinsettia, only to break off one of its brittle branches while navigating the driveway or popping groceries into the car. Here are a few tips to help you get your plant home in one piece.

Gently lay the pot down on its side with the bottom pressed against the car's seat back. Snuggle several small packages or a towel around the container to prevent it from rolling. And be sure to protect your poinsettia from freezing temperatures; don't leave it out in the car while shopping.

ELLEN RUOFF RILEY

Naturally
Beautiful Decorations

Bring nature indoors with these surprisingly easy arrangements. This mother-daughter team shows you how.

I magine turning your mantel or table into a winter wonderland brimming with Christmas spirit. This delightful idea is demonstrated by Molly Courcelle and Bee Sieburg, owners of The Gardener's Cottage in Asheville, North Carolina. Turning to the mountains for inspiration, they put together fabulous arrangements in a disarmingly easy manner.

Don't let the opulent look intimidate you—the best way to approach arrangements is to explore them in small steps. Both the mantel at left and the table on page 216 feature combinations of potted plants. Cut flowers, berry-laden branches, and fresh fruit round out the look. "This is very easy to do," Bee assures us. "Start with the plants, and go from there. The arrangement almost leads you along."

Understand the way these collections go together, and adapt the materials to where you live. Amaryllis, paperwhites, and cut flowers are available throughout the South. Go for a mountain look as Bee and Molly have, or celebrate your own region with greenery and berried branches unique to your locale.

left: This magnificent mantel can be assembled in simple stages. It combines potted plants, cut greenery, and fresh blooms. **right:** Molly Courcelle (left) and Bee Sieburg take a blank canvas and fill it with mountain treasures.

The Mantel

"We want the area over the fireplace to be a natural, casual reflection of the mountains," Bee says. Red is at the center of their palette, and they weave it through the arrangement. "When you pick a color, you're not limited to just flowers. You have plants, fruit, and berries to choose from as well," she continues.

Purchase potted plants in 4- and 5-inch containers, including ferns with soft foliage and ivy with long hanging tendrils. Use flowering kalanchoes and begonias,

BY ELLEN RUOFF RILEY / PHOTOGRAPHY JEAN ALLSOPP

above: You don't have to use the traditional red-and-green color scheme to create Christmas charm. This room is decked out in blue and green.

MOLLY'S TIPS

Whether you've been arranging flowers for eons or are brand new to the endeavor, Molly's tips are terrific.

■ Use different shapes and textures. Group similar forms—such as amaryllis blooms and apples, which are both smooth and rounded.

■ Begin with something large and solid, such as an amaryllis, or a collection of items, such as the concrete birds on the sideboard.

■ Include elements that will add texture and give a sense of flow. This can be achieved with potted ferns, trailing ivy, lush moss, or cut greenery.

■ Introduce items with strong lines, such as holly branches or bittersweet.

"All of these things complement each other very well," Molly says. "Your eye will land on a solid item, follow the texture, and move on to a linear item. It gives the arrangement order."

and add forced amaryllis bulbs for large, regal flowers.

"Begin by putting your plants on the mantel. Lay some on their sides so they're looking at you," Bee instructs. Use this potted material to determine the arrangement's length. Bee and Molly's creation extends the mantel's full span, but you can do it on a smaller scale. Some ferns need constant moisture, so slip their roots into sandwich bags containing soil to keep them damp. Place weighty plants toward the back for stability.

Next, center a moist florist foam bar—a long, narrow piece of florist foam wrapped in plastic—among the potted plants. Add greenery from the garden, using branches of various heights. "We cut cedar, pine, and other greens from the yard and used ivy with long tendrils too," Bee says.

Now, add cut flowers, fruit, and berried branches. Choose plants with sturdy stems, such as hydrangeas, roses, and ornamental cabbage. "Group items with similar shapes," Molly says. Push stems into the florist foam, placing some so blooms come over the mantel's edge. Attach

red apples with florist picks, clustering them for impact. "Just keep the whole thing loose," Bee says.

Table With a Theme

Molly and Bee use the same steps to put together a centerpiece. The homeowner's passion for birds is the focus of the dining room decor. "We want the room to be personal, so we use birds' nests, tiny eggs, and garden ornaments," Bee says. The arrangement meanders down the table, with fresh moss covering the pots and the florist foam bar. Paperwhites, ranunculus, ornamental cabbage, and ferns combine with lichen-covered branches for the look of a winter garden.

The sideboard takes simplicity into the realm of casual elegance. Garden ornaments flock around a bowl of green apples, and the ferns on the sideboard connect it to the table.

"Anyone can do this," Bee says. "When you're working with beautiful materials, you can't mess up. There are a ton of ways you can express your own style and feeling."

With a vote of confidence like that, we should all give it a try.

right: Nests, paperwhites, cut ornamental cabbage, and twigs nestle in a blanket of fresh green moss. **below:** The dining room decorations reflect the homeowner's interest in birds. The table arrangement, chandelier, and sideboard decor continue the woodland theme.

'Knock Out' Rose
(See page 225.)

Favorites

A Garden to Share

Look behind this small cottage where friendship and flowers bloom.

A garden should be a place where friends gather, a place that invites you in no matter what the season. Most importantly, it should reflect the personality of its owner. This is certainly true at Dan Franklin's small, in-town Atlanta home. You see, this garden is as colorful as the man himself.

I'll never forget the first time I met Dan. My wife, Aimee, and I were just married and had moved into a little house in Atlanta. One Saturday afternoon, I was trying to pull an old stump from the middle of the front yard, when out of nowhere this gentleman appeared. He introduced himself, told me it was about time someone pulled "that blasted eyesore" out of the yard, and let me know that his garden is open at five o'clock on Saturdays for cocktails. As quickly as he appeared, he was off. I stood there dumbfounded, thinking I had offended him. But how could I have? I had hardly said a word. Little did I know that this brief encounter would begin a long-lasting friendship.

Some weeks later, I mustered the courage to wander down the street and knock on Dan's front door at the appointed hour. His greeting was only to direct me to go around back and wait for him. As I walked around the side of the house, still thinking I'd offended him, the most glorious garden opened up. I would have never imagined that this small cottage would be home to such a wonderful garden.

As time passed, many things in my life changed, but I always looked forward to my Saturday afternoons at Dan's. We would discuss the politics of the day, I learned about what Atlanta used to be like, and almost as if through chance, I came to appreciate good landscaping and the beauty of wonderful flowers.

Dan's Design

This garden is amazingly simple. It's essentially a series of overlapping rectangles. You step from his back door onto a cobblestone patio, then up four steps to a rectangular lawn that's bordered by perennial and annual beds. Pots sitting on large square stones punctuate the corners of the lawn. In spring, pansies offer color, but Dan soon adds geraniums to carry the containers into summer. On axis with the steps, the rectangular fountain capped with a limestone ball adds a focal point at the end of the small lawn. Finally, the white lattice fence helps to define the formal part of the garden. Outside the fence, Dan has left the plants and design much more natural, providing a buffer between him and his neighbors.

On the highest point of the garden is "Franklin's Outhouse." The front and half of both sides are screened so bugs stay out, but the back is solid for privacy. Inside Dan has added comfortable chairs, a ceiling fan, and electricity for light so he and friends can enjoy the garden on hot summer evenings and during spring showers.

Dan salvaged elements from the wrecking ball of progress to incorporate into his garden. The cobblestones

above: Derick Belden and Dan Franklin
right: A lattice fence borders one side of a flowerbed with a cobblestone edge on the other. The double row of cobbles is set at lawn height for a mowing edge. The bed brims with Dutch iris, white tulips, poppies, and pansies.

BY DERICK BELDEN
PHOTOGRAPHY ALLEN ROKACH
STYLING LISA POWELL

top: The fountain is essentially a rectangular basin with a limestone ball perched on a stone pedestal. Water recirculates from the basin up the back of the ball, cascading back down into the basin.
above, left: Franklin's Outhouse is on the highest point in the garden. **left:** An ancient millstone serves as a landing for the steps to Franklin's Outhouse. **above, right:** A naturalized path with a lattice fence on one side offers a nice woodland walk and is a good buffer between the garden and neighboring yards.

came from an old house being torn down, and the steps were crafted from curbing found at demolition projects around town. Finally the stone ball on the fountain was salvaged from a nearby house.

Even new elements are built from easy-to-find materials using simple construction methods. The fence is made of 6 x 6 posts, 2 x 4s, 1 x 2s, and 4- x 8-foot lattice panels. And the walls Dan designed to help transition grades around the garden are common cinder block with a stucco finish.

Continuous Blooms

While Dan's genius lies in simple design, his passion is for plants. Anchoring the walk up to Franklin's Outhouse and in the corners of the flowerbeds are English boxwoods. Florida flame azaleas *(Rhododendron austrinum)* reach out over the stone patio, and a hedge of 'Mrs. G. G. Gerbing' azaleas lines one side. At the rear of the lot is a bottlebrush buckeye *(Aesculus parviflora)*, known to bear 18-inch-long, yellowish-white blooms. Other unique plants in the garden are a 40-foot-tall yellow wood and a tree-form Japanese plum yew.

The flowerbeds provide a symphony of color throughout the year. Dan has used perennials and bulbs to minimize maintenance. Starting in early spring with jonquils and narcissus, the garden transitions into full-blown spring with white tulips, Dutch iris, yellow flag iris, 'Newport Pink' sweet William, orange poppies, and foxgloves. Carrying it into summer are peonies, Shasta daisies, caladiums, cleomes, black-eyed Susans, bearded iris, perennial begonias, Japanese iris, reseeding impatiens, Oriental lilies, and garden phlox. In fall, goldenrod, asters, and sedum add seasonal color.

Time Well Spent

It's amazing how favorite places leave lasting impressions. Nearly 10 years after I first met Dan, I always try to build in some time to see him and his garden when in Atlanta. It's almost as if I'd never left. In fact, you'll see a bit of Dan's garden in my own. I've got a similar rectangular lawn, English boxwoods, 'Mrs. G. G. Gerbing' azaleas, and even a small bottlebrush buckeye that was a gift from Dan. Still, no matter how hard I try, there's nothing like the original. And that's what both Dan and his garden are—true Southern originals. ◆

Our Editors' Favorite Tips

Southern Living experts share a few of their secrets for success with plants.

Lawns
Steve Bender

▪ Water less often, but water well. Instead of watering for 15 to 20 minutes every day, do so for one to two hours once a week. Quick and frequent watering results in shallow-rooted turf that's prone to disease and croaks in a drought. Infrequent, thorough watering gives you healthy, deeply rooted turf that resists drought.

▪ Okay, I know it's Saturday morning, but surely there's something else to do before the sports come on besides scalping your lawn. Cutting it near ground level may make you feel manly and purposeful, but it's terrible for grass. It turns the lawn brown, so you have to immediately drown it with water. Afterward, the grass grows like crazy, so you're soon out there scalping again. This also increases problems with weeds, insects, and diseases. So cut off no more than the top one-third of the grass blades in any one mowing. If you need to feel manly, lift weights.

Annuals and Perennials
Gene B. Bussell

▪ When planting cell packs of annuals in borders, beds, or containers, keep a bucket of water nearby. With the plants still in the plastic packet, submerge the six-pack, and let it soak up water. Then remove the packet from the bucket, and allow it to drain before planting. Now you can loosen the roots with less damage, and the flowers will transition into soil better.

▪ Hanging baskets can be a bargain, as they may have more plants than you think. Purchase a basket with multiple plants, and when you get home, divide and repot. You'll save money and give your plants room to grow at the same time.

▪ By midsummer, some annuals have become tall, lanky, and less productive. It's time to cut them back. Water,

Vines such as this white mandevilla look great in hanging baskets. Buy a basket that's brimming with plants, and divide it into several containers to save money.

cut back by one-third, and apply a slow-release 14-14-14 fertilizer, such as Osmocote. Soon your plants will be covered with blooms again.

Watering
Edwin Marty

▪ Because most plants can't take up nutrients without water, dry soil actually starves them. Roots also need air to function properly. If soil is too wet, the tiny air pockets that allow oxygen to reach roots will collapse, causing them to rot. So let the top couple of inches dry out between waterings to allow air to penetrate the soil but still provide roots with moisture.

▪ If leaves begin to droop or if the tips start to turn brown, chances are the plant is not receiving enough water. Check the soil regularly to ensure plants are getting their needs met.

Vegetables
Charlie Thigpen

▪ Select a sunny site. Fruiting plants, such as tomatoes, prefer eight hours of sun daily, while leafy crops, such as lettuce, can get by with five to six hours.

▪ If you have poor or clay soil, add organic matter. Till it into the soil to a depth of 10 to 12 inches. Dehydrated cow manure can also be mixed into the soil to make it rich and fertile. If the ground is soggy, create a raised bed, which can be filled with topsoil to improve drainage.

▪ Make sure that your garden is located close to a water source. Dragging hoses all summer will get old very quickly. Lay soaker hoses down each row so that you can connect them to a hose bib and water efficiently. Spread a thick layer of mulch around your plants to keep out weeds and hold in moisture.

Cut Flowers
Ellen Ruoff Riley

▪ Gather blooms in the coolest parts of the day. Take a container of warm water to the garden, and place each cut stem immediately into it. Always snip directly above a set of leaves. If the plant is a rebloomer, this will force additional buds. Choose flowers with buds just beginning to unfurl.

▪ Indoors, recut stems at a diagonal. Place them in a bucket of fresh water in a cool, dark place for several hours or overnight. The fresh cut on the stems, cool temperatures, and darkness let flowers take up more water.

▪ Needle-holders are great to keep on hand. These weighted metal devices have sharp prongs to hold cut stems in place. Florist clay is also a must. A tiny piece under a needle-holder anchors it effectively in a vase.

To learn more of Ellen's tips on flower arranging, read "Quick, Simple Flowers" on the following page. ◆

right: Combine packaged bouquets with elements from your garden. **far right:** Look for flower and color repetition. This bouquet contains numerous yellow mums, red roses, and a leaf from an iron cross begonia houseplant. **below:** Four carnations, a pair of broad leaves, and a petite vase come together in an easy composition.

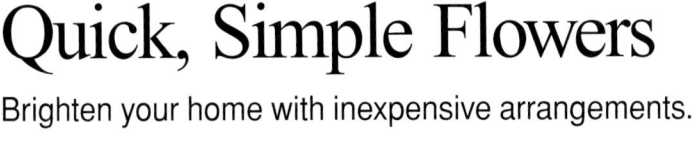

Quick, Simple Flowers

Brighten your home with inexpensive arrangements.

The beauty of flowers is that they don't have to be complicated, fancy, or expensive to work their magic. A packaged bouquet or several stems from a floral display are guaranteed to bring a smile.

The grocery store is a great source for fresh, affordable blooms. Choose bouquets with a color scheme suitable for your home and with multiple stems of the same flower. Avoid rainbow medleys containing only one of each type blossom—such assortments are difficult to arrange. And always ask for a packet of flower food.

Get Started

At home, separate your bouquet's contents. Throw away baby's breath and glossy, green leatherleaf foliage, grouping your remaining flowers by color and kind to assess your goods.

Next, condition your flowers to extend their lives. With sharp scissors, cut each stem at a steep angle, and put it in a container of tepid water mixed with flower food. Soak for several hours or overnight prior to arranging.

Go to the garden for greenery. This transforms a store-bought bouquet into a personal collection. Choose branches of delicate emerging leaves, boxwood tips, and foliage from perennials such as Lenten rose and Italian arum. Indoors, look to your houseplants for an interesting touch.

What's in a Vase

The best investment in flower arranging is not the blooms but the vessel. Bigger is not always better—a vase with a small opening requires few flowers and is easy to style. Choose one that complements your home.

Begin with a clean vase filled with fresh water. Remember this rule: Don't agonize over each addition. Recut the stems, and cluster like

above: Five white chrysanthemums are clustered for impact, while Japanese maple branches and Italian arum from the garden fill out this arrangement.

flowers together for maximum effect. Add greenery for height, texture, and fullness. If you spend more than five minutes placing the elements, you're missing the point.

Flowers are fun. Practice in small scale, and don't be intimidated by inexperience. With fresh blossoms, you can't go wrong.   ELLEN RUOFF RILEY

This Rose Is a Knockout

Meet our pick for the South's best landscape rose.
It blooms nonstop and never needs spraying.

When it comes to evaluating new plants, Garden Editors Gene Bussell, Charlie Thigpen, and I aren't exactly spring chickens. (We're more like summer turkeys.) It takes a lot to impress us. But impressed we were as we toured the production fields at Monrovia nursery in Azusa, California, looking for superior plants to add to our *Southern Living* Plant Collection. One in particular completely floored us—the aptly named 'Knock Out' rose.

Showers of Flowers

This All-America Selections winner might very well be the best landscape rose in existence. Three traits combine to win it high praise throughout the South. First, large clusters of lightly fragrant, cherry red flowers bloom from spring until the first hard frost in fall. Gardeners in the Coastal and Tropical South can expect year-round blooms. Second, it forms a compact, bushy shrub about 3 to 4 feet tall and wide. This makes it ideal for planting in containers, mixing with annuals and perennials in a border, or growing in a sweep as a low, informal hedge. Finally—and this is big—it never needs spraying for black spot. You don't have to drench it in fungicide every 10 days to keep its deep green foliage looking good.

Tips for a Fast Start

Like almost all roses, 'Knock Out' prefers full sun. In partial sun, it produces fewer flowers. It also likes moist, fertile, well-drained soil. Prior to planting, dig a hole as deep as the root ball and at least three times as wide. Work in lots of organic matter, such as garden compost, chopped

right: 'Knock Out' rose's compact, bushy shape and constant color make it a great companion for annuals, perennials, and bulbs in a mixed border.

'KNOCK OUT' ROSE
At a Glance

Size: 3 to 4 feet high and wide
Light: full sun
Soil: moist, fertile, well drained
Water: thoroughly during dry spells
Prune: late winter
Blooms: continuously in mild, warm weather
Spraying for black spot: not necessary
Range: throughout the South

leaves, composted manure, sphagnum peat moss, or ground bark. As you're working up the soil, mix in some slow-release rose fertilizer (available at any local nursery or home center) at the rate recommended on the label.

Remove the rose from its nursery pot, and place the plant in the center of the hole, so the top of the root ball is even with the soil surface. If the outer roots are wrapped tightly around the ball, use a pencil or stick to loosen them gently. Fill in around the ball with amended soil, tamp lightly with your foot to firm the soil, and then water thoroughly. Finally, cover the top of the root ball with a 1- to 2-inch layer of mulch.

Though an established plant tolerates drought, you'll get a much better show if you water regularly. Apply slow-release rose food each spring, along with two or three drinks of water-soluble blossom-booster fertilizer during the summer. Prune in late winter to reduce the plant's size or remove any dead wood.

'Knock Out' rose is just one of nearly 200 trees, shrubs, vines, perennials, fruits, and ornamental grasses that make up the *Southern Living* Plant Collection from Monrovia. Call 1-888-752-6848 for a participating garden center near you. Don't let your neighbors beat you to the punch.

STEVE BENDER

PHOTOGRAPHS: VAN CHAPLIN

above: Daily walks have become brighter for this family on a morning stroll.
left: Not all alleys are created equal. The typical one is accented by more trash cans than flowers.

Color Comes to an Alley

One gardener's abundance is a neighborhood's treasure.

Alleyways have a tendency to attract unsavory characters, things we'd rather our guests not see. Luckily for this Virginia neighborhood, one gardener's leftover plants helped to transform a typical alley into a flower-filled destination.

Calder Loth began taking care of

Calder deadheads his coneflowers to encourage an even more prolific bloom.

the alley that runs beside his home shortly after he moved into Richmond's Fan District 26 years ago. He started by simply mowing the grass and picking up trash but was eventually motivated to test a psychological hypothesis: "If something is taken care of, people will respect it." Using plants he divided or removed from his own garden, Calder began reclaiming the space between his fence and the gravel alleyway. By plugging in cannas, hostas, four o'clocks, and lilies, he created a bustling border of color and fragrance and quickly replaced the stark emptiness that had been a magnet for trash and neglect.

After a few years of "guerrilla" gardening in the alley, Calder noticed a marked change in the way the space was used. Instead of avoiding the alley, dog walkers and garden enthusiasts made it a destination. A stack of letters from neighbors attests to this trend. A fellow alley resident has even pro-

vided the most sincere flattery by joining him in his project. Between the two gardeners' work, they now have nearly 100 yards of alleyway planted in perennials and annuals.

How It All Started

Like many gardeners passionate about plants, Calder utilized every available corner of his small Richmond yard. He then leased an adjacent lot to continue realizing his gardening aspirations. Eventually, this also became crowded with colorful plants and unique garden structures. So he began again to look for homes for his excess plants. With a firm belief that "people have a right to use open space," he began transplanting surplus plants into the alley.

This quickly became a spectacular border of hollyhocks, caladiums, and hostas. The majority of plants used in the alley garden came directly from Calder's yard either as cuttings, bulbs, or transplants. However, because the alley provided a location with quite a bit more sun than the inner garden, he has been able to add sun-loving plants such as ornamental grass and coneflowers *(Rudbeckia nitida)*.

![Calder's plants float over and under the fence separating his yard from the alley.](#)

Calder's plants float over and under the fence separating his yard from the alley.

ears and perilla add texture and seasonal foliage color. Hollyhocks, cannas, and daylilies provide a big splash of spring and summer color.

All of these plants hold up fairly well with a limited amount of maintenance, and they also fit another of Calder's requirements—the ability to withstand community grazing. As in most public gardens, people act like insects, honing in on flowers with spectacular color and fragrance. Before long, the most desirable blooms find new homes in neighbors' vases. So start with plants that don't lend themselves to picking, or use reblooming flowers. That way you'll be more likely to keep all that spring color clear through summer.

The final suggestion Calder offers for an alley garden has more than a touch of irony. The transformation of a neglected alleyway into a spectacular public garden has increased foot traffic as well as the frequency of dog walking. However, what the dogs find attractive about the alley garden is a bit different from what the people find attractive. Therefore, he suggests using plants that are as dog proof as possible, avoiding annual bedding plants or edibles in the border. Because if you plant it, the dogs will come.   EDWIN MARTY

One of the advantages of using pass-along plants is the relative lack of maintenance. While the soil on the edge is certainly not desirable, it has been just good enough to allow the plants to survive without much more than a spring dose of slow-release plant food, such as Osmocote, and some hand-watering during droughts.

The City of Richmond regularly grades and applies gravel to such alleys but otherwise lets the neighborhoods of the Fan District do what they please with the areas. A number of formal community gardens exist in Richmond, either utilizing open space as Calder does or making arrangements with the city to take

> ## "If something is taken care of, people will respect it."
> —*Calder Loth*

over abandoned lots. Other neighborhoods are also taking note of his activities and planting alley gardens.

Calder's advice for those who want to reclaim an area through gardening is simple. The easiest way to keep an open space free of trash is to make it look beautiful. The rest comes naturally.

Plants That Make a Difference

While every region has plants ideally suited for its environment, Calder has found a number that seem to withstand Richmond's weather extremes and harsh alley conditions. Caladiums, hostas, and ferns create a solid border that seems to thrive despite neglect and competition. Then lamb's

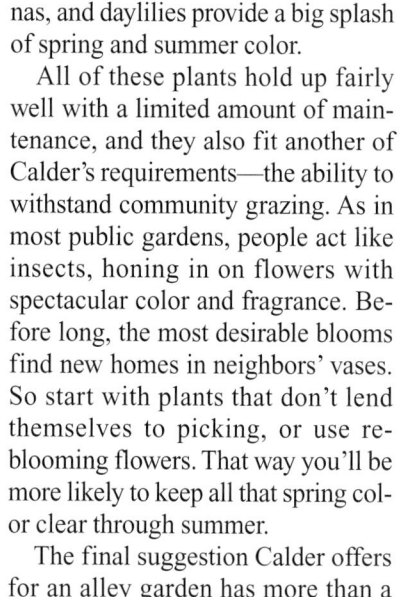

Daylilies and other flowers invite neighbors to enjoy the alley.

PINK SKULLCAP
At a Glance

Soil: any well-drained
Water: minimal
Sun: full sun to partial shade
Bloom: March to November
Range: Middle, Lower, and Coastal South

left: Loaded with pink flowers, mounds of skullcap soften steps of native limestone. This perennial can take Southern summers in stride.

Skullcap–A Tough Perennial

Pert and pink, this plant blooms vigorously all summer.

Up close, the flowers look flushed with excitement and ready to tackle garden boredom. From a distance, they turn into a handsome crocheted edging of matte green and dark rose. The neat, 8-inch-high mounds of spunky flowers are excellent in a low border, along a pathway, or in a rock garden. You have to appreciate the persistent, colorful energy and amazing toughness of these little perennials that bloom from early spring to frost.

Good drainage and sunlight are really the only requirements for success with pink skullcap *(Scutellaria suffrutescens)*. Once established, it will stay in bloom even through a drought, so there's nothing delicate about this perennial. If skullcap gets too woody or sprawls more than 15 inches wide, make it a little bushier with a trim in spring before the blooming season really gets going. Other than that, there isn't much you can do for such a tough little customer. It simply doesn't need coddling.

Pink skullcap socializes in the border with hardy, long-season bloomers such as gaura, lantana, Mexican oregano *(Poliomintha longiflora)*, salvia, and purple coneflower. In containers, skullcap's gray-tinged foliage and rich pink flowers bring out subtle shades hidden in agaves and other succulents.

Treat your skullcap well, and it will bloom happily. Abuse it with heat and neglect, and it will still bloom happily. So go ahead and try it. Make your day. ◆

Amazing Grace

Seasons may pass, and so may people, but the spirits of loved ones endure in flowers.

The Bible says we came from a garden. Perhaps it is to there that we long to return. These are my thoughts as I gaze in astonishment upon an old family cemetery outside Newnan, Georgia. Hundreds—no, thousands—of flowers rise in a chorus beside time-etched gravestones, as if to sing of all the joys, hopes, heartaches, and memories that human hands could not chisel into epitaphs.

The flowers serenade George and Liz Tedder, who bought land containing the cemetery and an old house 20 years ago. The cemetery was in need of attention. A rusting iron gate was all that remained of the ornate fence that once enclosed the hallowed ground. Beneath the stones lie 23 members of the Arnold family, most laid to rest in the mid-1800s.

The house and grounds were devoid of landscaping. So Liz created a series of beautiful gardens, but the thought remained that one day she'd restore the cemetery to its former dignity. In the meantime, George kept it tidy, mowing the grass around the stones and trimming the weeds.

Freeing the Flowers

Then a few springs ago, as George prepared to mow, Liz spied gladiolus foliage between the stones. "I told George 'We're not going to cut the cemetery this year; let's just see what happens,'" she recalls. Hundreds of hardy gladioli, also known as Byzantine gladioli *(Gladiolus byzantinum)*,

burst up through the soil. Spires of pink, rose, and magenta blossoms warmly hugged the graves.

Who had planted them? Probably an Arnold, marking the passing of a loved one. All those years, the glads' bulblike corms multiplied underground, unseen and untended, waiting for a day that would set them free. Apparently, their leaves had survived the mower just long enough each year to give them the strength they needed to survive and reproduce.

Legions of blue and white bachelor's buttons *(Centaurea cyanus)* now accompany the glads. These old-fashioned annuals bloom in spring and summer, drop their seeds, die in fall, and then sprout from seed the next spring. They were found in a country ditch and brought home for the wedding of Liz's daughter. Afterward, she threw the flowers in the compost pile, where the plants gave rise to thousands of offspring. Slowly, surely, they marched to the cemetery.

Liz still hopes to restore the cemetery. She has a way to go but is confident she'll reach her goal. In the meantime, the cemetery continues to bloom. "Descendants of the Arnolds visit occasionally, and they're so happy I'm taking care of it," Liz says. I'll bet those long-gone Arnolds are happy too.   STEVE BENDER

above: Hardy gladioli bloom gloriously each spring. **left:** For years, a carpet of neatly mowed grass surrounded the stones in this old family cemetery. When the mowing stopped, thousands of flowers revealed themselves.

Taller, darker 'May Night' and shorter, paler 'Blue Hill' grace Boone Hall Plantation's blue-and-yellow border.

Set the Scene with Salvia

For reliable garden performance minus the prima donna attitude,
choose 'Blue Hill' salvia or one of its close kin.

At South Carolina's Boone Hall Plantation in Mount Pleasant, gardener Ruth Knopf is an expert at casting flowers in their finest roles. Among her favorites for "Best Supporting Bloomers" is *Salvia superba*. Selections she has used include 'Blue Hill' and 'May Night' in the blue-and-yellow border and 'Snow Hill' in the white border.

"They don't make big, solid masses of color," Ruth explains, "but if you deadhead them, cutting off the spent bloom stalks, they just keep blooming from spring till frost. These are good all-season plants."

With budget limitations and lots of flowerbeds to keep full, Ruth faces many of the same problems that plague the average gardener. She prizes plants, such as 'Blue Hill,' that give their best performance with minimal pampering and cost. In her Boone Hall garden, raised beds help with drainage and keep roots healthy even with heavy rains. A winter top-dressing of dehydrated cow manure or compost, plus biannual mulching

with pine straw, keeps soil fertile. In spring, Ruth scatters a slow-release fertilizer such as Osmocote over the garden; that's the only other feeding.

"We just don't have any problems with these salvias," Ruth says. "They take the heat. They die to the ground in winter, but they've come back reliably every year since I planted them."

Ruth's tip to keep salvias at their best is simple. "If they look ratty in July, cut them back nearly all the way," she says. "Leave a few inches of stem with some foliage, and they'll be beautiful all fall."

Not every plant can be a superstar, but flowers such as 'Blue Hill' and the other *S. superba* selections hold every scene together. If you want your garden to put on a fabulous show, add some of these pretty and reliable salvias to the cast. LIZ DRUITT

SALVIA SUPERBA
At a Glance

Size: 1 to 3 feet high and wide
Bloom season: spring through frost, with deadheading
Soil: well drained, if possible
Light: full sun to light shade
Water: moderate
Fertilizer: minimal
Range: Upper, Middle, Lower, and Coastal South

'Snow Hill' (center), a sport of 'Blue Hill,' keeps up the family tradition beautifully in the white border.

One Easy Iris

Japanese roof iris make an attractive ground cover, but they're really too pretty to be classified as just that. This perennial will cover the garden at a speedy rate, and its spiky foliage provides interesting texture.

These iris *(Iris tectorum)* are a cinch to grow. (They are actually grown on rooftops in Japan, hence the name.) They prefer a fertile, moist, and slightly acid soil. They'll grow in sun or shade but bloom more in a sunny site. The neatly arranged foliage works well with hostas and ferns in naturalized areas and woodland settings. Mass plantings under deciduous shrubs, such as hydrangeas or native azaleas, look great too. They can also be used in containers.

Leaves have an exotic look, rising 10 to 12 inches tall and growing in a fan or whorled arrangement. New foliage stands straight, creating a jagged look, and old foliage flops or curls.

Blooms are about 5 inches across and appear in April and May on 10- to 12-inch stems. Each stem usually produces two or more blue or white blooms. The blue flowers vary from dark to pale; the white ones are pure white with yellow centers.

Don't remove spent blooms. Seedpods will appear where flowers have bloomed and can be collected in midsummer once they've turned brown. Pods have seeds, which can be sown in the garden or containers. Bury them about ¼ inch deep in loose soil. Seedlings emerge in a few months.

If you don't care to mess with seeds, your plants will still multiply. Established plants have creeping rhizomes that spread and form clumps, which can be divided. With the ability to multiply by seed and rhizomes, these iris will naturalize in the garden.

Many flowering plants bloom and have little to offer the garden once their flowers are spent. But Japanese roof iris just keep on giving by creating a leafy mass that covers the garden's floor. CHARLIE THIGPEN

PHOTOGRAPHS: VAN CHAPLIN

The exotic-looking leaves of Japanese roof iris produce a unique ground cover in this landscape. Beautiful white or blue flowers are a delightful bonus topping these spiky plants.

JAPANESE ROOF IRIS
At a Glance

Height: 10 to 12 inches
Flowers: blue or white, 3 to 5 inches across
Location: sun to partial shade, slightly acid, well-drained soil
Range: Upper, Middle, and Lower South

Go Outside and Play

Edith Eddleman allows her spirit to frolic in a garden overflowing with perennials.

If the ever-ready grin has vanished from Edith Eddleman's face, it's because she is waiting straight-faced for the moment to unfold for a guest. Her garden is for her delight, but of equal measure is the joy it brings visitors. Here Edith has fun, and the fact it amuses others makes it even better.

This garden designer has studied in England, toured gardens nationally and internationally, fulfilled commissions and presented lectures throughout the country, and been quoted and published in garden periodicals and books. But, despite her vast experience on the serious side of gardening, Edith is remarkably free in her own Durham, North Carolina, backyard. She admits, "There is a difference between my professional life and personal life." No rules of popular taste prevail here. If something pleases her, she probably needs several more. That's how it's been with the gazing globes that seem to have seeded about the garden in many colors and sizes.

Her original one was purchased 21 years ago as a joke, but it started her down a whimsical garden path. As the curator of the perennial border at the JC Raulston Arboretum at North Carolina State University, she set out to horrify then-director JC Raulston by placing a gazing globe, long a focus of condescension, as the centerpiece of his parterre garden—just in time for a tour group. "That was the same night that the flamingos made their first appearance in the perennial border," Edith recalls.

What began as mischief became a way of life. "JC tried to use reverse psychology, pretending that he liked them," she says. "But because I knew what he was up to, I just kept doing it. And he gradually came to like them!"

Edith didn't put these mirrored balls on predictable plastic or

PHOTOGRAPHS: VAN CHAPLIN

above, left: Edith Eddleman playfully arranges objects of her desire: gazing globes, spiral stakes, and dragonflies. **top, right:** Edith and collaborators Amanda (standing) and Mariah **above, right:** Nodding to folk art tradition, Edith created a bottle tree.

concrete pedestals in the center of the lawn. She accented existing colors in the plantings and nestled them into perennials to prompt a double take. They appeared to float in the tall ornamental grasses. Gazing globes reached new heights on pedestals of Edith's innovation.

Meanwhile, she also planted and nurtured her own garden, which boasts robust clumps of color that grow 8 feet tall or more by summer's end. "When you have plants the size of the ones in my garden, you need a lot a gazing balls," she instructs. "I am of the more-is-better school of thought.

"I realized that having them on the ground meant they would vanish in summer when the garden grew up. So if I wanted to see them, I had to put them up, hence the PVC pipe." Edith recommends using black PVC so the gazing globes appear to levitate. (She uses black spray paint to cover the yellow lettering.)

In her backyard, Edith is free from the constraints of popular opinion, so other spheres such as roof ventilators were put in place, adding the dimension of movement. Tin finials salvaged from Philadelphia row houses were set atop posts.

One of the latest innovations came with the help of her young neighbors Amanda and Mariah Dahill-Moore. Edith discovered that swimming pool noodles had holes in the center, allowing her to place them atop short pieces of concrete rebar stuck into the soil. Edith, Amanda, and Mariah made noodle sculptures in the garden, creating arches where rose-covered arbors might have stood.

Gardens have been recognized for their impact on both mental and physical well-being, but the truth came home to Edith when she learned the role her own had played. "When my friend's daughter was very sick," Edith remembers "they would come for consultations at Duke [University Medical Center] and then come over here and walk around the garden laughing." Her friend's daughter got better. "We don't know that laughter did it, but it didn't hurt," she says.

above: By midsummer when phlox is the major player in the garden, pink, purple, and blue ornaments prevail.

top: This red gazing globe is ready to spring from its pedestal.
above: Swimming pool noodles are a new addition to Edith's garden. With them came a colorful, oversize interpretation of the plant called horsetail.

Today, visitors to the garden laugh at Edith's flamingos—Cleopatra and her court, the Statue of Liberty, and Carmen Miranda. Another source of amusement is an assortment of things that are large or tiny. The gnome village has a life of its own. Then there is a salute to Georgia O'Keeffe—towering flowers made of streetlight reflectors. Edith explains, "Georgia O'Keeffe painted flowers really big. I decided we can make things really large because it pleases us. And that is what all this is about. I am offended by people who say, 'Obviously you were just trying to do this or that.' I want to kick them. I am just having fun!" LINDA C. ASKEY

Miss Eudora's Morning Glory

A novice gardener and writer gathers seeds of inspiration from Eudora Welty.

Like magic beans, the tiny black seeds tumbled into my hand, and I gasped out loud—right there in my flowerbed. Off and on for weeks, I had pulled and stored a green seedpod or two from the morning glory engulfing a too-small trellis in my garden, but something just didn't look right. Finally, with the luck of a novice, I accidentally got it right, pulling a pod that was dry and brown. It crumbled in my hand, spilling its ebony cargo into my palm.

These were no ordinary seeds, for they had come from the garden of Eudora Welty. A friend of mine had attended a garden symposium in Mississippi, where guests received a gift of seeds from a morning glory that belonged to Miss Eudora. (That's what I have affectionately and presumptuously called her since graduate school, when I studied her novels for my master's thesis.) Knowing how much I revere her work, my friend gave the seeds to me, offered a few planting tips, and reminded me to harvest new seeds once the morning glory had finished its show.

Now, here I stood in the scrappy flowerbed that was supposed to have been a symphony of flowering shrubs, vines, annuals, and perennials, feeling completely unworthy of Miss Eudora's morning glory. Gardening references pop up like daffodils all over her stories, and I feel sure that she would've been appalled at my scrawny rosebushes, poorly pruned gardenia, and, yes, out-of-control morning glory.

Although I never met the grande dame of Southern letters, I cannot bear the thought of a disapproving glance from Miss Eudora.

She's one of the main reasons I've always wanted not just to write, but to write in such a way that makes people think, feel, and remember; that makes them laugh and cry at the same time; and that makes them see that the ordinary lives of ordinary people are, at the end of the day, extraordinary. I look at the way she captured her native Mississippi on paper, and I long to fill books with my own unforgettable people and places, etched on the page in the red clay of my Alabama home.

So, like other writers, I attempt, I fail, I try again. I throw away three pages for every one I keep. I waver between wanting everyone to read what I've done and praying that no one *ever* sees it.

Truth be told, I garden the same way. I long for the vibrant roses, willowy borders of phlox, and giant begonias that my mother and aunts seem to grow so easily. I try my best to heed their wise horticultural counsel. I plant. I water. I celebrate success. (Or I plant. I forget to water. I mourn the loss.) I can't wait for the women of the family to see my hydrangeas—but I hope they don't drop in before I can get rid of that hanging basket showcasing a wilted petunia and a cluster of weeds.

I guess you could say that gardening, like writing, is an adventure. Both require a leap of faith, a willingness to try to create something out of nothing. Both have as much to teach through failure as through success. Both hold out the promise of a special kind of beauty that is, in a word, matchless. On behalf of writers and gardeners everywhere, Miss Eudora, thank you for that promise.   VALERIE FRASER

letters to our garden editors

I love hydrangeas and wonder if they would make a good hedge to go around my yard.
DELTA DATSIS
IUKA, MISSISSIPPI

A hydrangea hedge might work, as long as you don't plan on clipping it. Heavy pruning of hydrangeas results in few blooms. Keep in mind that hydrangeas lose their leaves in winter. If you're counting on the hedge for year-round screening, you should plant evergreen shrubs instead.

When is the best time to prune camellias? How should it be done?
JIM KERR
MARIETTA, GEORGIA

Camellias don't need much pruning, but if you have to, late spring is a good time. Prune individual branches back to a leaf, bud, or another branch. Use hand pruners or loppers, but never a hedge trimmer. Remove wayward branches, rubbing or crossing branches, and dead wood. Unless training them to grow flat against a wall, prune to maintain their natural, rounded form.

Nothing seems to grow in the shade of two large water oaks in my front yard. Can you give me a few suggestions of things I could plant that would give this area some color?
GLENDA BASS
MONTGOMERY, ALABAMA

Certainly. Probably the two surest sources of color in the shade for the South are impatiens and caladiums. Both come in a wide variety of colors and will put on a show as long as you give them decent soil and regular waterings. You'll have to plant new ones each spring, however. So you might want to consider perennial plants with colorful foliage. Good choices include 'Mr. Goldstrike' Japanese aucuba and variegated forms of hosta, English ivy, liriope, and golden sweet flag (*Acorus gramineus* 'Ogon').

I just purchased a dendrobium orchid. How do I care for it?
SHARON GABRIEL
NAVASOTA, TEXAS

Dendrobiums need at least six hours of sun a day. So place yours in a bright window or outside in dappled sun. While it is actively growing, keep the soil medium moist. Make sure the pot has a drainage hole. Feed monthly with a water-soluble fertilizer such as Miracle-Gro. After new growth matures, reduce watering so soil surface goes slightly dry between waterings. Also, quit fertilizing. Cool fall temperatures should initiate flowerbuds. Then, resume watering and feeding.

I need information about plants that like lots of heat and also grow in wet soil.
CHERYL CLEGHORN
FITZGERALD, GEORGIA

Many plants thrive in poorly drained soil and also take the heat. Trees to try include red maple (*Acer rubrum*), river birch (*Betula nigra*), bald cypress (*Taxodium distichum*), and sweet bay (*Magnolia virginiana*). For shrubs, consider wax myrtle (*Myrica cerifera*), Virginia sweetspire (*Itea virginica*), dwarf palmetto (*Sabal minor*), and buttonbush (*Cephalanthus occidentalis*). Perennials that like wet feet include Louisiana iris, cardinal flower (*Lobelia cardinalis*), canna, and elephant's ear. You'll find extensive lists of plants for wet soil in *The Southern Living® Garden Book.*

I planted two gardenias a couple of weeks ago. Now the lower leaves are yellowing and dropping. What is causing this, and what can I do?
CARLA MOSER
YADKINVILLE, NORTH CAROLINA

It's normal for a plant to drop leaves from time to time, especially lower leaves, which are older. Your plants may be responding to a change in growing conditions. As long as you take good care of them, the leaf drop should be temporary. Don't worry unless new leaves start dropping.

Can you tell me an easy way to root an azalea cutting?
DONNIE POUNCY
GEORGIANA, ALABAMA

Sure. Take a 4-inch cutting from the tip of a branch, dust the cut end with rooting powder, and then stick it in a pot filled with moist soil. Next, cut the bottom out of a clear plastic soda bottle, and place this over the pot to serve as a mini-greenhouse. Keep the soil moist but not soggy, and make sure the pot receives bright light but not direct sun. The cutting should root in one to two months.

A fungus is attacking my boxwoods. Sometimes the entire plant dies. Other times, whole sections of the foliage turn brown and die. The soil stays rather wet. What is the problem, and what can I do to solve it?
ANNETTE CROMARTIE
ALBANY, GEORGIA

Heavy, wet soil that contains a lot of clay is at the root of many a boxwood's demise. Poorly drained soil encourages a root rot fungus, for which there is no chemical control. We suggest lifting your boxwoods from the ground this fall and discarding any dead or diseased plants. Add organic matter and coarse gravel to the soil to improve drainage; then replant. Place so that the top inch of the root ball is above the soil surface, and then cover with mulch. If a downspout from the roof directs water into this area, pipe it away.

I've been told to put daffodil and crocus bulbs in the refrigerator for a month before planting. Is this correct?
DEE LOURENCO
BELLEVIEW, FLORIDA

Many spring-blooming bulbs, such as crocus and large-flowered daffodils, do not perform well in your area of Central Florida because they need some winter chilling. You can meet this requirement by putting bulbs in the refrigerator for six to eight weeks before planting. They'll bloom fine once, but probably not again, so you'll have to treat them as annuals. However, lots of other bulbs will do very well in your garden without any chilling at all. They include lily-of-the-Nile (*Agapanthus* sp.), crinum, gladiolus, freesia, spider lily, amaryllis, Easter lily, and tuberose.

Index

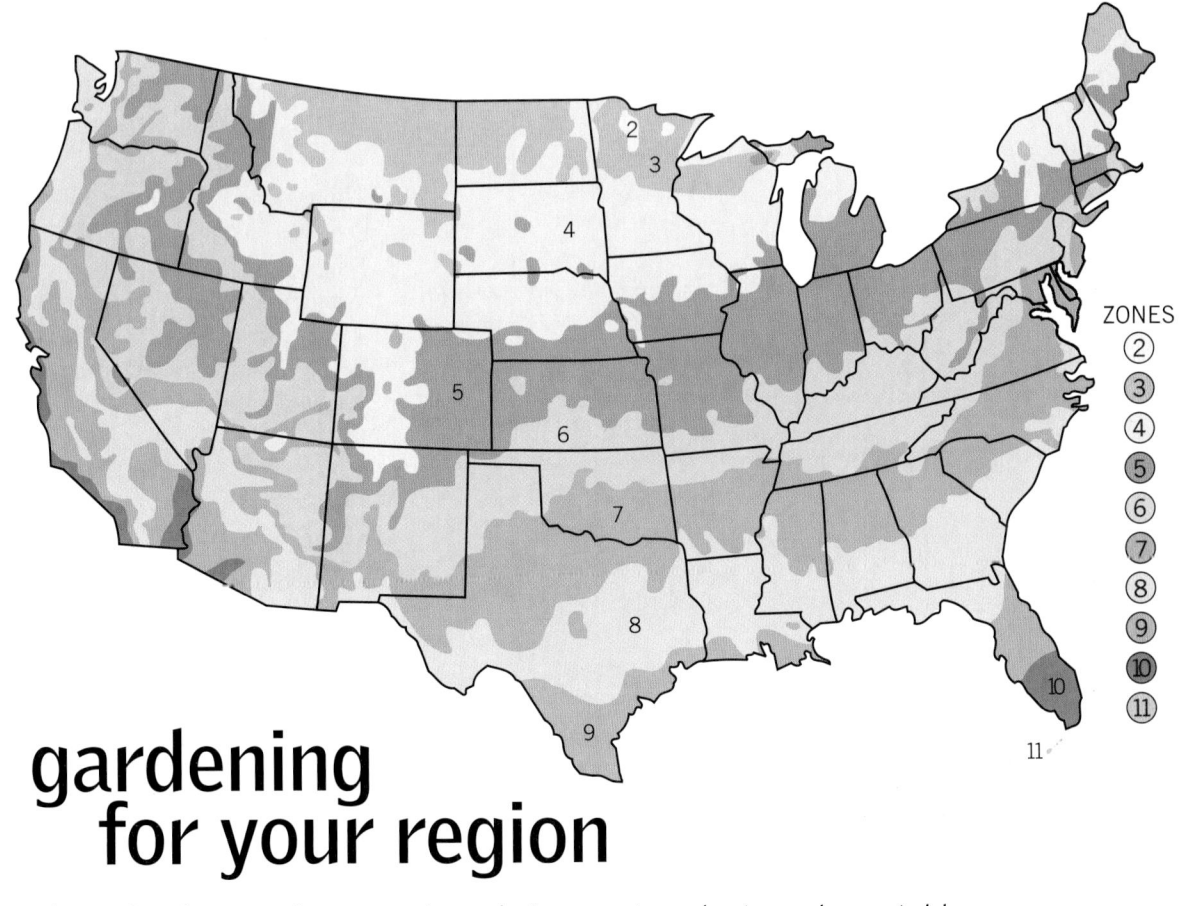

ZONES
② ③ ④ ⑤ ⑥ ⑦ ⑧ ⑨ ⑩ ⑪

gardening
for your region

The right climate plays a major role in growing plants and vegetables successfully. This handy map will help pinpoint your region in the South.

In discussing a plant's hardiness in *Southern Living*, we frequently refer to the Upper, Middle, Lower, Coastal, and Tropical South. We are referring to the geographical regions as they are shown on the map below, which appears here and in every issue of the magazine.

The map above is loosely based upon the USDA Plant Hardiness Zone Map. The United States Department of Agriculture bases this information on years of low temperature readings. Gardeners should note that it does not take into account summer heat, soil, and moisture extremes. It is intended as a guide rather than a guarantee.

For gardeners who are familiar with the USDA zone system and would like a point of reference, our regions are drawn as follows.

Upper South: Zone 6 (-10 to 0 degrees minimum) and colder

Middle South: upper region of Zone 7 (0 to 5 degrees minimum)

Lower South: lower region of Zone 7 and upper region of Zone 8 (5 to 15 degrees minimum)

Coastal South: lower Zone 8 and upper Zone 9 (15 to 25 degrees minimum)

Tropical South: lower Zone 9 and all of Zone 10 (25 to 40 degrees minimum)

UPPER SOUTH
MIDDLE SOUTH
LOWER SOUTH
COASTAL SOUTH
TROPICAL SOUTH

UPPER   MIDDLE   LOWER   COASTAL   TROPICAL